JUSTIN FOX

With Both Hands Waving

A journey through Mozambique

KWELA BOOKS

28 Wale Street, Cape Town 8001;
P.O. Box 6525, Roggebaai 8012

Cover design by Louw Venter
Typography by Nazli Jacobs
Set in Melior
Printed and bound by Paarl Print
Oosterland Street, Paarl, South Africa

First edition, first printing 2002
Second printing 2002

ISBN 0-7957-0144-6

http://www.kwela.com

For those who leave
and those who wait for their return

Revel and Ivy

ZAMBIA
TANZANIA
Cabo Delgado
Rovuma
Pangane
Ibo Island
CABO DELGADO
NIASSA
Pemba
MALAWI
MOZAMBIQUE
Lurio
TETE
Entre Lagos
Cuamba
NAMPULA
Nacala
Zambezi
Nampula
Moçambique Island
Tete
Blantyre
Alto Molócuè
MANICA
ZAMBÉZIA
Harare
Caia
Zalala Beach
Quelimane
Gorongoza National Park
Inhaminga
SOFALA
ZIMBABWE
Savane
Beira
Sofala
Indian Ocean
Bazaruto Archipelago
Vilankulo
Limpopo
INHAMBANE
Morrungulo
GAZA
Tofo
Inhambane
Guinjata Bay
SOUTH AFRICA
MAPUTO
Xai-Xai
Bilene
Maputo
Maputo Elephant Reserve
Johannesburg
SWAZILAND
Ponta do Ouro
0
300
km
Durban

O SUL

Chapter 1

We can go no further. This will have to be the end of the road. In truth, it is possible to continue the journey and strike north for the Rovuma. Our malaria patient could lie on the back seat of one Land Rover, our amoebic dysentery victim in the back of the other. So technically the expedition should continue. It's just that the stuffing has been knocked out of us during the past weeks of murderous roads, foul food and sleepless Larium nights. And I have a sandworm working its way through my foot.

We've also run out of time. There's the niggling issue of getting back to Johannesburg in eight days. At a rough guess, another 3 000 kilometres. If the trenches that pass for roads around here are anything to go by, it could take weeks.

I'm sitting on the sand watching a stormy dawn illuminate a bay dotted with dhows. A man wearing Islamic robes greets me cordially, 'Bom dia, tudo bem senhor?' *I return the greeting and yes, everything is fine, I suppose, considering. He looks at me for a long while as though he has seen something that disturbs him. Perhaps he has the answer to my travelling woes? Maybe he knows the meaning of the road?*

Then he takes a few paces, lifts his robes and, squatting down, empties his bowels loudly and copiously. I nearly throw up.

Back in camp I look at the motley band lying beneath the palms. On the face of it we are in paradise: Pangani Beach. The warm Indian Ocean lap dances on three sides of us, the Kusi trade wind rustles the fronds overhead and nudges a fishing dhow into the offing. Beautiful Hayley is making coffee over a camp stove. She looks a little worse for wear, worried about Dave who is lying on his back groaning in the corner of the barraca *or reed enclosure. Rob and Tank have headed off to the local fishing village in search of sunrise shots and Mike is staring into his bowl of muesli with the eyes of a ghost. 'I've got the shits and I've got 'em bad,' he confides. He's been irritating the shit out of* me *with his constant references to bodily functions, his symphonic burps and farts, but you have to feel sorry for him now. He looks rotten.*

We're all feeling crap, the journey has turned crap and, all told, Mozambique is crap. I want out. Now. Helicopter, submarine, dhow, just get me away from this god-awful country.

Cape Town. Monday morning, 09h15.

The editor strolled in, a mug of what looked like mud in his hand. Bristow sank into his swivel chair, crossed his feet on the desk and stared at us through narrowed eyes. 'Right. Mozambique,' he said.

David and I looked at each other and back at the editor.

'It's going to be the most important trip we've ever done. I want the two of you to go together,' he said. Outside the Cape rain was pelting, a grey mantle hung close to the ground. 'Think of it as a winter break: beer, girls and surf on an endless sunshine coast,' he chuckled, vindictively I thought.

'Sounds great, how far d'you want us to go?' asked Dave. 'Covering all the lodges around Maputo will take us ten days alone.'

'Actually I want you to do the whole country,' Bristow said.

You could have heard a fly land.

Bristow has a map of Africa on the wall behind his desk. I think of it as a sort of flight deck. At the beginning of each month journalists at *Getaway*, the travel magazine for South African readers where David Rogers and I were employed, gather here and are launched into Africa from our dot in the bottom left-hand corner that is Cape Town. Mozambique was largely uncharted territory as far as the magazine was concerned. A vast, white terra incognita.

Dave and I stared at the map in disbelief. Bristow had a faint smile on his face. 'I'll give you a month, tops. That's far longer than I've ever granted any journalist for a story.

'It's a piece of old tacky,' he said conversationally. 'Organise a couple of vehicles, head north from Durban along the coast until you hit the Rovuma River. Take a left and nip home via Malawi, the Tete Corridor and Zimbabwe. You'll be back with days to spare.'

'This is a joke, right?' said Dave, his bushy eyebrows drawing closer together. 'You can't seriously expect us to cover that distance on those kinda roads in under a month?'

'It's not, I can and I do. It's the trip of a lifetime and our readers are gagging to know what's in those remote northern regions. Tourists haven't been there since before the war. Actually, since before independence in 1975!

'Mozambique is going to be hot, hot, hot. Tourists are trickling into the south, to the old haunts like Ponta do Ouro, Bilene, Xai-Xai and Inhambane. But the more adventurous ones want to know what's up north. Are the roads passable? Where are the landmines? Will they get shot by bandits? We'll run the story over three issues and I promise you, we'll have over a million and a half readers. No question. Every oke with a 4x4 wants in.'

I looked at Dave who was distractedly ruffling his hair with his hand.

'Come on, what's your bloody problem?' Bristow barked. 'Now run along to the coffee shop and start planning. There are two of you, so the pressure won't be unrelenting – and if it is, hard luck. One can slack off while the other grafts. Justin, you write about the south. Dave, you do the rest.'

'This is too ambitious given the time allowed,' I mumbled. 'It's madness. Let me rather do the Seychelles cruising story you promised ...'

Dave and I talked of nothing else during our protracted coffee breaks, which extended into evenings of beer and pizza eaten over a table-size map of Mozambique. The itinerary unfurled. Five days for the south, a week for the centre, and about ten days for the north. Two vehicles, two journalists, four extra drivers. Maps, Portuguese phrase book, masks and snorkels. Mosquito nets, tents and plenty of chocolate. And I got reading, devouring whatever I could find about our north-eastern neighbour.

Like me, Dave had connections with Mozambique and a personal motivation for going. When he was a child his parents had brought back tall tales and tins of cashew nuts from holidays there ... and the spice of that never-never land had lingered through his childhood.

'Mozambique is scary 'cause of all the unknowns,' said Dave, 'and of course the rumours about bandits may be true. But, hey, that's what the adventure is about,' he added, brightening up. 'Once you're on the road, all the niggles evaporate. But doing it in such a short time will put a heck of a lot of pressure on us. It sucks having to work to other people's rules, but that's the price we pay, I guess.'

He'd neatly summed up the dilemmas of our job; in the end the pull of the road always won out.

Despite initial apprehensions, I was getting excited about the journey and inevitably began to regret that it would have to be such a rushed visit, and one following travel magazine formulae. This meant that some of the time, especially in the south, we'd be hopping from one South African owned lodge to another – and be mixing mainly with other travellers and expats. 'Give the readers what they want,' Bristow always demanded. The itinerary was too tight, our brief too narrow. There'd be no sitting in Maputo cafés chewing the cud with locals on this trip. Even on paper it looked like a Camel Challenge – hardly conducive to soaking up the atmosphere or meeting Mozambicans.

However, it was triggering all sorts of emotions and memories. I began to see the journey as tracing stories. Some of those stories intersected with my own, and that of my family. I thought of the country's narratives as sets of interweaving footprints, like those that crisscross Mozambique's dunes and sandy paths. On the one hand, I wanted to find points of contact established through familial nostalgia; on the other, to learn about the tempestuous history of this part of Africa. It was a country emerging from a mess rooted in centuries of conflict. It's not for nothing that one of the first things the Portuguese did when they arrived was to build forts, preferably on offshore islands. Heck, for all we knew, bandits were indeed still a problem.

My personal prints were in black-and-white images of my family living in Mozambique. But there were also historical texts, maps, shipwrecked sailors' logs, poet's laments, the last scrawled words of martyred priests. And the palimpsest volumes, those unwritten, never to be written stories of Mozambicans, leaving their imprints in a myriad of ways on the country's tale.

I was also in pursuit of the footprints of those who walked this country flat, in fever-ridden lands, through rivers patrolled by crocodiles, along tropical beaches. The first Bantu-speaking venturers from central and eastern Africa began arriving in the first millennium. They can be traced through paths of language and culture, coursing southward, and through a rich oral tradition. Later came shipwreck survivors, traders, refugees from tribal conflict, gold prospectors and ivory hunters. And there were the slave caravans: thousands who walked the breadth of the country on the way to the coast – the *pachiças*, chained walkers. Like all the others, they probably followed animal tracks, for elephants and hippos are the great road builders of Africa.

In recent years, during the country's civil war, millions of refugees had taken to the roads and tracks like the slave caravans of old. And then the footprints were removed altogether by landmines which had, in some cases, taken the feet with them.

Our Land Rovers would leave their tracks across that history. In our own way we'd dip randomly into lives and chronicles. For the period of a few short weeks we'd be wanderers following a great tradition pioneered by elephants and hunters, conquistadors and bandits.

As children we grow up with family legends, stories handed down through the generations that eventually become lore. Great uncle Ellis who stowed away on a ship in Southampton and arrived in Cape Town with no papers, no prospects and a dubious past ... you know the kind of tale. Every family is sown with them. They are versions of the creationist myth: who am I, where do I come from, which pieces of the jigsaw of lives make me?

My grandmother was the hander down of these myths. There was one period in her life that always fascinated me: her time in the neutral port of Lourenço Marques during the Second World War. Her husband, grandpa Bertie, was in charge of customs and excise at a time when German U-boats lurked offshore and spies from all corners of the Allied and Axis world would materialise in the Scala or the Continental Café to discuss sabotage, subterfuge and the remarkable texture of the best *pasteis de nata* pastries in town.

The Polana, that legendary Edwardian hotel, was a rendezvous for agents. The British spy Malcolm Muggeridge, author and one-time editor of *Punch*, posed as a consular official and lived there. Colonel James Stevenson-Hamilton, former soldier and conservator of the Kruger National Park, also showed up there while serving as an intelligence agent. His brief was to investigate reports that German spies were to be landed at Lourenço Marques and infiltrated into South Africa via Komatipoort.

One of the most dramatic episodes Granny told me about were the events surrounding the sinking of the *Nova Scotia*. The ship was returning from North Africa carrying nearly a thousand South African soldiers and Italian prisoners of war when it was torpedoed by *U-177* off the Zululand coast. The submarine surfaced to find out the ship's name from the survivors floating in the water – just for the record. 'No success,' wrote Captain Robert Gysae in his log, 'as they all shout and yell at the same time.' Italians who tried to clamber aboard had their hands stamped on by their German allies.

Then the U-boat dived and the sharks moved in, devouring many of the panic-stricken troops in the water. This went on for days, the few rafts being surrounded by man-eaters. Eventually the sloop *Afonso de Albuquerque* was alerted and rescued 200 men. The Portuguese sailors had to beat off sharks with boat hooks as they picked up survivors. Back in LM the men were interned, but most of the South Africans managed to escape with the help of Muggeridge who organised a fleet of taxis to drive the POWs to the Swaziland border.

As a boy I found the idea of the Foxes living in war-time LM extremely glamorous. Nothing to disturb the siesta stillness; no blackouts or fighting in that strange subtropical enclave of peace in a world at war. Granny's only son (my dad) was up north fighting the Ities and the Hun, but for the rest it was a lazy Portuguese colonial existence with four 'house boys' – as she insisted on calling them till her death in 1986 – in attendance.

I loved it when Gran described the big move to Mozambique from their home in East London when Grandpa was seconded to LM. The car was loaded to the gunwales and the roads were appalling. She told me about their journey through the Kruger National Park: having to wait for elephant herds to cross, sleeping in rustic bush camps. She described the vegetation as a 'jungle', which dovetailed with my favourite Kipling book. There was a particular incident, driving one evening on their way to the border, that caught my young imagination. I got Granny to tell this bit over and over. Coming round a bend in the 'jungle' they happened upon a huge black snake. Its head was in the foliage on one side of the road; its tail hidden in undergrowth on the other. The serpent was asleep, no doubt having recently devoured something weak and innocent, like Belgium. 'It was a black mamba,' hissed Granny. 'The most dangerous and most deadly snake in Africa. Führer of snakes.'

Somehow she created the impression that the whole Fox clan was in danger – which is nonsense, of course, but how was I to know? Grandmothers can be immensely deceptive. The Foxes sat quietly waiting for Herr Grim Serpent to wake, slither slowly into the jungle and then they drove through to the border and tropical sunlight beyond.

It was the dragon myth, repackaged for a credulous child in South African terms. Once past the snake they were into Eden and the riches of Gran's colonial Portuguese garden knew no bounds. You see she had all the licence she needed to crank it up, because Mozambique in the 1970s and '80s was as good as Atlantis. Given apartheid, Marxist Machel and a state of unofficial war, there was no way any of us young'uns were ever going to get there to corroborate her stories. The marrabenta dances went on all night, the prawns were the size of crayfish, the sea water as translucent as glass, the people the most charming on earth. In short: Lotus-land.

The time in Mozambique gave my family a passion for things Lusitanian and a host of Portuguese and Mozambican connections. The legacy passed to me. I studied the language at university and ended up on the replica of a 15th-century caravel bobbing down the Atlantic from Portugal to South Africa with a bunch of inept but lovable Portuguese mariners. We were a 17-man crew re-enacting the voyage of Bartolomeu Dias, first Portuguese navigator to round Africa's southern extremity.

Years later I wrote the script for a television documentary series on Arab dhow trade in the Indian Ocean. Being a Lusophile, I concentrated on Mozambique and managed to wangle a week-end in Maputo for 'research purposes'. The series never saw the light of the small screen, but it piqued my interest in Indian Ocean culture and the Asian maritime trade routes that stretched down the East African coast.

Southern Africa is bridled with a staid, paternal form of British colonialism. Whether you're in Cape Town or Gaborone, Harare or Blantyre, it's the same. It's conservative, Protestant, sober, eminently sensible. It's a game of cricket. Mozambique is different. It's lighter, less regimented, more chaotic, more passionate, more romantic (the climate helps), more plural. It has better rhythm. I suppose what I'm trying to say is that the Portuguese are temperamentally more African than the British.

My brother, Revel Junior, had one up on me. A serious one. He was born on the dance floor of the Polana's *boîte* (night-club) while my parents were visiting Gran and Grandpa for an extended vacation. Well, that's how they made it sound. They were keen dancers and although my mother was nine months pregnant, that didn't stop them. So to the *boîte* they went, perilously close to her due date.

Revel Junior wasn't actually *born* on the dance floor. Ma started having contractions while samba-ing and they rushed her to a little clinic nearby, staffed by nurses who spoke no English. Upon making his entrance into the world the first language my brother heard would have been Portuguese. I wonder if that experience left any unconscious resonance because 26 years later he married a Portuguese African.

That holiday of 1953 was important for our family in another way.

It was on the beach in LM that dad met Pancho Guedes, who became the doyen of Mozambican design, and later professor of architecture first at Wits, then at Lisbon university. They were both fiery young architects at the time, enfants terribles trying to make a name for themselves in Mozambique and South Africa respectively. They got on famously and the two families became life-long friends.

Living in Johannesburg after leaving LM in 1975, the Guedeses fuelled my interest in the tropical paradise turned to ruin. The tales got taller, the memories more frangipani filled. In Pancho's Johannesburg home were photos of old LM, great bug-eyed African masks that gave me the willies, Senufo fertility statues of hornbills, and the flotsam and jetsam of a Mozambican existence salvaged during their flight across the border, part of an exodus that saw most of the 200 000 whites leave.

'Uncle' Pancho had also brought his 17 Malangatanas with him. When Pancho met the talented black artist from Matola who was to become Mozambique's most famous artist, the young man was working as a waiter in a local club. Pancho got permission for him to be released from his contract and made his garage available as a studio from 1959 to '61. Pancho provided the materials and, over the years, bought the 17 early works. Today Malangatana's vibrant surrealist images are internationally prized and the Tate Gallery recently made a bid to exhibit Pancho's collection.

Pancho established an artists' workshop at his home on Rua dos Heróis de Navala. He's perhaps the most creative man I've ever met: always scheming, designing, drawing – mixing fine art, sculpture, architecture, engineering and urban planning like complementary colours on the same palette ... Our home in Cape Town was filled with artefacts – temples and galleons – created by wood carvers whom Pancho taught and nurtured. Uncle Pancho would buy a felled tree, draw plans for the sculptures and then, like a medieval patron, set his master craftsmen to work. By day they were cleaners in the next-door apartment block.

I had misgivings aplenty in the days leading up to the departure. Some of them involved my new girlfriend, Jennifer Mosely, a character who was to inform some of the proceedings, and be a bloody nuisance during Romantic Moments on tropical beaches and the like. She's half-British, half-American, fully New York Jewish and was at the time spending five months in London working on the movie adaptation of a Martin Amis novel. She left the week I set off on my Mozambican odyssey and we figured time apart would give us both some perspective on the infant relationship. Jenny is headstrong, difficult, intelligent, beautiful and I didn't really know it yet, but I was debilitatingly in love.

As a travel journalist my life had been essentially nomadic and the idea of settling down or having a home anathema. An intense period on the road could swing things one way or the other: reinforce my wandering inclinations or open me up to sedentary possibilities. As a singleton I'd been free to remain uncommitted. Jennifer posed a new dynamic: a serious relationship making a serious intrusion. The travelling groove I knew well, and loved. The other held a host of fears and unknowns, but also, I vaguely sensed, the promise of riches a wandering me could never reap. I had seldom felt as on edge about a journey as I did about this one. In a way it was Jenny and me versus me.

My travel compulsion was the outward manifestation of an inward nomadism that was rooted in the way I viewed the world. Cynical about society and its mores, politics and its shambles, family values and their perversions, I'd steered a course of scepticism and covert rebellion. I'd prided myself on the notion that I was able to escape. This had given me a sense of freedom and left me feeling I could elude society's pitfalls. Most alarming of the loomers was the idea of marriage and its horrific concomitants: two-point-two children and mountainous mortgage. The thought of white appliances left me nauseous.

Best stick with the simple solution I'd evolved: keep moving. My current job was the end result of years of diligently keeping the bonds loose, never committing fully to careers, countries or relationships. My motto had been '24 Hours' – the ability to leave town, permanently if necessary, with only a day's notice. This required careful planning and vigilance against the inevitable moss that gathers on a stationary stone. Indeed, it had taken me 13 years of studying, dithering, taking short-term employment and freelancing, before I'd found a job that factored in my nomadism. Until the advent of Jennifer, I had been highly successful at keeping my options open.

There were other misgivings about the journey at hand. Dave and I had plenty of second thoughts when bureaucratic obstacles began to threaten the assignment. Well, 'assignment' wasn't exactly the word: even Bristow – never one to exaggerate – was talking about 'The Expedition'. It was to be the 'last big one of the millennium'. The longest and most ambitious trip *Getaway* had embarked upon. It was the sort of thing that should get one excited, really pumped up. But in the face of the technicalities and logistics my negative side began whinging, inflating, deflating, poking holes. Looking at the distances and reading reports on road conditions only served to dampen any hubris about the ground-breaking nature – for magazine journalists, anyway – of the quest.

There were also the tedious hoops to jump through before we could enter the country. The simple matter of a visa was not so simple. It involved a journey to the nethers of Cape Town, a parking fine and a long wait for a neat gentleman who wanted to know what colour underwear Dave and I would be wearing in Mozambique and whether we, or any member of our families, had recently torpedoed a Mozambican warship or whether we had plans to do so in the future. Despite telling him all he wanted to know and me nonchalantly throwing in a bit of basic Portuguese, we had to return 'another day' with proof of having padded the consular slush fund with R130 each.

Then came the business of trying to get the vehicle papers in order for our two sponsored Land Rovers. Plenty of stolen or hijacked South African cars end up in Mozambique. All the red tape does nothing to slow the hijacking rate, but serves admirably to slow the tourism trade. We needed the vehicles' original registration certificates, letters of authorisation from the owners, temporary export permits, third-party insurance for driving Mozambique's notorious roads, temporary import permits, international driving licences. We'd also need to fill out re-importation forms for all expensive goods attached to the vehicles, right down to our photographic equipment. These mole hills grew tall with bureaucratic dung.

My misgivings were compounded by a visit to the British Airways travel clinic. 'For *how* long?' asked the nurse.

'Almost a month,' I repeated, 'and much of it in the far north.'

She looked grave. Had my inoculations for yellow fever, polio, tetanus, smallpox and cholera expired? I couldn't remember. I didn't know if I'd had half of them in the first place.

'By the sounds of it, you'd better get typhoid, TB and hepatitis as well. Just to be on the safe side,' she advised.

'You must take Larium or doxycyclin for malaria and I suggest you carry plenty of medication for dysentery. Oh, and Halofantrine or Fancidar to treat malaria if you start showing symptoms. You'll need antibiotic cream, antifungal cream, antihistamine cream ...' I lost track of the list. And condoms, she should have added, given the Aids epidemic and the encounter I was to have.

Her prescriptions were only the tip. Sitting with Dave in the coffee shop, guidebooks strewn across the table, I did a little medical reading. Mozambique was the perfect location for an ER horror movie, it turned out. There were torpedo-shaped bilharzia cercariae which would digest their way through my skin, then use my veins as supertubes to liver or bowel. Damage to my internal organs, noted one author, would be irreversible. More infectious than the Aids virus, hepatitis B was another nasty threat to my liver. Then there were tsetse flies that would give me sleeping sickness, ticks bearing fever and jigger fleas bent on making a home in my skin.

Meningitis would infect the membrane around my brain or spinal cord and kill me within hours – a cough or a sneeze from a carrier was all it took. The symptoms sounded like just about every other Mozambican malady: a headache and high fever. How would I know if it was a bad hangover or the death rattle?

My Bradt guidebook departed from its usual reassuring tone in its bid to get me immunised against rabies: 'Once symptoms appear rabies is incurable, and the way that you die is so horrible that all doctors advise a post-exposure boost.'

There was mosquito-borne dengue (no vaccine available) which would leave me with severe muscle cramps, high fever and nasty rashes. Oh, and leishmania (lovely name) – another difficult to treat disease affecting skin tissue, giving ulcers and disfigurement – was spread by sandfly bites.

I found out that going to a pharmacy in most parts of Mozambique wasn't necessarily of any use. Many dispensed medicines in brown envelopes without labels, leaving you to figure out your own dosage.

There were plenty of herbalists and *curandeiros* (traditional healers) whose medicines included hooves, hides and dried reptiles to give swift relief for maladies, as well as a range of roots to improve my sexual performance. I discovered that they used porcupine quills as syringes, that vulture heads would help get me into a trance and that puffer fish prevented theft. The lucky-packet brown envelopes were at least a step up from these cures, which would be my death's-door resort.

I had planned to pack little more than swimming gear and maybe a toothbrush or shaving cream, but clearly I'd have to make space for the portable pharmacy.

The guidebooks did little to allay worries about the terrain we were to pass through either. 'Assume that all man-made structures outside of the towns, such as bridges, wells, pylons, lighthouses, pump stations, abandoned vehicles, footpaths and reservoirs are mined,' one of them warned. Oh that's just great, I thought. As a photographer I'd learnt that the easiest way to get an arresting image was to find an unexpected angle. That meant getting high, like a pylon. Bridges offered great photo opportunities of rivers or the lie of the land, while abandoned vehicles always made interesting shapes. And lighthouses – of which Mozambique has many beautiful examples – are a particular obsession of mine, one of the most photogenic human-made objects. Taking photos in Moz was going to be no fun at all.

I read further: 'It is not advisable to travel after dark, due to the presence of people, animals, broken-down trucks and vehicles without lights on the pot-holed roads. Armed hijackings (especially of new 4x4s) are a real threat.' I had just received a fax saying we'd been offered a brand new, signal red Land Rover TD5, straight off the showroom floor. A new model with all the bells and whistles was bound to attract admiring glances. I could just imagine a hopeful band of hijackers oiling their AK47s in anticipation of our arrival.

As if bandits weren't enough, we were warned about frequent police roadblocks where the slightest supposed misdemeanour – not carrying hazard triangles to place in the road at the scene of a breakdown was specifically mentioned – could see you wasting half a day, paying a hefty fine; or worse, getting hauled back to the police station.

Landing in a Mozambican prison didn't bear thinking about. I'd heard about five Zimbabwean gold panners who'd been caught on the wrong side of the border. Four of the five had died in a local prison before the Zimbabwean authorities found out they were there. The fifth was so traumatised by the events that had taken place, he refused to breathe a word about it afterwards. I made a mental note to buy two hazard triangles.

The sun had not yet risen. Mid-June, the dead of winter, and rain bucketed out of the sky. It was bleak outside Cape Town International. I stood waiting with a mound of luggage at the check-in desk. A treacly voice announced our flight and I looked around anxiously for my three flying companions.

Suddenly they burst though the revolving doors like a Marx Brothers act, trailing half-open luggage, tents, sleeping bags. Dave had on a big floppy hat and baggies for the tropics. Rob, dapper and well-turned out for the expedition in matching khaki, was sharp on his heels. Trailing them was Derrick with red eyes and reeking of alcohol. He looked shattered. 'Late night,' he mumbled and leaned against a pillar to regain his breath. The lurid neon lighting didn't help his cause.

Derrick and Rob were to be our two extra drivers. Rob Ross, the oldest in the group, was a mutual friend from New York living in South Africa, working part time as a retail property consultant and getting to know the continent. He was soft-spoken, level-headed and a calming influence when things weren't running to plan. He was a keen photographer and had jumped at the chance of an expedition to the remoter parts of Mozambique.

Derrick Mills (better known as Tank) was a sea kayak manufacturer. He was also Dave's half brother and my colleague assured me Tank was as fun a guy as you could wish to have on a trip like this. Tank had a wicked streak and a talent for coming up with the right joke when others had long since lost all sense of humour.

'Do you smell something?' asked Tank when we neared the head of the queue.

Actually, yes, we had to admit.

'Sort of like alcohol,' Tank took a wild guess.

We couldn't fault him on his powers of deduction.

'It's almost as though the smell is coming from me,' he decided finally.

No getting away from it, we had to confess.

After protracted investigative sniffing, he opened the top of his rucksack and we all reeled back. Our pre-breakfast stomachs weren't prepared for the stench of Tequila Gold which had marinated his clothing, from underwear to woolly jersey. The celebration bottle – destined to toast our arrival on the banks of the Rovuma a few weeks hence – had cracked. It's a bit like breaking the champagne bottle on the bows before the ship's ready for launching, I thought. Talk about a bad omen. But I didn't.

Dave and I kept well clear of the reeking Tank. Besides, we had sponsored seats in business class – a trade-exchange arrangement that left Rob nursing the overhung Tank onto the plane, through the roller-coaster air pockets of a bumpy flight and the final hiccoughs as we approached Durban. Out of the porthole a patchwork of sugar cane was rising fast. The journey was upon us.

Our disjointed but cautiously merry band gathered in the parking lot where we took delivery of one of the Moz-bound Land Rovers. It was an ageing TDi supplied by a local rental company. The owner brought the vehicle in person and showed us around his 'baby': rooftop tent, fold-out tables and chairs, extra fuel and water canisters. He paused frequently, seeming to size us up, and stroked the bonnet absent-mindedly, expressing his apprehension about the journey.

'Take care!' he yelled as we pulled away.

The air was thick and muggy and we shed jerseys and long trousers as the TDi grumbled up the N2 sounding like a tractor. Dave was driving with Tank and Rob recumbent in cattle class. Our pace was sedate: no need to rush things at this stage. If necessary, we'd take all day to get to the border, where we were to meet the second Land Rover.

As we headed north I played through the two contending images I had of Mozambique. The first was rooted in family folklore. One of my favourite stories is of my dad coming home in 1945 after serving in North Africa and Italy. He'd been away for years and his parents had had no word from him. Dad managed to catch an unscheduled flight out of Egypt some months after the hostilities ended and when he landed in Pretoria, didn't know for sure whether his parents were on holiday in South Africa or at their new home in LM. He gambled on the latter and took a train through the night to the border and down to the coast, taking off military gear as he went (men in foreign uniform were liable to be arrested in neutral Mozambique).

Only mildly disguised as a civilian, he stepped off the train in downtown LM on a Sunday with no money, no clue where his parents were – if they were indeed in the country – and speaking no Portuguese. After tramping the streets for a while he stopped a man who spoke a bit of English. Yes, some new people – South Africans – had moved into a grand house on Rua Infante Dom Henrique, near the Cordosa Hotel. No, he didn't know what number.

I see it as a scene from an old movie, in black and white. Dad walks down a palm-lined street. He's come out of a bleak northern winter, having left his Sherman tank on a wharf in Genoa. The foliage is rioting and he's shedding army kit, stuffing it into a duffel bag. It's a cicada-shrilled, mid-afternoon: siesta time, so he can't knock on doors. He looks over walls, peers into driveways. He stops outside a house. There's a hat which he thinks he recognises hanging on a stand in the open doorway. The soldier decides to try his luck and walks up the path of a tropical garden. He hesitates at the door. There are muffled voices coming from the back. He ventures in, picking his way like an intruder through to the kitchen and out the back door. His mother looks up, says nothing. Her eyes well with tears. He drops his duffel bag ...

Perhaps because I'm a traveller I hold this story dear. Perhaps also because I too did this kind of prodigal arrival once, repeating it on a smaller scale after my long voyage on the caravel. Homecomings are half of what journeys are about. Without them the travels and travails have no raison d'être, the protagonist turns to jelly. He becomes a Vladimir or an Estragon, stuck on an open stretch of road for eternity. The journey wobbles, loses its internal logic. Ask Homer.

But there was a dystopian vision of Mozambique that vied for contention while I was growing up in a country severed through apartheid from the rest of the African body. Moz was a place of destruction and mayhem, of Marxism and the *rooi gevaar*: the Vietnam of East Africa. Officially, it was the poorest country on earth.

In South Africa, our neighbour's woes were blamed on commie Frelimo (Frente de Liberação de Moçambique). The country was a basket case because of a Marxist dictatorship. Simple. But even as a child I had an inkling that things were more complicated than that. Frelimo's track record in health, education and social reform were admirable. The Portuguese had left a shocking education system and the legacy of five per cent literacy among black people. During the first five years after independence secondary-school enrolment increased sevenfold while Frelimo's programme of immunisations reached most of the population and drastically reduced infant mortality. Gender equality was another victory with women making up nearly a third of those elected to popular assemblies.

However, Frelimo's economy was a shambles. Stalinist grand plans, collective farms and state-owned industries – everything, from coffee shops to barber shops, was nationalised – drove the country further into ruin. Frelimo's cause was not helped by the global depression of the mid-1970s, the exodus of Portuguese skilled labour and capital, and years of flooding and drought which brought on a famine that left 100 000 dead. But worst of all was the Renamo factor.

Hard upon the heels of the war of independence came Mozambique's far more destructive civil war, fuelled first by Rhodesia and later the South African government. The Machiavellian plan was designed to render the country ungovernable so that no concerted effort could be made by Frelimo, or the ANC cadres it harboured, to take on their Big Brother neighbour. Renamo was fed just enough weapons and supplies to keep the country in a state of paralysing guerrilla warfare for well over a decade. Soviet intervention on behalf of Frelimo exacerbated the situation and it was not until the mid-1990s that the country began to claw its way out of a mire of self-destruction and poverty.

In South Africa we grew up hearing horror stories: Renamo troops amputating the recently vaccinated arms of children who'd sought government medical aid, Soviet firepower wreaking havoc in remote villages and gross administrative incompetence. The peasants who remained on the land eked out an existence at starvation level and the cities became Frelimo enclaves. The infrastructure was shot, trade and industry came to a halt and Maputo harbour was clogged with sunken ships.

Renamo approached its policy of rendering the countryside ungovernable in Pol Pot style. Schools and hospitals were razed; teachers, doctors and educated leaders were executed. Ill-disciplined guerrillas would make their presence felt in an area by mutilating civilians, cutting off ears, noses, genitalia. Travel writer Nick Middleton recounts the story of a woman from Tete Province:

> Renamo soldiers arrived in my village saying they were extremely hungry. We told them we had no meat to give them with their *nsima* (mealiemeal). So they grabbed my child, chopped it up, and forced me, trembling, to cook it. They even forced me to eat some. I have vowed never to eat meat again.

Renamo's savage and random acts left a traumatised rural population. A million Mozambicans died as a result of the war and a further million and a half took refuge in neighbouring states.

But who was Renamo? Initially the Mozambique National Resistance Organisation was a military unit of dissident Mozambican soldiers controlled by the Rhodesian army to help in its anti-terrorist war and to destabilise Mozambique, where many of Robert Mugabe's Zanu camps had been established. For instance, Renamo forces aided the Rhodesians in the daring commando raid on the Beira oil depot in 1979. After the fall of Ian Smith's government, Renamo found a new patron in the South African Defence Force (SADF) and was given two bases, Savong and Zobo City, in the Northern Transvaal, now Limpopo Province. From then on its units were supplied from land, sea and air by the South African military.

In the early years Renamo appeared to have no real political policies or motives, other than opposition to Frelimo. In time it learnt to exploit differences between Frelimo and traditional leaders, between city and countryside and tap into resistance to socialism, particularly the system of 'communal villages'. Renamo slowly won over the rural population, largely by coercion or terror, swelling its ranks by kidnapping young men and boys. Children were forced to commit horrific crimes – often inflicted on their own families – as part of their initiation into the guerrilla bands.

One of the strangest twists in this plot was the alliance between Renamo and fundamentalist Christian churches in the West, particularly in the anti-communist US Bible belt. Organised by elements in South Africa, missionary front organisations raised huge sums of money for Renamo warriors who were presented as religious revivalists carrying the New Testament into battle for Christ's cause against an atheist and Marxist foe. Extremist American organisations such as the 'Believers Church', 'Church for the Nations Inc.' and the 'End of Time Handmaidens' sent their money and their blessings to a generation of adolescent serial killers.

Historians in the English-speaking world have steered clear of Mozambique's complicated misery. Malyn Newitt is one of the few to offer a comprehensive analysis of the country's past. In his seminal *A History of Mozambique* Newitt writes about the country in terms of a series of what he calls 'dis-integrations', its history seen as a dialectic between forces of integration and disintegration. By integration he means forging peace, creating larger scale polities and widescale trade, and the spreading of Islam and Christianity. Against this process he poses the forces of disintegration: drought, famine, floods, banditry, warlordism, the creation of monopolies (colonial and post-), slavery and the export of migrant labour – all of which have plagued Mozambique down the centuries. This force has been the doppelganger, the shadowy Mr Hyde ready to destroy all that is constructed.

Today Mozambique is in the process of integration, its Jekyll phase, after a long reign of glorified banditry. During this period of growth, there were many things to be positive about. The years of war kept developers away from one of the most beautiful coastlines in the world. Over a 25-year period when many of the best beaches on the planet – from the Costa del Sol to Phuket – had been ravaged by realtors' dreams, this stretch had remained pristine. Here were nearly 3 000 kilometres of white sands with few footprints ... and if you added dhows (unmotorised, due to fuel shortages), the odd deserted Portuguese fort with seaward pointing cannons or overgrown ruins of Muslim origin, it's the stuff of travel-brochure romance.

Rob wanted to pee, so we pulled off and stretched our legs in a pineapple plantation. Tank bought one of the fruit from a woman who'd built a pyramid of pineapples at a wayside bus stop. Out came his Swiss Army knife and back on the road the cabin was filled with it's tropical scent.

I hauled out an old guidebook, *Holiday in Mozambique* by Douglas Alexander, that I'd bought at a second-hand bookshop in Cape Town. It was published shortly before the Portuguese evacuation in 1975 and would help inform my journey back and forth between the past and the present, between the dream and reality, between inherited nostalgia and current conditions.

'Coral-rimmed, palm-fringed Mozambique, that sizeable piece of the jigsaw map of Africa, lures more holidaymakers than any other country in southern Africa.' That's how Alexander starts his book and the opening statement could not have been more revealing about how quickly things changed: civil war effectively put an end to holiday making. From almost 100 000 visitors a year in the early 1970s the figure was down to 1 000 in the early '80s. Tourism had died. But we'd been told the industry was up again, bouncing on its toes and ready to deliver.

So there we were, sidling towards Mozambique in the TDi and these contending notions were banging about in my head. I anticipated that reality would to be somewhere between my dreams and the dystopian vision. What I never expected was that it could be both, often at the same time.

Chapter 2

It was warm for the dead of winter and even with the Land Rover's big front vents open, we were feeling sticky. The undulations of cane had given way to bushveld dotted with yellow fever trees. The Lebombo Mountains rose in the west like a fleet of battleships. Our TDi crossed the Mkuze River and headed past Lake Sibaya, bobbing with hippos, deeper into rural Maputaland.

We drew up at the Engen petrol station in the border town of Kwangwanase, the rendezvous point with our other Land Rover – the new TD5 sponsored by the manufacturers. Our guide, Mike Slater, and Hayley Retief, Dave's girlfriend, had left Johannesburg that morning and were due to meet us in Kwangwanase. We'd hardly ordered our chicken and chips from a café pumping maskanda music, when the scarlet TD5 pulled up beside us.

I knew Hayley well from Cape Town, a teacher at the Waldorf school with an even temper and a gentle manner. She was a petite and pretty 27-year-old blonde with intelligent, sparkling eyes. I saw cover material in Hayley; getting her to pose would prove more problematic.

'So all four you boys made it here in one piece,' she said with a smile.

I gave her a hug and reached out a hand to the driver, a short man with hair shaved almost to stubble. 'You ready for this one, bru?' he said in a Jo'burg drawl.

'I suppose we could have waited five years and done all the newly opened resort hotels,' I said.

'Nah, that wouldn't be the real Mozambique,' he answered. 'By the way I'm Mike. You must be Justin.'

Mike was a geography teacher and the author of *Guide to Mozambique*. There was determination in his look and he had an air of resourcefulness. He looked like a guy who wouldn't mince words, which had its pros and cons on a trip like ours. He was also a bush doctor and paramedic.

We mopped up the vinegary chips and took the road as the sun began to redden. It was 16h00 and the border closed in an hour, so the drivers stepped on the gas.

We were up to our full complement: two 4x4s and six drivers. The idea was that we'd be three in each vehicle which left the back seats for sleeping or convalescing. Given the 17-hour driving days that lay ahead, this set-up was ideal. The drivers never got too tired, and there was always the chance of a back-seat nap after a long stretch at the helm. That was the theory, at least.

As we neared the post the road began to deteriorate, slowing our progress. The local municipality had obviously deemed it appropriate to prepare drivers for what lay across the border. Perhaps it was some kind of unofficial warning to the would-be crosser: Thither Be Potholes Far Bigger Than These.

We reached Kwangwanase border control – if you could call the two run-down buildings a border post – with ten minutes to spare. There was a line of 4x4s towing ski boats queuing to enter the land of bounteous kingfish, barracuda and mackerel. The boats were bristling with rods like amphibian porcupines: a maritime slaughtering spree in store. The manne were already drinking, standing in the passport queue with cans of Castle Lager.

A man with a belly peeping between T-shirt and shorts strolled up to inspect our 'scarlet lady'.

'*Nuwe model*?' (new model) he asked in Afrikaans, without introducing himself.

'Ja,' said Dave.

'Don't know why you bother with anything other than a Toyota' said our new friend.

We made non-committal noises.

'The five got any balls?' he asked, taking a long slug from his beer.

'Seems OK,' said Dave.

A desultory technical conversation ensued until suddenly the man looked at his watch and exclaimed: 'Bliksem, we've been here 20 minutes already. These brain-dead munts couldn't organise a piss-up in a shebeen.'

He turned on his slip-slops and waddled back to his Land Cruiser.

There are stereotypical tourist punch bags: loud and brash Americans, swarms of Nikon wielding Japanese, soccer-hooligan Brits … South African men on 4x4 sorties into Africa deserve a special place on that list. It's as though the racism they have to keep in check in post-apartheid South Africa is given Lebensraum when transposed to neighbouring states. Revving 4x4s, bullish shouting, loud music, alcohol indulgence, and copious amounts of meat, occasionally shot or caught en route, complete the picture. It's not for nothing that some of the disaffected have taken to calling southern Mozambique Boerassic Park.

As much as one can distance oneself from queuing companions, we did. The group ahead of us broke into an Afrikaans *treffer* called *'Liewe Lulu'* and we were subjected to the chorus sung in three-part disharmony: *'Liewe Lulu, sal jy vanaand met my kom doedoe?'* (Lovely Lulu, will you sleep with me tonight?).

I suppose I found them so offensive because in a way they were an extension of us. Would Mozambicans make any distinction between our group and theirs – both come to exploit the country in different ways? The one lot looking for fish and fun, the other, photographs and text for a foreign travel magazine. Modern conquistadors. Was it enough that my personal journey was all about comprehending if and how I fitted in?

By the time we'd crossed into Mozambique the sun, now as red as the TD5, had bled into a bandage of clouds and was making a mess of the horizon. The Landies were soon grinding along a gravel road and I noticed that Mike was quite transformed. There was a wide grin on his face: the man had come home. He began talking enthusiastically about his 'first time' and how passionate it was, how tender She had been to him. He admitted that although he was now married, She had become his mistress. About twice a year his wife let him visit Her, to maintain the bond and renew the affection. 'I've got a long-suffering wife,' he said.

It took me a moment to realise he wasn't talking about some ebony princess with whom he was fulfilling erotic fantasies, but the country itself. 'When I first came here in the early nineties it was a wild place and there was still sporadic fighting,' he said. 'But I fell head over heels in love. The countryside, the people – just couldn't get enough. Still can't.

'Hey, it's like a phoenix rising. When I came back after the 1992 cease-fire there was such a positive vibe. Farmers were preparing to plant their first crops in over a decade, markets were buzzing. Musicians and dancers were jolling in the streets. The place was bursting with confidence. Man, you can still feel that energy.'

I saw no sign of phoenix-like infrastructure. Not even anything that could be termed a road. The contrast from one side of the border to the other was more startling than I'd expected. The 'road' had petered out a few hundred metres after leaving South Africa and we were driving north over dunes. Soon the TDi was stuck, wheels flicking sand high into the air. Two 4x4s raced past, their ski boats bouncing along behind. The occupants waved carelessly.

We bailed out and used twigs to depress the tyre valves, releasing pressure to get more bite in the soft sand. By the time we were up and growling again it was dark and the headlights probed a path through dune scrub. Mike drew us to a halt and shouted to Dave, who was at the wheel of the other vehicle: 'Plenty of landmines around here buddy, so keep your tyres in the ruts made by other vehicles. Whatever you do, don't venture off the road.'

What road? The main route from South Africa to Ponto do Ouro was a confusing series of unmarked sand tracks. They all headed north and ostensibly all ended up in Ponta, or thereabouts. Relatively simple in daylight, I would guess, but less than pleasant for landmine-nervous rookies like ourselves. Nightjars flew from under our tyres and flitted along in our headlight beams to settle further ahead, only to be disturbed again. In parts of Mozambique the nightjar, usually a difficult bird to spot, was one of the most common species we saw. A regrettable conclusion is that in some areas 'day fowl' had been hunted for the pot. This bird's nocturnal habits and exceptional camouflage had spared it. In this part of southern Africa I'd rather be a sparrow than a lilac-breasted roller (to borrow from Simon and Garfunkel).

Although it seemed an age, it couldn't have been more than an hour of dune sledding before we spied lamps in the distance. Soon we were coasting up the main street of Ponta. Mbaqanga music issued from a ghetto blaster at an outdoor restaurant where tables were laid under big-leafed, subtropical trees. The sound of surf echoed at the end of the street. The air was warm and windless.

We found Casa Azul, also known as Blues Beach House, on a dune above the beach. Jon and Bonny Sawyer were waiting in the driveway, a fire going and drinks in hand. '*Boa tarde* and welcome to Mozambique,' said our host in a Yorkshire accent. Jon and Bonny had come here in the bad years and had their share of scrapes, but had created a New Age-style guesthouse and were thriving in Ponta.

Despite the Bohemian atmosphere, Jon and Bonny weren't throwback hippies living on love and marijuana. An industrious team, they'd worked hard to renovate an awkwardly designed, Modernist building. Bullet holes had been plastered over, the garden replanted, walls painted in pale washes of green and blue, the colours of the ocean, and a windmill and solar panels stuck on the roof for eco-energy. The furnishings were simple and elegant, the fabrics tie-dyed. Even their home-made garments reflected shades of sea and sky. Marimba music filtered through the spaces, the moon rose out of the ocean and the lights of Ponta samba'd in the shore break.

'Things were pretty wild when we first came to Mozambique in a beach buggy with our long hair blowin' in the wind,' said Jon over a spicy curry on the deck, the candle flames standing firm in the stillness. 'There'd be columns of smoke from ambushes behind and ahead of us. But we smiled and waved and must have looked unthreatening, 'cause we never had a bad incident.'

Jon was an anomaly in Ponta. I can't imagine what the Pontaloons made of him when he first arrived. A slightly effeminate Yorkshireman with a mop of blonde hair and a handsome face arrives by buggy to settle in a war-ravaged village on the Mozambique coast – you can't expect the locals to get the entire picture.

'Around here it was Renamo territory during the war, hence all the landmines,' explained Bonny, dishing seconds for everyone. 'Frelimo only just managed to keep the town. The surrounding area was held by the rebels who could be easily supplied with weapons and provisions from across the border in Es Ay. At times it was only a Russian warship in the bay that prevented the town falling to Renamo.'

Although she looked Portuguese with her mane of brown hair, dark eyes and olive skin, Bonny was an Afrikaner. But she found that some conservative South African visitors were rude and even aggressive when they heard she was from the highveld. Her bohemianism, New Age leanings, marriage to a 'lefty' Englishman and emigration to what was, until not so long ago, an enemy state put their noses out of joint.

'Until recently I let most South African visitors think I'm a white Mozambican and pretended not to understand Afrikaans,' she confided. 'Things are better now.' I marvelled at what strange shades the chameleon Afrikaner sometimes turns when 'deserting' the tribe.

It was late and the moon lifted higher in the sky casting a shimmer across the wave crests. One by one we stole to bed.

I woke early from a night of stormy Larium dreams. New Age ocean music wafted from somewhere in the house. Sunlight splashed Casa Azul and illuminated the *ponta do ouro* (point of gold), lending an added dimension to the name (derived from a mistake on an early

Portuguese map which suggested gold could be found there). A lighthouse stands on the headland marking the border with South Africa. During the war this 'hot spot' was a place of minefields, skirmishes and smugglers. Nowadays you have to make do with fishing rod or surfboard to get a kick at the golden point.

I stepped off the deck into the face of the light and strode over a dune where turtles lay summer eggs, and into bath-warm water for a long, slow swim out to the where the waves hollowed. I could see humpback whales blowing and the 'dolphin encounters' boat heading out to give patrons a chance to swim with the gregarious cetaceans. Down the beach divers were preparing for the trek out to Pinnacles, a legendary spot four kilometres offshore frequented by hammerhead sharks.

Over breakfast Mike hauled out a map and with a pencil Jon traced a shorter route past Ponta Malongane north to our next destination in the Reserva Especial do Maputo (Maputo Elephant Reserve). 'I think the road's still passable,' said Jon. 'In the wet months you'd have bugger all chance of getting through. Wouldn't even find the thing, it gets so overgrown. But you should be OK at this time of year.'

Driving over Cell-Phone Hill (so named because of its good cellular reception) to the north of Ponta we came across a Toyota Land Cruiser whose occupants were seated in camping chairs enjoying a breakfast Klippies and Coke. We stopped and warned the four Gauteng fishermen not to venture off the clearing. We'd heard that a man had recently triggered a landmine with a back wheel of his bakkie while making too wide a turn there. Judging by their saucer-like eyes it seemed likely they would respond appropriately to this titbit of information.

We made what was intended to be a short toilet and reconnaissance stop at Ponta Malongane (which means 'the place of the man who fixes everything'), a resort and camp site snug under a canopy of dune forest. The owner, a burly man who looked like he could fix – or break – anything, showed us round. When he heard Dave and I were from *Getaway*, he got his claws into us and we were subjected to The Grand Tour.

Time was a commodity we couldn't waste. We'd been warned that driving after sunset in Mozambique is dangerous and to be avoided. The first night had put us at risk and we'd been forced to negotiate bad sand tracks in the dark. Our crazy schedule didn't leave margin for slack days, bar one in the middle. These thoughts were running through my head as we inspected the bathroom tiles of a new chalet. 'What lovely towel rails,' I found myself saying, ridiculously, the map of south-east Africa filling my head. Eventually, after much clandestine gesticulating, everyone was back in the vehicles and we took off with unseemly haste.

At Jon's recommended turnoff, we halted for a rethink. A track would be too grand a name for Jon's route. We doubled back and rechecked his map: surely this couldn't be 'the road'. Alas, it was. The path snaked through marshy grassland, often vanishing completely. At times we sunk to our axles, grinding through mud with water coming over the bonnet. It would have been odious if either vehicle had stalled in those conditions. It was frying pan and fire stuff: the hard ground spelt mines and the swampy ooze could mean days of waiting for a tow truck.

I think everyone, cucumber-cool Mike included, heaved a relieved sigh when we cleared the wetland and meandered along a track towards the park entrance. The gate-post was served by a derelict house out of which four startled guards emerged. From the looks on their faces no-one had come this way for months. The men had pitched a tent inside the leaky building and were living rough. They wanted R80 per person – and a little bread, if we had any to spare. Mike thought this extremely pricey, so he settled into an elaborate bargaining discourse in broken Portuguese.

'Come on, senhores, you're being unreasonable,' he argued. 'You're asking a small fortune for one night in a park with practically no animals.What do you take us for?'

'What's up with Mike?' muttered Rob in his nasal New York accent. 'We haven't got time for haggling. Night's coming on. When's this guy gonna get with the programme?'

Rob was right. Our brief was to get the feature, not save a few rand here and there. We finally convinced Mike that it was OK to spend the R80, but I had to agree with Rob when he foresaw that our two contending philosophies of African travel would knock heads again soon.

Once through the post, vervet monkeys munched on *masala*, or 'apple fruit', and green pigeons flitted through the clearings which undulated towards a series of freshwater lakes loud with the grunt of hippos. We kept an eye out for elephant, but, alas, were not rewarded. There wasn't another vehicle or soul in sight. The park seemed to be ours alone.

I'd hoped for more wildlife, especially elephants, but we discovered that much of it had been poached. The rhinoceros population (65 white rhinos relocated from Umfolozi Game Reserve in 1967) had been wiped out altogether. Of course large-scale hunting in this area long predated the civil war. I checked in my prerevolutionary guidebook by Alexander and found he contended that Mozambique offered some of the best hunting in Africa. He enthused about conditions and noted that rates charged by Mozambican safari companies, although high, included the services of a professional hunter, gun bearers, skinners and porters, but unfortunately, not the taxidermists who prepared and packed your trophies. Each hunter was limited to 'only' one 12-bore shotgun, two rifles and 500 rounds of ammunition when visiting the game concessions. Even in the 1970s there was a certain nostalgia for the glory days of mass slaughter.

In this part of Mozambique, the big prize was elephant. When the ivory trade was at its peak, Delagoa Bay (now Maputo Bay) was an important export centre. Bands of hunters tracked the herds and singled out the great tuskers for killing. They only became protected game here in 1960, and during the civil war they were again put to the sword. The reserve's current generation of nervous elephants are descendants of creatures which have been hunted for centuries.

We'd planned to meet park-manager Richard Fair at the gate and he was going to show us to our overnight spot at Ponta Membene, a rustic coastal camp that sleeps just eight guests. Richard was missing and we'd have to find our own way to the camp using a hand-drawn map and dodgy GPS (global positioning system) co-ordinates. Soon night began to fall and the cryptic directions were failing us.

In the twilight we blundered down a side track I thought might be the right one, into a family of Germans pitching tents on a sweep of beach beside a point with the melodic name of Milibangalala. Mike apologised and our circus turned and headed north.

We halted beside a lake and waited for the satellites to line up before taking our GPS co-ordinates. From the look of it, we had to roll a log out of the way, slash an entrance and head down a tiny overgrown track. Richard had mentioned that Msala Bush Camp had been closed for some time and was not due to be reopened until the following year, but we hadn't expected such a bundu-bashing approach.

Trees closed overhead to choke the last of the light. We were driving through marshy terrain again and Dave was worried about getting bogged down. With hippo, crocodile and swarms of mosquitoes around, it wasn't a very healthy spot to try digging ourselves out. Lost and chasing nightjars on bad roads again ...

The track came to a dead end beside a lake which sparkled with moonlight. A hippo snorted in our direction. From over a dune we could hear the ocean breathing heavily against the shore. Very enchanting, but where the hell were we? Mike flicked on the GPS and stared at the co-ordinates, looking doubtful. '*É pá*!?' he said finally. It's one of the most expressive Portuguese exclamations, denoting a combination of 'hey', 'say what?', 'gosh' and 'excuse me!'

Then, after some time: 'Well boys, believe it or not, this is it. We're there!' We looked around in disbelief.

'Richard must have given us the wrong co-ordinates,' said Hayley.

Then Dave spied a glint of white in the moonlight. Upon closer inspection we found it was a hippo rib bone marking the beginning of a path into dune forest.

'Let's see where this goes,' he said, disappearing into the bush.

I could just make out the white sand of a path that led up through thick vegetation. We entered a clearing and came upon Robinson Crusoe-style Msala Camp with its four tents set under trees and a simple wooden structure in the centre which acted as a living-dining area. It was perfect.

We chose tents and unloaded our gear. Once we'd lit a few lamps, Tank started a fire and before long chicken was sizzling on the grill. Rob popped the corks of two bottles of Thelema Merlot and even a sudden tropical shower couldn't dampen our elation at being in such a seductive spot.

When the rain ceased, the moon opened a crack in the clouds and rinsed our camp with light. Night creatures regathered composure and began their symphony. We sat in silence listening to a crescendo. Later the green eyes of a spider stared at me down the beam of my torch as I passed the skulls of small animals which decorated the route to my bed and a date with Larium. Tomorrow we'll track elephants. If only Jennifer could be here, I thought as I drifted off.

I woke early, slipped from my tent and climbed to the dune's crest. An unspoilt beach curled to the north in a golden arc. Below me in the surf were two naked figures. A man and a woman. I sat and watched as they gambolled out of the water and hugged each other. Then they stood holding hands watching the sun come up. I retreated to camp, leaving Dave and Hayley alone.

Due to persistent poaching, the reserve's battle-scarred pachyderms are nervous of humans and tend to keep to the thick bush. There are about 200 survivors and they migrate along the Fúti Channel to South Africa's Tembe Elephant Reserve. They're allegedly the last remaining elephants in southern Africa able to follow their ancient migratory routes and Dave had recently visited Tembe to try to photograph them.

'They are some of the most cantankerous animals in Africa and have a reputation for charging vehicles,' he said pointedly as we drove out of camp. 'At one stage I got to within 100 metres of a herd and they buggered off into the undergrowth. I couldn't get a closer look. You can't blame 'em. In 1989 a quarter of the elephants had wounds from snares or bullets. They were all seriously traumatised.'

We took a short cut to the main gate and trailed through sand forest resplendent with wild mango and Mozambique coffee trees, pausing in clearings to switch off the engines and listen for the telltale sound of breaking branches, but no luck. Indeed there was very little game to be seen at all. Snares and AK47s had stripped the park of its fauna during the bad years. Although the flora was better able to withstand the war, illegal forestry and slash and burn subsistence agriculture also threatened these last wilderness areas.

A marshy flood plain blocked our way. The road disappeared into swamp, but, after inspecting the water obstacle, we decided to risk traversing it rather than turning back, which would have added another hour to our drive. Dave didn't get up enough speed and his TDi got hopelessly bogged down, sending a shower of mud over the onlookers. The TD5 didn't have enough space to pass by and pull its older cousin through. Stuck.

Half an hour later a Land Rover with two Germans in matching khaki found us digging at the axles and poking logs under the wheels for traction. In their dapper safari gear they could have been part of Rommel's Afrika Korps on a scouting mission. With hardly a word they sprang into action. Rope was passed between the vehicles and all spare hands were marshalled to help push. Hayley at the wheel hit the accelerator and with a mighty heave the vehicle lurched free of the mud, whining shrilly.

Our band was a wretched sight, bespattered from hair to toe in mud – eight studies for an Abstract Expressionist series. We felt for the Germans, whose outfits were now a mess, but I think they secretly enjoyed the mud and guts.

At the main gate we met with Richard Fair, who had been waiting there since the previous afternoon, not figuring that we'd enter through the little-used southern gate. 'We've started reintroducing animals,' he said as he showed us around his camp. 'Soon the park will be able to compete with its more famous neighbours across the border in KwaZulu-Natal and Mpumalanga. We've also got to preserve the unspoilt coastline here, but that might be an even tougher task than saving the reserve.'

He explained that already big industry had come snooping and there were plans for a major harbour within the reserve's borders, an ecological disaster if it came to pass. Even in the short time we spent with him it was apparent that Richard had tremendous drive and was determined to 'get things right' in his reserve. He saw it as his duty to make the place shipshape for animal and tourist alike. Putting a stop to poaching, creating a feeling for conservation among subsistence-level villagers, replacing fences, building camps, training game guards and marketing the park as a holiday destination were among the projects he'd set himself. Crippling bureaucracy, insufficient funding, distrust and a lack of manpower were his obstacles.

As we neared the southern shores of Maputo Bay the dirt turned to pocked tar. We pulled up beside Catembe's ferry jetty amid a flurry of activity. At the embarkation point we stepped from our 4x4s onto a bed of fish scales where township jive eddied on a breeze heavy with the smell of petrol and sewage. Across the water, downtown Maputo glistened.

Choral African voices filled the air as we lounged around our Landies waiting for the slow boat to the capital. Wrecked vessels lay scattered along the beach or half submerged in the bay. Street vendors offering eels and oranges wove through the throng. A woman in a bright red and yellow *capulana* (sarong) joked with us: '*É pá*! Why you guys so dirty? Just because you're on holiday doesn't mean you don't have to wash.'

I looked around at my fellow travellers. The woman was right. Already we appeared rougher than when we'd crossed the border: an unwashed and unshaven lot, our clothes filthy from the mud bath. The vehicles also looked the part. Mike decided he'd pay parking attendants – who we knew would crowd around our vehicles in Maputo – *not* to wash the Landies. We were into the overlanding groove.

Hayley was wearing rather skimpy shorts and I noted that Alexander's guidebook had lots to say about appropriate attire for women. 'Portuguese men are ardent 'bird-watchers' – that is, they like to admire the passing parade of girls,' it commented coyly. 'But unlike the Italians they are not bottom-pinchers. While on the subject of posteriors, visiting girls should remember that although shorts are allowed on the beach they are taboo in town.' All that had changed and the only harassment Hayley seemed likely to pick up was from the odd tourist.

It was going to be a long wait for the ferry, so I found a place to sit on a stranded fishing boat and surveyed the bay so full of history. Portuguese maps originally referred to it as the Baía da Lagoa, the bay of the lagoons, because early navigators believed the rivers flowing into it originated from a large, inland lagoon. The British were responsible for corrupting this to Delagoa Bay, a name which so displeased the Portuguese that a law was passed in the 1920s prohibiting its use.

The bay of the lagoons was first properly explored by the Portuguese in the 1540s during the trading voyages of Lourenço Marques and it became apparent that the area would be fruitful for commerce. The bay – nowadays named after Chief Maputa, who governed the region when the Portuguese first landed here – was frequented by fishermen, farmers, ivory traders, and whalers who targeted cows returning each year to calve in the shallows. For a vast hinterland encompassing Zululand, Swaziland and what was the Transvaal, Delagoa Bay became a focus for trade and provided a link with the trans-oceanic world of Asia and Europe.

By the end of the 16th century Portuguese ships were calling here every year, often setting up temporary camps on Inhaca or Xefina islands from where they'd send boats venturing upriver to barter their wares. The sailor-merchants were after ivory, and offered in exchange beads and cloth, but ambergris, slaves, honey, rhino horns and the tusks and hoofs of hippopotamuses were also on the Portuguese shopping list. In the 17th century English and Dutch ships began muscling in and the three European contenders jostled for regional power. In 1721 a Dutch expedition landed in Delagoa Bay and rounded up 200 African women labourers to help build a fort. But the Hollanders suffered badly from fever (malaria) and their numbers dwindled. The following year English pirates attacked and razed the settlement. Although the Dutch rebuilt it, trade didn't produce the hoped-for riches and the pocket colony was abandoned in 1730.

The Austrian-Asiatic Company sponsored by Empress Maria Theresa – who also wanted a little piece of Africa, poor dear – established a fortified trading post here in 1778. Under the leadership of an Englishman, William Bolts, the stockade was given the grand name Imperial Encampment of Fort St Mary. But by now the Portuguese were losing patience with foreign interference. Bolts was sent packing by a military expedition in 1781 and the Portuguese established their first permanent settlement in the bay. They set up their post on the site of the abandoned Dutch stronghold, roughly the spot where Nossa Senhora da Conceição Fort now stands.

That initial, rudimentary stockade surrounded by swampland was the embryo of what was to become Lourenço Marques. Portuguese soldiers dreaded being posted here because of its isolation – more than 1 500 kilometres from the security of Moçambique Island – as well as the heat and tropical diseases. The place was fever ridden. Indeed, Afrikaner Voortrekker leader Louis Trichardt later died of malaria in a room inside the fort after his long trek from the highveld to the coast.

Although the town was harried by French corsairs during the Revolutionary wars and sacked by Dingane's Zulu impis, the Portuguese hung on grimly. With the formation of the Transvaal republic, Delagoa Bay took on renewed significance as the Boers' outlet to the sea, and eventually replaced Moçambique Island as capital.

But the British, intent on ruling the Indian Ocean waves, were never entirely comfortable about the Portuguese owning such a prize anchorage. In 1823 Commodore Owen raised the British flag on the south shores of the bay, near the spot where I was sitting, and his claim was reasserted in the 1860s in an attempt by the British to maintain paramountcy over the Transvaal Boers.

This led to a heated tiff between Britain and Portugal, which was finally settled by arbitration when French President MacMahon decided in favour of Portugal. So grateful were the Portuguese that they seem to have named every second street, building or *praça* after him. But the greatest honour accorded old MacMahon was to have Mozambique's most popular beer named after him: Dois M (Two Ms). MacMahon was obviously too much of a mouthful, especially after a Dois M or two. Or maybe it was only after a few Dois Ms that the Frenchman's name rolled easily off Luso-African lips.

We boarded a clap-trap ferry along with an assortment of unroadworthy vehicles and villagers bound for the city. Our lookout on the bridge wing took in life on the river. We watched as a beautiful woman with long braided hair came up the gangplank, a bucket brimming with prawns balanced in her head. Beside us a baby in a sling clung with both hands to the orb of his mother's breast, drinking greedily.

The ferry swung away from the Catembe shore in a shroud of bilge fumes and pointed its prow at the capital. Maputo is no longer the beautiful city of the history books and my family photo album, but from the ferry I could already make out renovations and new coats of paint since my last fleeting visit three years previously. Three pretty children in their Sunday best stood side by side, staring wide-eyed at the buildings. Out came my camera: in close, wide-angle, click.

The ferry had a gung-ho helmsman whose idea of mooring was alarmingly close to ramming. The vessel scraped the pier to the sound of tortured metal. Paging through Alexander later, I found some things hadn't changed:

> Our crowded ferry glanced off the pierhead as the skipper took her through the narrow entrance of the Doca da Capitania. On the return trip he grounded the craft on a mudbank just off Catembe jetty. Buckled guard-rails and chunks out of the concrete are evidence of occasional collisions suffered by this jetty.

Perhaps it was the same captain; more likely his son honouring a proud tradition.

As soon as bow and stern were secured passengers streamed ashore, disappearing into the lanes of *baixa* (downtown) or hopping into *chapas* (minibus taxis).

We made a hasty circuit of the city to give the two novices – Hayley and Tank – their first taste of the capital. Maputo was not in the brief for our overlanding story, but I had happy memories of my previous visit and wanted to look around. While writing the script for the documentary series about the East African dhow trade I had spent a weekend with the television team in Maputo interviewing historians. But it was really the night-clubs, opulent Polana and dhows themselves that excited us.

We drove through the city centre past the dive in which our TV crew had stayed. The company had rented an apartment on the top floor of the tallest skyscraper in Maputo, known as the Trinta-e-três and named after its 33 storeys. The lifts were broken and the lights in the stairwell had blown, so it was an agonising climb back home after a night on the town. The ascent was made more hazardous by the habit of residents using the steps as a toilet. On one occasion the elevator did actually work, but after a hell ride to the basement we vowed never to use it again. The lift car had no door and the crumbling fabric of the building hurtled past at stomach-churning speed. We bounced to a halt at a level that required us to climb out of this cunningly disguised coffin waiting for occupants.

Those were still early, post-war days and Maputo had looked devastated from the recent civil strife. The drive to the capital was in itself frightening. Ambushes were still a problem and burnt-out cars dotted the roadside. Every kilometre or so we'd come upon heavily-armed soldiers patrolling for bandits. We had foolishly accepted the producer's offer and borrowed his BMW. In *baixa* it was like a red rag to a herd of bulls. The street kids swarmed all over the thing. The trick was to break a piece off the vehicle and then sell it back to us a few hours later. It was no wonder local car owners used to have 'loose items' – headlights, hubcaps, number plates – soldered, riveted, glued or bolted down. Sometimes owners deliberately cracked the perspex to reduce their resale value.

When the Portuguese left in 1975, Lourenço Marques was, many claimed, the most beautiful city in Africa. But the settlers took everything with them. They cashed in what assets they could, threw their telephones into the harbour, emptied bank balances and loaded their cars with valuables. There were many instances of sabotage: cement poured into engines, buildings burnt and documents destroyed. If we can't have it, the *pretos* sure as hell can't either.

Tank swerved to avoid a *chapa* pulling into the traffic and narrowly missed another. '*É pá!*' he shouted, getting into the lingo and sporting his cheeky grin.

The whip around *baixa* was proving as treacherous as the elevator of the Trinta-e-três. But there were many improvements: sewage no longer ran in the streets, potholes had been filled in, electricity and running water were reinstated, and *salões* (sidewalk cafés) were opening everywhere. There was no mistaking the optimism of the Latin African city.

A left turn took us past the green-domed, Victorian station with its marble arches and wrought-iron work, the very spot my father stepped off the train more than half a century before. Then we drove through the small red-light district, the so-called 'Street of Trouble' in the old days, centred around Luso Striptease and adjacent Portuguese buildings – double storied and tiled – which reminded me of coastal villages north of Lisbon. There was that same sleepy feel – siesta-filled afternoons, the wail of fado singers, the sense of *saudades*, that peculiarly Lusitanian version of melancholy. We passed the red-stone fort where the remains of the last great Nguni chief, Gungunhana, are buried. The 'Lion of Gaza', as he was known, proved a powerful adversary, but was finally defeated by the Portuguese in 1895 after a series of bloody battles.

We headed along avenues Ho Chi Min, Mao Tse Tung and Vladimir Lenin. The old indunas would have frowned on the tide of free-market decadence sweeping the avenidas that bore their names. The Land Rovers crossed Praça da Independência to the white cathedral of Nossa Senhora da Conceição. The construction of the latter is shrouded in shame: apparently the authorities used to pick teenage girls off the street and have them examined to establish whether they were virgins. If not, they were labelled prostitutes and given the option of paying an exorbitant fine or providing labour for the cathedral construction site. I wonder if the fingering officials understood any of the ironies, this being the cathedral of Nossa Senhora, the head Virgin.

We cruised along the Marginal, Maputo's grand promenade punctuated with breezy palms and marinated in a rich yellow light; past the Feira Popular where, on my previous visit, I'd watched an unforgettable sex show. It was my friend Ross Douglas's 30th birthday and we were celebrating in one of the restaurants of the Feira when a teenage boy called Orlando sidled up to us and asked if we wanted to see a show.

'How much?' we asked.

'That depends,' he said. 'You want kung-fu or porno?'

'Porno,' we both said, without needing to consult. It was Ross's coming of age party after all.

Once we'd agreed on a price, the lad fetched his theatrical contraption: a cardboard box with the bottom removed. It had a proscenium arch and a backstage area in which he lit a candle. His tiny shadow theatre glowed and with a roll of drums and trumpet fanfare (produced by the boy without instruments) the protagonists – cut-out silhouettes of a man and woman – entered the scene. There followed a bedroom farce conducted in high-pitched, colourful Portuguese interspersed with steamy sex scenes. Orlando had the dialogue of rapturous 'oohs!' and 'aahs!' down pat. The conquistador's penis was half the size of the man who sported it and Dona Maria's orgasmic squeals drew a crowd to our table. Our rapturous encore elicited an implausible threesome during which Dona Maria's ostensibly jealous husband rather enjoyed it up the arse.

The Landies headed past the neo-Manueline Natural History Museum which houses a collection of elephant foetuses representing each stage of the animal's 22-month gestation period. Why, one wonders? If I were curator I'd be content with a few jars of snakes or the odd drawer of colourful butterflies with pins through their thoraxes (even that's a bit gruesome). But what on earth possesses someone to say to themselves: wow, 22 formalin jars stuffed with baby elephants will make a smashing exhibit?

We refuelled at the petrol station beside Sir Herbert Baker's majestic wedding cake and site of my brother's coming into the world, the Polana Hotel. Tank and Rob shooed away the rag-wielding car washers, and tried to discourage the over-priced wooden trinket sellers. 'If you want diesel, ask for *gasóleo*, not *gasolina*, which is petrol,' cautioned Mike as the attendant filled the vehicles. 'The worst would be to ask for *petróleo* – paraffin. I've seen guys make that mistake coupla times!'

Then out of town through bustling *favelas* and onto the EN1 (*Estrada Nacional* 1), the great north road which was to take us to Beira. Fumes and smoke from fires hung in the air and doused the sun. The headlights of approaching vehicles probed the gloom. After a shaky patch of dodgem driving we pulled up at Casa Lisa, a wayside motel run by South Africans, where the car park sported a few boat-trailing 4x4s. Owner Paul Hallows was behind the bar regaling a pod of ample-bellied fishermen about how bad publicity 'back home' could knock the area. 'Floods, droughts, corruption, hijackings are all reported with glee in Sith Efrican newspapers and the result is that tourists stay away. It's criminal what those bleddy journalists do to us,' he railed.

The ruby-faced boatmen at the Casa Lisa bar looked relieved at having made it from Komatipoort to another South African Safe Haven without incident, and before nightfall. Tomorrow would be their last leg to Bilene or Praia do Xai-Xai, Guinjata or Barra – names that had been lodged like grails in their highveld minds for months. You couldn't fault their excitement, just the occasional sailor-on-shore-leave behaviour.

It was soot black when we crept into Bilene, known to old timers as the holiday paradise of San Martino, a resort town on the shores of

Uembje Lagoon. Long before that, it had been the residence of the Gaza king, Soshangane. The Gaza monarchy was the most powerful Nguni state in Mozambique and its raiding parties exacted tribute from as far north as the Portuguese *prazos* on the Zambezi and inland as far as Zimbabwe and South Africa's Limpopo Province. Its army's structure was similar to that of the Zulus with warriors divided into age-group regiments. In the 1830s Soshangane chose Bilene as the location for his royal household and place for his burial. In the tradition of Soshangane, Mozambique's current leader, President Chissano, has a residence there.

It wasn't going to be easy finding Praia do Sol in the dark, so we flagged down a boy on an antiquated BMX bicycle and asked for directions. 'Follow me, amigos,' he said and pedalled ahead, using our beams to guide him as he weaved between bushes, splashed through puddles and dismounted to shoulder his 1x2 over boulders.

'Sorry we're so late. We got way-laid in Maputo, stopped at Casa Lisa for a drink …' Dave started what was becoming a habitual litany before we'd even stopped the vehicle in Praia do Sol's driveway.

'*Boa tarde* and don't worry,' said manager Leo, who'd been waiting for us at the bar. 'Let me show you ous around the place before dinner.' Water lapped a moonlit beach lined with casuarinas. Hobie cats waited on the shore like seabirds with folded wings. Our tents were tucked under trees behind a dune and the ablutions were unpatriotically spotless.

'This place is awesome,' said Tank as we unpacked. 'I'll just stay here for the next fortnight then. You lot can pick me up on your way home.'

'It's a local fish – tastes just like barracuda,' said Leo from behind the bar as we dug into platteland-size plates of fish. A bunch of boitjies stood resting their boeps against the counter and talking about fish size and breast size. They'd long since kicked down the inhibition barrier. The music wasn't helping. Leo's tape deck oozed a string of come-sit-with-me-by-the-fire-baby songs.

'I bet the next song's going to be "Careless Whisper" by Wham,' I said. To my utter amazement, I guessed correctly. The others just stared, mouths full of fish, like I was some kind of psychic psycho. I did feel a bit queer. As though I'd brushed the supernatural or swallowed a fish scale.

When our band headed for bed, Hayley got some bleary, unmitigated stares. The DJ was playing an old singles-bar classic with a desperate chorus that goes something like, 'I don't care who you are, where you're from, as long as you love me.' Judging by the thrust of conversation at the bar, the song's sentiment was being interpreted as something more along the lines of: 'I don't care how you smell, whether you still have teeth, as long as you bonk me.'

The dome tent was snug as a womb and Jennifer seemed only a breath away. She'd been knocking around in my head all day and the cheesy music had only made matters worse. Would I swap this journey, or even all journeys, for her bed, I fretted? Maybe, probably? Heck, I didn't know what was what anymore.

Next morning Leo was at the helm of the barge and the sun had just lifted from a duvet of cloud. It looked and felt just like Knysna on the Garden Route – the lagoon, the light, the headland were the image of the southern Cape lakeland. 'It's the inshore counter-currents of the Mozambique Channel that create these lagoons and dunes,' said Leo as we slid across Uembje's mirror. The bow of the barge bit into the beach and we ran across the sand bar to where the ocean chided the shore with a cuffing break. Ours were the only prints on an interminable strand. At one end of the lagoon, beneath a golden cliff, fishermen aboard the rowing boat *Cuidado* (take care) unpicked crabs from their net.

'Unfortunately these ous are indiscriminate in what they haul out: morays, lion fish, you name it,' said Leo. Like most of the lodge owners and managers, he had a fiercely protective attitude to the threatened wilderness – both marine and terrestrial – of Mozambique.

Soon mango and russet-coloured cashew trees, the latter imported by the early Portuguese from Brazil, were again flashing by. A man waved a pair of live chickens by their claws at us. The things flapped pathetically. We saw a sign for Zongoene, a posh resort. Its glossy brochure had landed on my in-tray some months earlier, so we took the turn off and drove a long, lush track down to the coast. The road curled across the alluvial grasslands and marshes of the Limpopo River flood plain, soon to be under water in the next summer's catastrophic floods. Subsistence farmers were everywhere at work delving in the rich soil. The fringes of the plain were strung with huts shaded by palm and banana groves, a scene that could hardly have changed much in centuries.

In 1891 the lower reaches of the Limpopo witnessed a curious episode of colonial folly. Cecil John Rhodes – that artful rogue – had sniffed an outlet to the Indian Ocean for the landlocked country that bore his name. In order to obtain concessions from, and a treaty with, the Gaza king, Gungunhana, Rhodes sent a 100-ton steamer, *Countess of Carnarvon*, up the Limpopo with a gift of rifles and ammunition. But the Portuguese despatched a gunboat, ordered the vessel to lower its red ensign and escorted it back to LM. After a diplomatic dustup Rhodes was forced to abandon his interest in the area.

Three years later Portuguese paranoia about Gungunhana had reached such a pitch that Governor-General António Ennes sent a force to capture the king and crush his Shangaan impis. Gungunhana was the last surviving independent African monarch in southern Africa and the Portuguese were determined to follow the example of the British South Africa Company, whose troops had successfully crushed the Ndebele in 1893. A force of 2 000 men, many armed with machine guns, marched on the Gaza armies while an armed flotilla entered the Limpopo in an outflanking move.

When Gungunhana, the Lion of Gaza, was finally run to ground at Chaimite, he was put on board a Limpopo gunboat, destined to be paraded through the streets of Lisbon – the lion tamed. Then exile and death in the Azores. Ironically, the gunboat carrying Gungunhana passed the *Countess of Carnarvon*, now flying Portuguese colours, which carried orders from Ennes not to risk capturing Gungunhana lest failure cause a setback in public morale.

Zongoene's thatched chalets rose from manicured lawns like the prows of ships. The river muscled past the front of the lodge, built from mahogany, and swung between dunes towards the ocean. We entered the 'court' beneath a thatch archway, with the TDi behind. Suddenly we heard a bristly crunch, a few shouts and the sound of an engine in quick reverse. The roof-top tent had got jammed and the thatched eaves looked like ruffled feathers. None of the staff had noticed, so the TDi was quietly parked out of harm's way and its occupants strolled nonchalantly into the lobby a few minutes later.

I gave the others 15 minutes to have a swim or cold drink or whatever, and did the journo reconnoitre, jotting and shooting on the hoof. What looked like Maputo's 'in' set were lounging round the pool. Loads of pendant gold. After completing my circuit I found the others on the front lawn staring at the river. 'Why didn't you guys have a dip to cool off?' I asked incredulously.

'Sharks,' said Hayley disappointedly.

'And crocs,' added Tank.

'Oh.'

Later I was told that sharks had been spotted more than 100 kilometres upstream. Some people even claimed that alleged crocodile attacks far in the interior were in fact the work of sharks. What a nasty combination. Where I come from, the most menacing thing about rivers is their temperature. At Zongoene, river swimming was obviously a no-no, so guests had to take boats or quad bikes to the beach for bathing. However, most of them didn't look like the energetic type. We looked longingly at them. We were all dying for a brightly coloured drink with an umbrella in it and an hour or two to work on our suntans, but the clock was ticking ... and there were 8 000 kilometres still to cover.

Chapter 3

Monotonous northing ... we crossed the Limpopo's suspension bridge where naked children chanced their luck with the crocs; then down to Praia do Xai-Xai. The resort has legendary status with misty-eyed old timers in Johannesburg bars. Alexander's guidebook had also fuelled my imagination:

> Xai-Xai (pronounced 'shi-shi') is one of the loveliest beaches in Africa. Golden sands, a long coral reef barely 180 metres offshore, and calm, limpid blue water against a backdrop of lush tropical vegetation, combine to make Xai-Xai a dream resort.

Not only is Alexander's pronunciation iffy (it's 'shy-shy'), but when I got there I failed to see the attraction. The place was architecturally challenged and the beach looked uninspiring. The caravan park was empty; along the beachfront groups of listless teenagers went through the motions of flirting.

As we chugged through the scruffy town Mike held forth on the area's less tangible assets: 'The African Pentecostal Church conducts the most bizarre rituals just south of here. They hold baptism ceremonies at a tidal pool fed by an underwater tunnel – a place they call "Jordan". The priests dress in bright, Catholic robes and wear amulets made from herbs and animal entrails. They dunk initiates under water, then pour chicken blood over them. Apparently this cleanses you. For instance, it makes a widow shipshape for the next marriage.'

My, how African religions placed their prints in the spoor left by Christianity ... and Islam for that matter. Traditional beliefs were mixed in with the imported faiths. In this way ancestors became transmogrified into saints in the Mozambican spiritual cauldron and pagan rituals found a home in the Church (nothing new there).

We pulled up at Mike's favourite restaurant, Golfinho Azul, the blue dolphin. Marine murals adorned the walls and Angolan pop music bubbled over onto the deck where we found a spot in the shade of an awning. Waves licked the reef-line beyond the shallows. Two teenagers in Rio-style bikinis watched a group of lads keep a soccer ball suspended between them. Chests, heads, thighs, feet. Shouting, bravado, stolen glances.

The scantily clad girls got me thinking about the former name for Xai-Xai: Praia de Sepulveda. When the galleon *São João* was wrecked on South Africa's Wild Coast in 1552, Dona Leonor Sepulveda was cast away along with her Portuguese nobleman husband, their three children and hundreds of others. Knowing that a Portuguese trading vessel called at Inhaca Island once a year, Dom Sepulveda decided to footslog it northward, leading the band of survivors. After an arduous journey up the KwaZulu-Natal coast they reached Inhaca only to find that the packet had already called.

Despite the fact that his party was almost at the end of its tether, Sepulveda urged them to press on to Mozambique Island, a march of more than 1 500 kilometres. Chief Inhaca warned the *dom* of a hostile king in the region of Xai-Xai, but they set off regardless. Sure enough, near the spot where we were enjoying lunch, the band was waylaid and ordered to hand over arms and possessions. The warriors, so the story goes, stripped the Portuguese of their clothes. Dona Leonor was so ashamed of her nakedness in the presence of commoners that she buried herself up to her neck in sand and refused to take another step. There she remained until she died. Many others were murdered and only a tiny group eventually reached Moçambique Island.

The story of the *São João* is typical of many other wrecks along this coast. South of Inhambane the shoreline becomes increasingly treacherous, with barren stretches pounded by surf and few natural harbours. The monsoon winds of the tropics give way to the gales of the Southern Ocean. Portuguese carracks often left Goa late in the season, having hung on for the best pepper cargoes. Ship design – basically great cockleshells with high fore- and stern-castles – did not develop to keep pace with the increased tonnage. The replica caravel I crewed on in 1987 from Portugal to South Africa was 125 tons and sturdily built, while some of the 16th-century Indiamen were over 2 000 tons, undermanned and rotting from teredo worm. The ships were overloaded by avaricious captains, rudders came adrift in heavy blows, top-heavy masts had to be cut down in storms and, although often built of India teak, the ships usually leaked badly. To make matters worse, cargo cluttered the decks, preventing efficient handling of the rig, while below, pepper clogged the pumps.

In the heavy seas off southern Africa carracks frequently foundered and the harrowing accounts of survivors who sometimes spent months walking the beaches of the subcontinent bear testimony to folly and greed. Their tales, often compiled by professional writers back in Lisbon, form some of the most compelling accounts that we have of conditions in contemporary south-east Africa. They are similar to the great shipwreck yarns of the English tradition, like the first-hand accounts by castaways that inspired classics such as *The Tempest* and *Robinson Crusoe*.

'Are you going to Scarborough fair? Parsley, sage, rosemary and thyme.' Simon and Garfunkel – ubiquitous in Mike's tape box – sang us out of the valley and up to the EN1 through a world which would, in a few months, be underwater and filling world television screens. Clouds slid overhead and the light went liquid amber as we coasted through Mozambique's lakeland, the topography bearing witness to millennia of geological confusion as the coastline advanced and receded, creating dunes, lakes and islands. At Chidenguele we took a winding sand track down to the beach where we found lovely cottages, landscaped on a dune in a garden of cycads. The beach was wild and coursed with tyre tracks, testimony to the fact that South African holiday makers thereabouts paid scant regard to the restriction on beach driving. To hell with the crabs, nesting turtles and seabirds.

Onward. Lake Inhampavala was invigorated by late afternoon sunlight, its shores lined with lush vegetation. Quissico passed in gloom, Inharrime in darkness. Then there were only the speedometer, odometer and occasional item snared in the beams for distraction on the road to Inhambane. It was late when we reached the region's vast coconut-palm groves and took the turnoff to Guinjata Bay, our destination for the night. The road disappeared into a sea of stems and Tank and Rob slewed the vehicles through slippery sand. It was endless and mesmerising, like being trapped in some demented computer game, doomed to course through dodging trees forever. In the end, it began to look as if the palms were moving and we were stationary.

The kitchen was long closed when we drew up at the restaurant and lobby of Guinjata, but Dave talked the staff into rustling up a mountain of *camarões* (prawns) and a few frosty Manicas. We settled in the bar where long-liner buoys and nets from pirate Chinese and Japanese trawlers were strung up like trophies.

'When someone spots an unlit trawler sneaking inshore under cover of night, the locals gather on the beach and launch the boats,' the bar tender explained in Portuguese I could just understand. 'We go to the spots where the trawlers have sown their long-lines and cut the buoys free, letting the line and hooks sink to the bottom. Sometimes we bring back a few scalps for the bar.' He gestured to the décor. '*Porra*, we're hardly Greenpeace, but I think we're just as effective.'

We woke at dawn in a thatched hut above the sweep of beautiful Jangamo Bay. The sun was just making an entrance and lithe lads were suiting up, grabbing spear guns and heading for the point. We joined a bunch of early risers, all hastening for the water.

I could make out a circle of Chope, a tribe of the region, wading waist deep in the shallows – like some kind of trance dance to issue in the new day. Upon closer inspection I saw that the men were beating the water with sticks, driving fish into the heart of their circle. As the tide receded the fish were trapped in shallow rock pools. One man stripped bark from a branch and tossed it in the water. He wrapped more of the vegetable matter on a spear and rammed it into the crevasses where small fish were hiding. Soon the bark's poison began to take effect and silver ingots floated belly up to be harvested. The rest, inedible creatures and a mound of tiny tropical fish, bobbed in the shallows or were stranded to rot.

Further up the beach a man wheeled a microlight onto the hard sand. I strolled over and introduced myself.

'Want to get some lekker photos from the air?' said Ben Cilliers in a thick Afrikaans accent, even before I had a chance to ask. Ben was from Hazyview, a part of the game-rich lowveld that I'm particularly partial to, and he looked like he knew what he was about. This was a helpful conclusion for me to have arrived at so rapidly because I'm a nervous flier. Even the 'fasten your seat belts' and 'stow your tray tables' announcements make me uneasy. And when the flight attendant pretends to drop the oxygen mask, then smiles blandly as she places it over her nose and mouth, my imagination runs riot. In my mind I practice the aisle dash, removal of high heels, slide into icy ocean blue with whistle clenched in my teeth. My job finds me on dodgy aircraft flying out of grass or gravel runways around the continent – something I'm never comfortable with. My fear wasn't wholly unfounded. The previous year fellow journalist Patrick Wagner was killed along with four other *Getaway* associates in a light-aircraft crash while coming in to land in Nairobi.

So I don't easily take to the air. But it was windless and Ben ran his hand along the wing in a manner that inspired confidence. He was a big man with a gentle touch.

'Come for a flip, man. The coast here is so bleddy beautiful,' said Ben. 'The developers haven't buggered it up yet.'

Bug-eyed goggles in place, I felt like a baby mosquito strapped to mother as we buzzed along the sand. Then, with surprising acceleration, we rocketed skyward and in an instant Hayley, Tank and Rob were reduced to tiny inter-tidal creatures. It was a startling sensation. There hadn't been time to get nervous.

Guinjata's thatch chalets were huddled behind a dune and beyond them were palms, blanketed to the horizon. To the south lay Lighthouse Reef and the green promontory of Cabo das Correntes. Beneath us I could make out the sinuous shapes of bottlenose dolphins breaking the surface in synchronised dips, a lone shark on patrol and the glint of game fish catching the low rays as they rode the crests.

'Hey, Justin, look there!' shouted Ben. He pointed to port and there was just time to see a turtle, disturbed by our noise, dive with a splash. 'Man, isn't that something!' he howled.

'Fantastic,' I shouted back, hardly able to contain my excitement.

Dark Indian blue bent eastward to starboard. The shallows were rich emerald. When we swept lower, the coral reefs spooled kaleidoscopically through the colour and light spectrums. My flying fears were back there somewhere, doing their ritual jig, but the spectacle kept them at bay. Having been rewarded with turtle and dolphin, I felt we were on a winning streak and kept my eyes alert for elusive dugong, those strange herbivorous, seal-like creatures (of the family *Sirenia*, referring to the sirens of Greek legend) thought by early mariners to be mermaids. This misinterpretation is partially attributed to the fact that dugongs suckle their live-born young from teats on the mother's 'chest'. But no luck. Alas, trawler lines and nets have cleared these parts of comely babes with fishy nethers.

On the trail once again. Hayley sat at the wheel of the TDi and Mike was back-seat driving. It was a tricky stretch of road that threaded between palms. Deep sand ruts made steering difficult. 'Take it easy, Hayley. Let the thing drive itself. Just let it go with the tracks,' cautioned Mike. 'C'mon don't fight it!'

I could see Hayley was struggling, but largely with irritation at Mike. On one sharp corner she let the Landy slide from the tracks and nearly scraped a palm. 'That's it!' she snapped, slamming on the breaks. 'I'm not driving this damn thing anymore.' She was flushed and angry. Mike took the wheel.

At my feet was a gash in the cliff's side. Nearby stood the remnants of a vandalised socialist monument, its freedom fist having disappeared. 'This crevice was once a torture-chamber-cum-execution cave,' said Nick Tasioulas, owner of Turtle Cove Lodge. Far below in the gloom was a patch of sand washed by waves. It was low tide and, driven by morbid curiosity, I asked if we could climb down the chimney's ladder to examine the cell.

'Victims of Portuguese kangaroo courts and enemies of the state – Frelimo guys – used to be thrown in here,' said Nick as we descended. 'When the tide came in, they'd be bashed against the rocks. They're like knife edges.'

It was a place of evil, a site to raise the hairs on the back of your neck. Crouching in the back corner I tried to imagine what it would be like at night with a big swell running. The chamber would be flooded with water dashing the captives against the roof and walls, then suddenly drained to leave them stranded, awaiting the next wave. 'Apparently, if you dig around you can still find the odd femur or skull,' Nick offered.

'Let's get out of here,' I said.

Nick is a surfer who worked the barrels of Tofo's point break long enough to set down roots and finally opened a backpacker's joint at a spot that's become legendary with the young trekking fraternity. We headed back up the hill towards Turtle Cove passing fishermen perched on rock ledges. Pausing on Tofinho promontory, Nick pointed to the take-off spot. 'When it works, this is an absolutely classic break,' he said. 'Clean, smoking tubes, man! Do you surf?'

'Yup, love it,' I said.

'Ah, should'a been here yesterday, bru. Six foot and no-one about – you'd've had the wave to yourself.'

It was the old story and I didn't want to hear it. How many times had I arrived a day too late. The tale of my surfing life.

Turtle Cove sits under a canopy of palms and we found our huts in a clearing behind the main, outdoor activity area. Laid-back young folk lounged about, playing drums, backgammon, or braiding each other's hair. Above the bar were photos of Tofinho going off – it looked like Hawaii or J Bay. There were surfboards stacked on exposed beams and boogie boards piled against reed walls. A couple of lodge dogs lay at the bar and Tank suggested we photograph them. 'How 'bout a book about the lodge dogs of Mozambique?' he joked. Bright capulanas served as table cloths and a cat lay curled on a wicker sofa. An overlander in tie-dye shorts scratched its ear while puffing on a joint.

'I've planned a bit of a full-moon party for tonight – kind of to celebrate you lot being here,' said Nick. 'Should be a gas. We'll start with a seafood buffet at around seven.'

'Cool,' we said in unison. The mood was catching.

Early evening found me at palm-tree height on the star-gazing sofa atop a wooden scaffold. I was peering through fronds at the strange assortment of guests materialising out of the foliage. The sofa was an ideal spot to chill out with a companion, preferably a romantic one. Green nuts hung like testicles suspended beside me and mauve clouds coursed overhead. The fronds sighed. Reggae music throbbed from somewhere beneath a *makuti* (dried palm frond) roof punctured by palm stems. As the light drained I started to feel a touch sorry for myself. My thoughts were filled with Jennifer and how badly I wanted her to be on this trip, to be there in the palm fronds with me. It was beginning to ache. I didn't wait for the moon and clambered down the over-sized ladder rungs to join the others.

Hayley and I got talking to some of the travellers at the bar. One guest had been at Turtle Cove a month waiting for a spare part for his boat, and didn't seem in a hurry to leave.

'It's coming on a ship from Durbs. Who knows when it'll get here,' he confided between drags. The barman was a similar case. 'I came here six months ago to surf. The water was warm, the wave glassy and consistent. So I stayed.' Tank was sitting on the sofa chatting to a bunch of surf rats up from Amanzimtoti. He looked in his element in his board shorts, strops, surfer T-shirt and sunglasses perched on top of his head.

Nick called me into his open-air kitchen where chefs were cooking over coals. Dozens of fat prawns sizzled in frying pans. The things were unnaturally orange and looked succulent. 'These are my famous peri-peri *camarões*,' he said with a flourish. 'I learnt the recipe from a Mozambican sailor, and no, it's a secret.'

Over drinks I met Alison, a young American with blonde dreadlocks who was travelling through Mozambique, living on mangoes and positive vibes and learning Portuguese from a string of lovers. The flavour of the day was an ace coconut harvester. She was like from New York and 'doing' Africa: really digging it. A vision of a slightly altered Jennifer, or rather the things that irritated me about Jennifer, flashed before me. It was disconcerting. And Alison talked too much. A naive, credulous drone – probably mildly doped – pitched at a level that, over time, can drive a hole in your head like a gentle jackhammer.

Suddenly Jenny was there, almost palpable. I registered a deep longing, but felt her Northernness acutely. 'I can't make South Africa my home, Justin,' she'd say in her husky, emphatic way. 'You know that my base will have to be London or New York.'

'But my roots are here!' I'd say accusatorily, not completely sure what or where 'here' meant. Her words in my head tore anew at my heart. It was as if our angry conflicts only served to heighten the passion I felt for her.

Pre-dinner drinks were getting raucous and backpackers were putting away *cervejas* as well as some more dubious local brews at a prodigious rate. Compared to what I'd read about alcohol abuse, it seemed the boot was now on the other foot. In the old days it was the locals of Inhambane district who were known for inordinate consumption. Bootleg liquor was apparently a big problem. Villagers distilled moonshine from any plant that could serve the purpose – pineapples, mangoes, cashew nuts, cassava, sugar-cane.

Governor Ennes, writing in the 1890s, called the cashew a tree of vice and ruin: 'In the season of this accursed fruit when the atmosphere is poisoned by the resinous odours of the fat jugs displayed in the markets and in the taverns, native labourers leave the hoe, carriers abandon their loads, servants flee their masters, soldiers and sailors desert. Vagrancy and saturnalia continue so long as the supplies of drink last. When they begin to be scarce, they command higher prices than that of the best port wine!' He seemed to be as indignant about this last point as he was about the bacchanalian goings on.

Over a rowdy supper – a three-course affair of prawns, prawns and prawns – I was regaled with Alison's experience of this 'ah-some continent'. She'd been trekking through southern Africa for months and had recently lost her sister at Praia do Xai-Xai. Well, not exactly lost: they'd both been swept across reef by a 'tidal wave' and been badly cut up, her sibling worse than she. The sister would convalesce while Alison pushed on. They were to meet the following day, or thereabouts, in Vilankulo. Given the distance still to cover, Alison was way behind schedule. The Lotus-land of Turtle Cove and the lures of a coconut brandishing paramour had obviously set her back.

'Do you think you guys could give me a ride north tomorrow?' she asked. 'I'd be sooo grateful.'

'I don't know if my boss would approve, um, you see it's a sponsored vehicle and all that. But I'll chat to the others and let you know in the morning,' I said as non-committally as possible. But her effusive thank yous rendered the ride a virtual *fait accompli*.

Nick had organised a group of Chope dancers to perform for us after dinner. The air was thick with the scent of rain and, as the women began swirling before us, the stars were doused by clouds. It was not a form of dance we were familiar with. Most of the group kept time with clapping and hypnotic chanting while a few spun like whirling dervishes, driving themselves into a virtual trance. It felt as though the audience were completely excluded, seldom even acknowledged by the dance leader and MC.

The performance became more and more frenetic, the air increasingly heady. A young woman was spiralling out of control, a baby tied to her back wide-eyed but silent. It seemed certain the child would sustain whiplash injuries, such was the ferocity of the spinning, but never a peep. As long as they're strapped to mother, babies will endure almost anything. She lost her epicentre and appeared destined to land in the fire or among the seated guests, but two older women leaped forward to grab the dancer and twirled her back into the fold. Then a new set of tops were spun into life.

Suddenly there was a flash and a loud explosion. The firmament opened. We scrambled for shelter as the ground turned to mud before our eyes. Although some revellers tried valiantly to keep the party going, it was clear the rain would get the better of festivities. Even Bob Marley cranked up full volume on the ghetto blaster couldn't drown the downpour's din. Things were not, it appeared, going to be as saturnalian as Nick had hoped. Perhaps cashew wine was the missing ingredient.

Next morning, Alison's departure was difficult: lingering moments with Mr Nuts – showered kisses, fingertip parting. Then she joined the leading Landy. 'Thanks, you guys. This is so neat!' she said as she tossed in her rucksack and climbed aboard the TDi. First we headed north along Inhambane Peninsula where Dave wanted to look in on the folks at Barra Lodge, a place he'd spent a memorable assignment. The resort is on a long sandy spit surrounded by coconut groves.

'I had some awesome dives at Barra,' said Dave. 'Deep Forest, a reef at a depth of 34 metres. Superb. The gullies and overhangs were packed with moray eels and some enormous tropical crayfish. If only we could chill out here a bit.'

While we were looking at rooms for an update in the mag, Alison found herself a pair of local boys who were, when we joined them 20 minutes later, transfixed by her breasts (she had, I noticed, dispensed with a brassiere, for which the teenagers were obviously grateful). She was valiantly trying to practise her new Portuguese phrases on them, but their attention kept dipping. Rob had to lean on the hooter to drag her from her new friends. 'Why can't she get with the programme?' he muttered.

Our other New Yorker represented a very different breed from Alison and the well-to-do, Jewish yuppie in him was railing against the loose-cannon nature of the woman's undiscriminating pluralism, her pretentious heterodoxy. I could see Rob was keeping his distance and I felt a little guilty about letting her join us.

On the way into Inhambane we passed signs for a number of new developments and evidence of foreign investment in the area. *'Pas op*, the South Africans are coming!' I said and expressed my fear that the barbarian element among our compatriots could easily destroy the fragile ecology of a peninsula such as this one.

'Last time I was up here I went sailing with David Law, the owner of Barra Lodge,' said Dave, his khaki cap pushed back on his head. 'He told me that only five years ago these beaches were untouched. But now 4x4 tracks scar the sand, get-rich-quick poachers are stripping the reefs of shells and tropical fish, and freezer-loads of catches are being hauled back to Gauteng by overzealous anglers.'

'Gawd, that's awful,' interjected Alison.

'But Law said the government was bent on protecting the coast round here and he felt they were getting there, albeit slowly,' said Dave.

Inhambane – home town to Graça Machel, former wife of President Samora Machel and now married to Nelson Mandela – began inauspiciously with a graveyard of vehicles destroyed during the war. Town folk used to try to run the gauntlet of Renamo ambushes – with little success, it seemed. Some were bullet-holed, others had triggered mines or simply rusted away in the years of fuel rationing. In those days, Renamo bandits could turn your Sunday outing to visit granny in a nearby village into a life-threatening event. But the town itself, when we reached its heart, was unscarred. A piece of 18th-century Portugal.

Inhambane was probably the southernmost point of Arab trade settlements at the time the Portuguese arrived in the Indian Ocean. Although the peninsula fell outside the reach of monsoon navigation, there is evidence of extensive oceanic trade, and cotton was being grown here for textile production long before the Portuguese arrived. Probably since as early as the beginning of the last millennium Shirazi (Persian) and later Arab traders had visited Inhambane Bay exchanging items such as cloth, salt and beads for slaves, ivory and gold.

The first permanent European settlement dates from 1727 when a Portuguese vessel found a Dutch ship, the *Victoria*, trading with Tonga chiefs. The commander sent a message to the fort at Sofala calling for military reinforcements in order to teach the locals a lesson for consorting with foreigners. After a march of more than 400 kilometres Commander Rebello's force set to work: chiefs were executed, villagers rounded up and killed or sold into slavery, cattle were confiscated, huts and farmland set on fire. The usual thing.

Henceforward there was a continuous Portuguese 'presence' in the bay. A fort of earth and stakes was built, then a church and a few houses for the *mestiços* (half-caste Afro-Portuguese) and Christian blacks who formed the garrison. Inhambane became an important commercial centre, particularly for slaves and ivory, and attracted a growing number of Indian settlers, often trading from their 'mother houses' on Ilha.

Our contact in town was Richard Bartlett, who ran a backpackers lodge on the shorefront promenade. We found Richard out back chatting to some German tourists.

'So where's the dugong biltong and Dois M beers?' exclaimed Mike, holding out his hand to Richard.

The proprietor was a short, bearded man, thirty-something, soft spoken and burning with enthusiasm for his adopted town. 'I'm from Joeys, but after visiting here and falling in love with the place, I came back to start the backpackers lodge a couple of years ago,' he said.

'My passion for things Portuguese started a decade ago when I studied Portuguese literature at UCT. I became fascinated with Mozambique through the writing,' he said.

'Not with Carlos?!' I exclaimed.

'Yes! How did you know?' asked Richard.

It transpired that both of us had studied under the urbane Portuguese lecturer, Carlos da Silva, at the University of Cape Town back in the '80s. Richard had concentrated on literature, while I had muddled through the basic language course.

'It was Carlos who inspired me to read enough Mozambican literature to end up editing a collection of stories translated into English,' he said with his back to me, rifling a bookshelf behind him. He handed me a copy of his *Short Stories from Mozambique* which was to be my bed-time reading for the rest of the trip.

'Now I want to write something on Inhambane. It's such a fascinating place – the cultural centre of Mozambique. But come, let me take you guys on a quick whip through the old quarter.'

As we strode round the esplanade, Richard explained: 'The EN1 bypasses Inhambane and goes inland 30 kays west of here. The authorities effectively cut the town off and it's been left to rot. Which is, if you're conservation conscious, not a bad thing. It's laid back and sleepy and most of the old buildings haven't been messed up.'

We passed mosques, curious pavement sculptures and elegant, decrepit Portuguese villas. I couldn't believe how spotless everything was: the cleanest town in Africa. No doubt prosperity will bring the dreaded plastic bag. A former colonial hotel was roofless with trees growing in the rooms. An old man, semi-toothed, greeted us warmly at reception. Some of the buildings even showed neo-Manueline influences, that magnificent late-Gothic style incorporating nautical and colonial themes developed during the time of the discoveries.

Wandering through the back streets we came upon a statue of Vasco da Gama (which formerly adorned the main square at the foot of Avenida da República) surrounded by broken machinery and a rusting Model-T Ford. The explorer was staring intently at a pile of rubble – vestiges of the colonial legacy he has left us.

It was somewhere on this stretch of coast, probably near Inharrime, that Da Gama landed on 10 January 1498, marking the start of Portuguese presence in Mozambique. He was well received by the inhabitants, people wearing copper ornaments in their hair and carrying daggers with tin scabbards and ivory handles. Da Gama named the place *terra da boa gente*, land of the good people. At least he got that right. A pity their reward would be centuries of slavery, or versions thereof.

Further on we came to the railway station. 'Until recently the ticket seller still worked here, collecting his salary every month from some ossified bureaucratic agency that didn't realise a train hadn't reached

Inhambane in over a decade,' said Richard. 'Sadly the old boy is no longer with us ... gone to sell tickets at the great station in the sky.'

The building was immaculate, its platform neat and ready for the next train from Inharrime. A cluster of what looked like would-be commuters sat on benches. After a tortuous haggle with a station official, Richard obtained permission for us to look around the railway yard – as long as no pictures were taken. Richard led us between rows of rusted rolling stock – carriage after derelict carriage – eyed by railway security personnel. We hadn't seen this level of protection since the president's residence in Maputo.

The rust created abstract patterns over bodywork. I hauled myself up into one of the coaches only to find that the floors had rotted away revealing tracks beneath my feet. When I raised a camera someone started shouting from 50 metres away and I quickly pouched the Nikon.

Rob drew back the sliding door of a huge hangar and we peered into the darkness. There was a hollow hammering sound coming from within. We stepped into the gloom and waited for our eyes to adjust. The sight that exposed itself out of the acid darkness was astonishing.

So this was the 'military secret': a Victorian locomotive workshop of startling proportions. The centre piece was a steam engine propped up on stocks, its wheels – gleaming with the glint of loving polish – laid out and ready to be reassembled. Grease-covered men were discernible in the deeper shadows. Some had stopped their hammering or welding, and were staring at us with hostile looks. Others continued without glancing up. Where was Dickens? Where was H G Wells? Rob and Dave had those hungry eyes photographers get when thwarted.

The narrow-gauge line from Inharrime to Inhambane was completed in 1912 and in the early seventies the line, despite having been superseded by road transport, still retained the loyal support of the locals. The 'Inhambane Flyer' was fuelled by logs and, far from what its name promised, would make unscheduled stops so that the driver could fell wayside trees for fuel.

As we tramped back to the station Richard told us about Inhambane's railway school (designed by my 'uncle' Pancho Guedes, I later discovered), explaining that these men were keeping their engines ready for the day the line re-opened. What Sisyphus-like dedication! Surely if the Inhambane line was ever re-instated it would be with modern locomotives and these old steam engines would be destined for the scrap-heap. You didn't want to think about the trauma to those railwaymen when their engines were hauled away.

The most striking thing about it was that during a long period of civil war, when almost everything in the country had gone to pot and most public services had ceased to exist, these men had kept their engines ready. They'd held back the chaos, the forces of disintegration, in the only way they could. In its own way, theirs had been a heroic defence.

We wended our way to the harbour along Avenida Revolução past Restaurant Tic Tic (the best fish and chips in Mozambique, Mike assured us), the *machimbombo* (bus) terminus and Grafico Sul do Save, the old printing press. 'The guys here still use presses dating back to the 1940s,' said Richard. 'Each character is fixed on brass blocks by hand.' I could just imagine editor Bristow's eyes light up: 'That be nothing! When I were a junior journalist we carved every character with our teeth …' Etc.

Back at the waterfront I scaled the clock tower of the 200-and-something-year-old Cathedral of Our Lady of the Conception. On the lower levels you had to hold your breath as the basement was being used as a public toilet. Someone had also defecated, with considerable dexterity and a good aim I imagine, on the rungs of the ladder, making the ascent hazardous. The summit offered tantalising views. Below, clustered around the old church, lay the pleasant, tree-lined streets and elegant colonial buildings that held memories of the north of Portugal. Behind was a wide bay flecked with dhow sails and, beyond that, I pictured the great north road bending into the distance.

Once free of the tourist south ('the south's for sissies' Mike kept on saying) we knew we'd be in for the trip of our lives. To the north lay burnt-out Russian tanks, derailed trains festooned with creepers, bridges whose spans had been washed or blown away, roads that could hardly be graced with the name and mosquitoes the size of bats. There would be toilets that defied belief, meals that crawled with the creatures of decomposition and water to turn our stomachs inside out.

Bloody hell, I thought.

'Dude, come on, it's getting late and we need to catch the ferry,' called Dave from below.

What on earth were we doing?

'Just-in! DUDE! …'

NIDO
MANIC
vite o sida

O CENTRO

Chapter 4

Mike and Tank headed round the bay to Maxixe (pronounced like 'hashish') in the vehicles, a distance of more than 60 kilometres. The rest of us stood in the rain waiting for a ferry to take us across, a distance of four kays.

'*Quando é o próximo barco para Maxixe*?' (when is the next ferry to Maxixe?) I tried my Portuguese. Blank looks from the other passengers. Was it my accent, or the idea of a ferry coming at a particular time? Then a woman with a sleeping child tied to her back pointed beyond the becalmed dhows to where a water taxi – hopelessly overloaded – was chugging towards us. Oh God, not that thing.

Locals were crammed into a bus shelter, collars turned up in what must have seemed Arctic conditions to them. The rain was actually fairly warm, but we were anxious about how wet our camera bags were getting. When the vessel docked, thudding against the jetty, it still took an age for the Maxixites to disembark. Not only did they do it in slow motion, hardly breaking the stride of their conversations, but an inordinate number of passengers kept pouring out of the Ark. The ticket collector-cum-guarda must be a magician, I decided, when another woman with a flock of children and tethered chickens emerged. It was getting ridiculous. The situation was neither quaint, nor picturesque, nor colourful and water was trickling down the back of my neck and coursing down my spine. 'Move, morons, time is money!' I muttered flamboyantly.

Just then a young girl held up a 100 000 metical-note and asked whether anyone had dropped it. We were standing in a throng and no-one owned up. So she offered it to us, the only whites, assuming it to be ours. We shook our heads and she pocketed it, beaming. It was the equivalent of R50, enough to pay for half a paperback novel, and probably as much as an adult in her village earned in a week. She smiled all the way to Maxixe, leaving me ashamed of my earlier impatience. Why hurry? This was, after all, the land of the good people.

We filed down the weed-covered steps, with chickens and ducks being passed hand over hand above our heads. Inside the cabin were rows of wooden park benches. We found a seat at the stern and waited for the entire population of Mozambique and its neighbouring states to board. As in any East African train or bus, luggage and livestock were tossed on the roof, while humans were sardined into the motor-dhow's stinky bowels. My comrades looked queasy as the boat nudged back and forth against the pylons, settling deeper. At this rate we'd soon be taking water. The cabin smelt stale, but most of the fogged-up windows were nailed closed.

At last we pulled away from the jetty. As the vessel turned to port the deck tilted alarmingly and we held our breaths as the craft swung back onto an even keel. Then momentum heeled it over in the other direction. A groan went up from the human cargo. I looked at Dave and could see he was thinking the same as I.

'*Somos jornalistas, fotos faz favor*,' (we're journalists, photos please) we called as we elbowed through the crowd and up the ladder to the 'roof'. An officious looking man shook has head as we emerged into clean air and indicated that we should return to our seats. '*Foto, foto, da licença, senhor*?' (photo, photo, may we take your picture, mister?) we said and made a big show of photographing him, then settled down to the complicated task of recording every aspect of the voyage. We sure as hell weren't going below again.

'Bru, this dhow's less sea-worthy than a bath tub,' said Dave. 'When we turn it feels like the thing must capsize. No-one below will get out alive!'

'I can't help thinking of my girlfriend's sister, Gillian,' I said morbidly. 'She was one of the last people saved from the sinking *Marchioness*. D'you remember the incident? A barge on the Thames hit a party boat packed with trendy Londoners. The people on deck survived. Most of those below died.

'Jenny's sister was near a hatch when the barge struck. A hand just reached down and grabbed her. Her best friend was standing beside her ... she didn't make it.' Sometimes life is very simple. A hand reaches down and you snatch it.

We swerved to avoid a slack-sailed dhow propelled by oarsmen and the ferry slewed over again, giving us that gut-twisting feeling. It was to our considerable relief that the mooring lines arced onto Maxixe pier and we scrambled ashore. *Capitão* Noah had brought us to land against the odds of physics. In an hour or so he'd be tempting God's grace again.

'That was totally cool,' said Alison as she emerged from steerage. 'I just love doing this African public transport thing.'

A flotilla of dhows with unbrailed sails lined the water's edge. The calm waters of Inhambane Bay have possibly the largest fleet of working dhows in Africa. These *ingalões* or *barcos a vela* symbolise this part of the east coast. They're the living incarnations of ancient trade routes, emblematic of the continuity of civilised habitation hereabouts since long before the advent of European navigators. I so wanted to sit and gaze at the furling and unfurling of their butterfly wings, to watch their coming and going. But the Land Rovers were revving at the top of the beach. The great north road beckoned. With a storm of hooting from Tank and Mike we drilled out of town.

David changed into *Getaway* mode and scribbled away in the passenger seat. Thankfully my job as magazine journalist was largely over, as my article was about the south. Now I could concern myself exclusively with personal quests. I was looking forward to taking a break from the fact gathering, but it felt strange being a passenger. Something else was happening in my head too. I'd been complementing my journalist jottings with private observations and a chronicle of feelings. Should I keep going with them? Maybe there was, well, a book in it? Perhaps the journey led that way? The very notion brought a wave of anxiety ...

The Landies headed down a branch road to some nondescript ex-Rhodesian haunt, deserted of course – probably been so since 1975.

'This place is charming,' said Dave, 'like something on the upper Zambezi'. Was Mike's value system rubbing off on him? Would it be bully-beef sandwiches, enthusiastic roadside camping, cold showers with inspections and corporal punishment at dawn from now on? Frankly I'm of the school that says: if there's a five-star lodge begging to roll out the red carpet and lick the soles of your feet, why not indulge them? Mike would rather die than be pampered, but I had hoped Dave was on my side. If this was 'charming', then the rest of us were in for a hard ride.

'There's a magical spot near here,' said Dave as we drove back to the EN1. 'I spent a night there last time I was in Inhambane. We took a rubber duck from Barra to the northern point of Inhambane Bay. The boat stopped along the way on these excellent little sandbars covered with pansy shells. We got to a point called Linga Linga as the sun was going down. It was such a lekker place. Dolphins surfing the waves, men tending their fish traps, boys paddling about in dug-out canoes ...' Dave was in lyrical mode.

'Sounds like bloody paradise, boet,' said Tank.

'Ja, it was kinda. We'd been told about a nice camp to stay, Casa Lucia. It was very basic: three tents and two hammocks round a fireplace in a clearing beneath palms. The guy running the joint kept fussing that we were going to be killed by falling coconuts if we slept under the trees.

'He gave us chicken for supper – man that bird was tough – then he led us through the forest to a hut packed with bleary-eyed locals. That's when the real jol began. The local poison is a palm wine called *soura*. It means "happiness", but man, it tastes like battery acid. The evening went by in a blur.'

Dave's reverie was interrupted as we pulled off the road for the first of our scheduled Radio 702 interviews in which we'd report on the progress of our trip to South African listeners. Out came the satellite phone for a celestial link-up with talk-show host Alan. Reception was good as long as we didn't walk too far into the palm groves.

'So, what you boys been up to?' Alan asked in a cheesy, chat-show voice brimming with enthusiasm to keep his listeners awake. I warbled on about the trip, the road, the full-moon party, the cassava plants through which I was strolling. 'If you want to discover the *real* Mozambique ...'

'Sorry Justin, what was that?' cut in Alan.

'I said, the secret to ... '

'You're breaking up ... ' His voice dissolved. The satellites had moved on.

We'd heard that Morrungulo was a fine resort, a bit like Inhambane's Guinjata Bay, with plenty of beach toys and hot-and-cold running servants, so we took the turnoff and zigzagged through palms again. On the way we met the baker.

Dave is mad about 'African characters' and he 'collects' them for his portfolio. I'm landscapes and architecture, but Dave loves meeting and photographing interesting people on the road and is putting together material that will make a wonderful book one day. This particular contribution to his collection occurred when we pulled up to photograph a curious-looking signpost planted in the middle of a palm grove.

It was Hayley who sniffed out the bakery in a nearby hut and met Senhor Sabão. The old man emerged from his home bidding us the traditional Inhambane greeting of open hands in front of the chest, a sign that you come without weapons. Being a baker he didn't see any disjunction between his name and his profession (*sabão* means soap), so we didn't pursue it. His wife was rolling dough into buns while Sabão tended a primitive oven made from a tin drum.

The baker's sons sat in the shade decorticating a sea of harvested coconuts. Alison wanted a drink and befriended the eldest boy who deftly lopped off the end of a *lanho* (young green nut) with his machete and handed it coyly to her. She drank in long draughts. Coconut water trickled down her chin and into her cleavage.

'Ahsome!' she said. The boy agreed. She handed back the drained nut and said, 'That was neat, dude, thank you sooo much.' The boy blushed. Well, he would have if he could.

The rest of us began tucking into the bread rolls. 'Aren't these just the best rolls you've ever tasted,' said Hayley, wiping flour from her lips and beaming her infectious grin. She got carried away and bought 20, which would have been fine if we could've eaten all of them immediately, but the buns didn't 'translate' well the following morning. Alison was a vegan, so predictably she was in her element when we were out of ours. How could anyone travel through Africa on a backpacking trip, and survive without meat or dairy products?

We pulled up at the bougainvillaea-covered entrance to Morrungulo for a quick look around. A Burchell's coucal, or rain bird, gurgled the odds from a tree. The entrance was on a low cliff overlooking a complex of chalets, campsites and *barracas* set among palms along the curl of a lovely beach. White horses flecked Nelson's Bay, named after the Zimbabwean family who have owned Morrungulo since before the revolution. They'd managed to hold onto the place during the dark days by buying all the coconut palms, this being a more effective form of ownership than land tenure. Beyond the point was a nice little break, glassy and hollow. I glanced at Tank and he smiled. No words required. If only there'd been space for our boards.

Manager Jorge showed us round. It was a fine spot: comfortable chalets above the beach and good, clean camping facilities. Big tick for *Getaway* readers. Dave was jotting furiously while Mike had an intense discussion with the manager. Then a man in blue overalls with a semi-automatic rifle stepped out of the foliage. Now there's something to put a dampener on one's holiday, I thought. Jorge greeted him and pre-empted the image problem: 'We have three armed guards here. It's purely precautionary you know. We don't want to have any incidents, and besides, it makes the guests feel safe.'

'What was that about?' Hayley asked Mike when we were back in the Landy.

'Ah, *nada*. There were a couple of hijackings round here a while back,' he said. 'They're just being cautious.'

Hayley blanched.

We'd all heard stories about bandits, ex-Renamo types with too much time and ammunition on their hands. Hayley asked Mike what our options were if we encountered hijackers.

'Well, if you see a dubious-looking obstruction, like a tree across the road, in time, stop and check out the situation. If it looks dodgy, back off and drive to the nearest town. If there's clearance to one side you could have a bash at going round it.'

I figured we might have a chance if we hit the obstacle – provided it wasn't too hefty – at speed. If it was another vehicle, we'd ram it at the lighter end, where the engine wasn't. Land Rover South Africa would be proud of us and a few bullet holes would add panache.

'If they manage to bring us to a halt, we should bail out. Run like Frankie Fredericks for the bushes and let them have the vehicles. It's all they want. When you see an official-looking guy holding up his hand, stop only if he's wearing a white shirt, police cap and dark trousers. And never hand over your passport,' Mike continued authoritatively, running his hand over the stubble on his head. 'Rather hold your documents open against a quarter rolled-down window. Also, remember that the amount you pay for a fine – often for an imaginative list of offences – is inversely proportional to the length of time you're willing to spend haggling. If the cops see that they're missing out on easier pickings, you know, like other, less patient drivers, they'll let you go soon enough.'

Best-case scenario: no bandits and no bad cops. To that end it would be prudent not to travel on remote roads at night, as this was asking for trouble, not to mention the *covas* (potholes), *trincheiras* (trenches), animals and other hazards. Reaching our destinations before sundown had been an unattainable goal thus far. We'd have to improve. Alas, it looked as though that night would be no exception. There was still a long way to go before Vilankulo and what with a couple of wrong turns in the palm maze, we were heading for another embarrassingly late arrival at a swish lodge.

We thundered on and Mike resumed: 'A few years back I worked for the aid agency Care, first in Somalia, then the Sudan. *É pá*, it was wild stuff. Once an RPG was launched at our aid station and once we drew anti-aircraft fire while flying over a Sudanese town. I was with a bunch of South African pilots making a food delivery in a Hercules

C130. Next thing there's puffs of smoke around us and this crackling sound. We were flying low to have a squiz at the town – that's what saved us. If we'd been any higher, they would have had a chance to find the range.'

Mike filled the empty hours, regaling us with his more curious episodes. 'There were some funny scrapes too. I was once attacked by a mob of cripples and paraplegics when I wouldn't hand over the food in our store,' he chuckled. 'I had to climb onto the bloody aid-station roof as they crowded around waving crutches at me. The buggers wouldn't let me come down, so I called in the US marines.'

The Landies rumbled into the darkness. A sign marked the Vilankulo turnoff.

'Then there was this *Playboy* bombshell ...' Mike was at it again. 'She was gorgeous. A centrefold. Tall, blonde, big breasted. She stepped out of a tent next to this remote runway where we'd just landed in the Sudan. She was working all on her own in the mountains, the only foreign woman in a 200-kilometre radius, tending to the needs of thousands ...'

'I think what you guys are doing is just ahsome.' It was Alison. The New Yorker had been quiet for a while, but now she was ready for a good natter. Her contradictions irked me: the dreadlocks and unshaven armpits juxtaposed uncomfortably with First World fastidiousness about things like food. Her patronising, Waspy pseudo-promiscuity with Mozambican lads and naive assumption that she was making 'meaningful friendships' after a few hours with locals also grated. If only she'd talk less and softer and with less of a whine and stop popping infernal garlic cloves in her mouth.

She chattered on aimlessly, 'You know, the simplicity of tribal life shows us up ... our big-city rat race, our obsession with money and material possessions. We Americans can learn so much from this continent.'

But I couldn't help feel there was something fine and intrepid about her adventure. She smiled at misfortune, saw the best in every incident and was determined to do some 'good work in Africa'. She also kept reminding me of Jennifer, bringing me closer in the most tenuous form of vicariousness. The accent, the altruism, my own exasperation: it was a familiarity, tinged with irritation, that made my longing more acute. But she also reminded me of the things about Jenny – and myself – that would make a settled existence difficult.

We reached Vilankulo, gateway to the Bazaruto Archipelago, and dropped Alison off at a backpackers hostel. 'Good-bye you guys and thanks a ton. Maybe we'll bump into each other again up north.'

At the Beach Lodge a guard with beaming torch and face led us to parking bays, then to reception. The air was still. Water brushed the shore. The following day was to be a non-driving day, our first and last R&R stop. Two nights in one place and a chance to rest aching bones was just what we needed.

The boardwalk led down a slope through trees to the main lodge, a thatch-roofed, wooden structure with paths branching to chalets raised on ironwood stilts whose pitched *makuti* roofs could just be made out against the starry sky. Beyond the two illuminated swimming pools was a beach and the silhouettes of dhows. Dinner was served in an open-plan living area, one of those buffets that go on forever, and it was all safe! No gippo guts here, so we tucked in – perhaps a little too heartily as we drew alarmed looks from a table of more refined guests. In truth, our troop couldn't have made a good impression.

After dinner we had a drink at the bar and the brave among us tried a mild version of Mozambique's national poison: tontonto. I abstained, not wanting to have my head blown off. The stuff the locals brew is often not properly purified and actually *does* kill people. I could see the epitaph: 'Taken before his time by tontonto.'

I decided on a post-prandial turn along the beach and soon regretted it. An all but full moon, scarlet as I'd never seen it before, rose out of the ocean and regarded me with a sort of come-hither look that left me feeling quite ill. Jennifer filled the emptiness and the ghastly romance of the moment had me by the throat. I felt tempted to run back to the chalet, drag David and Hayley out of bed and force them to ambulate, arm in arm along the sand, just to take advantage of the celestial seduction. It was wasted on me. The moon had no right to lay it on so thick, I thought, as I stomped off to bed, cursing the hole I felt inside. Dragging the mosquito net over my head, I lay back and thought of England.

Next morning David beat me to the beach by half an hour and got some classic pre-dawn studies. The ocean was mercury and fishermen poled their dhows towards the horizon, looking for wind. By the time I reached the beach, the sunlight had lost much of its richness.

After breakfast we gathered for a day of knocking about the islands.

Parts of the archipelago were joined to the mainland only a few thousand years ago, but tectonic movements and rising sea levels resulted in lowland flooding. A number of mammal species, including samango monkeys and bushbucks, were trapped on the newly formed arks as they 'sailed' towards the sunrise. Given a few extra millennia without human intervention, these creatures would no doubt have begun to evolve curious life forms, as happened beyond the eastern horizon on Madagascar. When that pocket continent snapped off from Africa it turned into an evolutionary laboratory throwing up the strangest species: giant chameleons, pygmy hippos, and Aepyornis, the largest bird on earth.

In a more recent era, legend has it that the Queen of Sheba's Ophir pearls came from Bazaruto. By the time the Portuguese first navigated these waters, the islands, then known as the Hucicas, formed part of a chain of Muslim trading settlements and Bazaruto became associated with a love affair between a Portuguese trader-explorer and a beautiful Muslim woman called Mariame.

This corner of the Indian Ocean was known to the Arabs by the ancient name of Bahr-el-Zanj, the Sea of the Zanj, a fabled realm sprinkled with magical islands. Sinbad-the-Sailor knew its winds and ways. South Africa's doyen of travel writing, T V Bulpin, conjures the mystery:

> It was a sea which nursed a lost world inhabited by nightmare creatures wandering through a whole greenhouse of fantastic plants. It was a sea of legends where dwelt the Roc, that monstrous bird which, it was whispered, could carry an entire elephant in its talons. It was a mysterious wilderness of waters, a backblock of the Indian Ocean where the great rollers came sweeping in towards the shores of Mother Africa.

We boarded a Beach Lodge ski boat which was to ferry us the 15 kilometres to Benguerra.

'*Como se chama*?' (what's your name?) I asked the skipper after we'd stowed our gear.

'Vasco,' he answered.

'Your surname's not Da Gama?' said Tank.

'*Não*! you got to be joking,' chuckled Vasco.

Our skipper was in his thirties and had grown up in Vilankulo. He was a Frelimo supporter and had hardly ventured beyond the town limits during the war. Instead he'd spent his teenage years on dhows round the islands, learning how to fish, sail and negotiate the archipelago's channels and currents.

He kicked the engines into life and our ski boat tore towards a gap between mirage-like strips of sand flecked with palms. We raced past a becalmed dhow being rowed towards Magaruque, its occupants singing as they dipped triangular-shaped blades in perfect synchrony. I read its name on the green, yellow and blue hull: *Dianora João*. A naive image of a crocodile was painted below the bowsprit, the Mozambican version of a figurehead.

We raced past Meu Sócio Sandbar, only visible at low tide. 'It's also known as Thieves' Island,' shouted Vasco above the engines. 'In the old days criminals used to be left there at low tide to drown when the water rose. Today we call it Meu Sócio (my partner), because it's a place we can land in bad weather or if our dhows are damaged.'

Our boats took a wide sweep to avoid luminous green shallows where starfish dotted the seabed like an underwater sky. Humpback dolphins rose and dipped in our bow-wave, doing victory rolls beneath us. This was more like it, I thought! Sedentary Land Rover days had ground away at our nerves and the sinuous movement of the ski boat's twin hulls was an exhilarating antidote.

To the north I could make out Paradise Island, also known as Ilha da Santa Carolina, hull-down with just its casuarinas shimmering in the horizon haze. Due south lay Magaruque with its pretty anchorage. In the 1960s both isles had been playgrounds for the famous and prosperous. The resorts were owned by Joaquim Alvez, a local businessman who'd acquired his wealth from shops, shipping, hotels and other business enterprises in and around Vilankulo. Rumour had it that he'd also made a fortune supplying German U-boats. He held the tourist concession for the entire archipelago and opened luxury hotels on the islands – exotic destinations for southern Africa's jet set.

Today Alvez's big concrete resorts are in ruins. On Paradise Island the dance halls, villas, bars and street-lamp lined avenidas designed for golf carts are crumbling to dust. Even the chapel where the Portuguese said their vows in Eden is derelict – windows shattered, concrete streaked to look like a machine-gun pill-box and the crucifix broken to reveal rusted reinforcements. Mike had heard there were plans to restore the Paradise and Magaruque resorts. A wealthy businessman had secured the concessions and work would 'soon' begin. But these things take years and the pitfalls, both bureaucratic and logistical, are big enough to sink a bank. When it came to business in this part of Africa, it's best not to hold one's breath.

Two teenagers had joined us on our trek out to Benguerra. They were visiting Beach Lodge on their winter vacation from a posh private school in Cape Town. One was related to the owner, the other a friend who'd come along for a fortnight in the sun. They wanted to be dropped off on one of Benguerra's northern beaches for a day of saltwater flyfishing. The friend was clearly in his element. Being marooned on a deserted shore with a big grass hat, fishing rod and little else, was as close to heaven as he could imagine. His party-pooper friend was blasé (spoilt kid, done it all before, yawn) and so the talkative one had to rein himself in.

The boys were dropped at the sandy point where Benguerra is separated from Bazaruto by a narrow channel – known as Kingfish Alley – famed for dugong sightings. Then we cleaved across to Bazaruto where Vasco negotiated the craft into a small bay and we waded ashore. 'Hey guys, watch out for giant razor clams,' David called cheerfully from the boat. 'I once had my foot shredded by one.' He'd definitely got Mike's disease.

I cajoled Hayley into some comely, bathing-blonde-on-deserted-tropical-island shots, for which she berated me. I claimed it was for the punters, that it wouldn't take long, that it could make the cover (which it did). She scowled at me as I snapped away like a Jack Russel, feeling guilty at forcing her to pose. 'Come on Just, you know I can't stand having my picture taken,' she said. 'Why not shoot the boys instead.'

'Ag please Hayley, the guys won't cut it on the cover.'

I also hated trotting out stereotypes, but alas, that's what magazine covers are all about.

I was rather hoping for a picnic lunch and a swim, but Vasco, bristling with enterprise, suggested we scale the mountainous dune. We reached the crest after a calf-burning climb to find gorgeous views in every direction. To the north were dunes and resorts, and lakes filled with crocodiles. How they got there is something of a mystery: perhaps they swam from the mainland or were marooned by tectonic upheavals. Over to the west lay the continent, shrouded in haze, while in the south we could make out two dhows picking their way between sand banks whose shallows rendered the sea the palest green. To the east were expanses of coral upon whose outer reefs the surf was pounding, creating a chalky line scribbled through the blue.

A southerly wind had got up and the ride to Two Mile Reef was bumpy. We hit a tricky patch where currents came together forming pyramids of water that behaved without rhythm or reason.

'*Segurem-se*, hang on tight!' shouted Vasco as we leapt off a crest. The propellers chewed air, whining hysterically before they found their bite. A comber came raking towards us, kicking spray before it. We turned and ran from it, waiting for the wave to lose its force before carving round and punching through the white water. Then we were gliding easily over longer swells again.

'Kingfish, *estibordo*!' shouted Vasco, pointing over the starboard bow. He banked hard to chase the silver shapes, throwing Rob and me off our feet. The fish were all about us and Vasco's eyes were on stalks.

'If only we had a spinner, we'd catch plenty!' cried Tank.

But the wind was freshening and some of us were more interested in seeing what lay beneath the surface. We anchored in the lee of Two Mile Reef at a spot known as the Aquarium. Dragging on masks, snorkels and fins, we tipped backwards into warm, translucent blue. There is something thrilling about snorkelling kilometres off-shore. I suppose it's the remoteness, the knowledge that if the boat weren't there you'd be in serious trouble. Coming from the freezing and comparatively steep-shelving Cape of Storms it was also a novelty to be in warm, clear shallows far out in the ocean.

The undersea world enveloped me. Fish of every shape and hue drifted by as if on parade. A clownfish came over to see whether I was for real; groupers grouped about me. Schools of goldies, threadfin butterflyfish, Moorish idols and parrotfish cruised through forests of staghorn and plate coral. Two blue-spotted ribbontails, smaller cousins of the manta ray, lay doggo, hoping they hadn't been seen. A green turtle – that strange aquatic tortoise – ghosted by. I took deep draughts of air and dived, equalising pressure as I kicked down to the ocean floor where I lingered, surrounded by the spectacle, before crying lungs forced me to the surface. Tumbled by swells and showers of air bubbles I moseyed through the surge, ever closer to the reef.

Suddenly Tank loomed into view swimming fast by me, wide eyed. He pointed to a hole in the coral wall and kept on going. I followed in haste. When we reached open water, he slowed, plucked the snorkel from his mouth and yelled, 'Big shark taking an interest in me … probably just a white-tip reef, but I don't think we should hang around to see if he's friendly!' I concurred, trying not to let anything in my voice show. We rounded up the others and swam to our boat.

The ski boat glided back past Benguerra Lodge. Chalets on stilts were set among milkwood trees and a double-masted dhow was drawn up among palms. Guests lay on wooden chaises longues under thatched umbrellas spaced at regular intervals along the beach. It looked like the perfect romantic getaway. Apparently the owners had started the lodge long before the civil war ended. As always in the long history of armed conflict, Mozambique's islands had provided havens of peace, free of mainland strife. Even for tourists.

Back at Vilanculos Beach Lodge we had a couple of sunlight hours left to see and photograph the town. Dave also wanted to check out places of accommodation. Casa Rex was a posh restaurant and guesthouse near the town centre. That morning Mike had mentioned to the staff that we might be popping in for lunch. Unfortunately the manager – a lanky and aristocratic looking, but uptight, Dane – had rolled out the red carpet for a group of six lunch guests who had been disposed somewhere on Two Mile Reef. By the time we arrived – gates swinging open to reveal cascading bougainvillaea, cool blue views of ocean and Arab-style elegance – our host was seething.

'We expected you three hours ago ...' he said through his teeth. Then, 'Do you still want lunch?'

At this point I melted into the bougainvillaea. Dave is a diplomat and a gentleman: 'I'm so very sorry. We did leave a message with the people at our lodge that we wouldn't make it for lunch. They must've forgotten to call. I feel terribly guilty. Is there anything we can do?' he asked, back-pedalling graciously.

This only seemed to goad our host into making an even bigger meal of our missed date. 'Perhaps you should come to dinner and buy some of our expensive wines to make up for your faux pas,' he said. Now this was going a bit far, I thought, but kept in the shadows as I know my fuse is shorter than David's. My friend was doing good work with a range of innovative apologies, interspersed with utterances of appreciation for the fine restaurant. It *was* a lovely, open-plan space, furnished with antiques and fine Makonde sculptures: grotesque figures of the spirit world carved in ebony. A piece commissioned by absent-owner Rex featured a departure from the usual Makonde subject matter – it was a slave caravan heading for the coast with white slaver in pith helmet borne aloft on a bier by four black attendants. I found it a little chilling.

The Rex garden was loud with birdsong and rolled down the bluff towards the beach. A boardwalk led to a platform with views of the archipelago. The main guest rooms had the feel of a sultan's palace: simple 'Moorish' interiors, Afro-Asian fabrics, Spanish tiles and stained-glass windows. When Dave asked if he could photograph the interiors, the great Dane reluctantly agreed, but wouldn't lift a finger to help rearrange the furniture so as best to show off the rooms. So it was window dressing by Dave, art direction by Rob, styling by Hayley.

Tank and I retreated to the car, cursing Vilankulo's Hamlet, and revved the engines. As soon as the shoot was over, we skidded out the gate, Dave calling his profound regrets saying we unfortunately had another important engagement that evening, and could thus not make dinner. Alas, maybe next time.

We cruised between reed houses with brightly painted doors, then past a mosque and Methodist church competing opposite each other for clients. A couple of guys strolled by carrying a portly parrotfish on a stick between them. Down at the waterfront we came to Hotel Dona Ana where vehicles were guarded by a parking attendant armed with a bow and arrow. The ugly 1960s edifice was another Alvez project, a concrete bunker with curious marlin and sailfish reliefs on the seaward wall. We checked out the campsite (clean but unremarkable) along Bimbi Beach and a local B&B where the owner was busy fleecing two long-haired Germans. They merely wanted to leave their BMW motorbike in his garden overnight, but the wily old shark was insisting on Berlin rates. His reed-hut accommodation was so-so, but we couldn't recommend it to our readers, so high-tailed it out of there to go and meet John of The Last Resort fame.

We passed the mayor's house, which would not have been out of place in Beverley Hills: long winding driveway, clipped hedges, garages for a fleet of vehicles and enough rooms to house all the town's orphans. It made me sick and angry. Like I wanted to knock on the door, take him – his excellency the f'ing mayor – by the throat and sock him one. How could an elected representative in a one-horse town make that kind of money without being corrupt, without having leached the locals; and how could he erect something so ostentatious in the heart of abject poverty? I cursed the pocket Mobutos thriving all over our subcontinent.

Then again, who am I to speak as a white South African who has benefited from all the spin-offs of grand, late-colonial corruption?

Or maybe I'm perfectly qualified to speak. (I later discovered that the mayor, an Indian businessman, had done a lot for the town and wasn't as mean as I'd thought. But my sentiments about corrupt officials stood for many other fatcat Mozambicans who seemed to have prospered because of, rather than despite, the civil war and the destitution of the locals.)

We headed up the main street to a bustling market thronged with evening shoppers and parked beside a traffic jam of carts loaded with amputees, victims of Renamo and mines. Stepping out of the vehicle we were accosted by children offering to show us around the stalls, to be our interpreters, to bargain for us. A teenager with earrings, gold chain and fake-leather jacket with no shirt sidled up to me and asked if I needed to change money.

'*Como se chama*?' I asked, and he told me his name was Santos. He was a hip looking kid and as streetwise as they come. I told him how many dollars and rands I wanted to change and he replied instantly with the exact amount of meticais he'd offer me. When I looked startled he hauled out a calculator, sighed, and did the sums slowly so that I could see how he got his total. Santos was spot on. His mental arithmetic was light years ahead of mine. '*Tudo bem*,' I said and we did the deal.

'Senhor, if you want alcohol, I can organise,' said Santos. 'Very good price. You'll see.'

I didn't doubt him. When Santos grows up he's likely to be the next Joaquim Alvez, I thought as I meandered through the low-roofed market stalls. Bananas and oranges were piled in small pyramids; boxes of Kingsport cigarettes from Zimbabwe stood stacked like Lego impressions of architectural classics. The guitar strains of Mozambican jazz musician, Jimmy Dludlu, rang from a boom box and people greeted us warmly, inviting us into their enclosures. Two girls plaiting each others' hair looked up and smiled when I passed, but shook their heads when I asked to take a photo. The guy making girls' dresses on an ancient Singer sewing machine was more obliging. A beautiful woman in capulana and Calvin Klein vest leant over the counter of a makeshift bar, her cleavage distracting the patrons' view of an array of bottles lined up on crooked shelves.

I bargained for capulanas with a man wearing a beret cocked jauntily on his head and toe holes in his shoes. I couldn't coax him below 60 000 meticais (R30) per sarong and time was short. I bought two – one for Jennifer and one with big red hearts and the word 'Moçambique' emblazoned along the bottom for my office wall – and headed back to the vehicles.

Finally we found John's Place and pulled up in a swarm of street kids who promised the kind of security service you'd expect in downtown Johannesburg on a Saturday night. It was obvious they were offering us protection from themselves, so to speak. We were to pay them to show restraint and not strip our vehicle of the 'loose bits' (wipers, number plates, aerials). 'Senhor, I will be guarda. Nothing will happen to your car,' they chorused. Most of the young people here spoke at least some English, much of it learnt in Malawian or Zimbabwean refugee camps during the bad years. I shouted, '*Não é preciso, não quero* guarda!' (it's not necessary, I don't want a guard) as we muscled through the gang. In any case, choosing a particular boy would have started a mini civil war.

We found John in the kitchen, where he looked perfectly at home whipping up a prawn dish big enough to feed a street of urchins. It was a ramshackle place where overlanders pitched tents in his yard and street sounds echoed through the restaurant. John told us he'd left England many years ago and come to Mozambique with high hopes of adventure and $80 in his pocket.

'That was long before it was safe to visit here, mate,' he said. He started The Last Resort, which became a legendary home from home for wayfarers. Now he owns and runs John's Place, which is congenial enough, in a rundown, African sort of way. Unfortunately, there wasn't time to sit down, enjoy a plate of prawns and discuss the merits of London living versus Vilankulo chilling.

Rob ran his eye over the vehicle for damage: one Land Rover insignia had been prized off. We'd come off pretty lightly. Then we checked out a few mosquito-ridden establishments that were more up Mike's backpacker alley than ours, and ended up at Na Sombra Restaurant, a reed-walled eatery with large 'portholes' for windows.

Our party proceeded to get merry on Mozambican beer. This was in celebration of the first and last rest day of our trip and the official end of comfort travelling, but also due in part to the terribly slow service that saw us through quite a few *cervejas* before even the hors d' oeuvres arrived. At one point Rob came back from the bathroom looking pale. 'Don't go there,' he said. 'Just don't go there.'

But after my umpteenth Dois M I was bursting. The *casa de banho* was worse than I'd expected. A jug of dirty water (the flushing system) stood next to an overflowing toilet, the floor was awash and the bath was blackened as though a trainload of Welsh miners had just visited. I retreated holding a hanky over my mouth and exited through a porthole to relieve myself against the reed exterior, watched by a group of bemused villagers. Back at our table the crew were stuffing their faces and preparing for a hasty departure. The Dane had arrived – clearly no clients for dinner at Casa Rex – and was regarding our table with stony silence from his perch at the bar. He looked ready to swoop. I saw what was required and devoured my tough *bifesteque* (steak) with immodest haste.

I knew I was pushing my luck choosing meat. All the others stuck to seafood, which was almost guaranteed to be fresh along the coast.

'If you don't know for sure the beef has recently come across the border from Zim, it's usually best not to risk it in local joints,' Mike had warned. 'You don't know how long ago it bit the dust, or even what animal it is.' I was reminded of the rat kebab a boy had offered me in Lesotho, and downed another Two Ms, trying not to think about it. My luck was holding ...

But Dave's was about to run out. That night he slept with one leg protruding from the mosquito net and got royally bitten. We thought nothing of it at the time, but later realised it's probably what did him in.

The following day was a big drive and we should have started far earlier. But there was the usual faffing after breakfast: interminable packing, loading, good-byes, photographing. It was 10h00 when we finally pulled away, but before we'd even left town there was a pit stop for more dhow on beach shots, then a protracted refuelling halt during which everyone vanished on short sorties.

At last we hit the EN1 and turned north towards Inhassoro through a landscape dotted with mopane and silver cluster leaf trees. We shot past picturesque wayside chapels (the light, I noted with relief, was dull, preventing long photo sessions) and traversed the kilometre-long suspension bridge over the Save River. Some of us decided to walk it, as the crossing seemed somehow symbolic.

'*Oiçam*, this is where the *real* Mozambique begins,' said Mike with relish when we reached the north bank. I detected something maniacal in his look, something that said no more pussy footing around in luxury lodges. It bears repeating that I don't see anything intrinsically wrong with luxury lodges and fine restaurants.

Glancing at Mike's book for guidance as to what lay ahead on this leg I read the following:

> Apart from the EN1, roads between Inhassoro and Beira are in very poor condition and impassable after rain due to mud and damaged bridges. There are presently no facilities and the ferries which cross the mouths of the Save and Buzi rivers are not operational.

It didn't sound promising, but at least the EN1 would be our saviour. Hopefully, if we just stuck to the national highway all the way up the length of Mozambique and didn't stray too far from it, we'd be OK ... How wrong this assumption would prove to be.

North of the Save we were indeed in a very different Mozambique. Not only had the vegetation turned to wild and unspoilt miombo woodland, but the mood had changed. Rusting Frelimo tanks of Russian origin guarded the road on the far side of the bridge and pointed their muzzles to the north. 'That way danger lies,' they seemed to say. 'Beyond this point we can't help you anymore.' Just a few years earlier, driving this road into Renamo territory would have been a terrifying experience, the rap of machine-gun fire a possibility at every turn.

The drive to Chimoio took most of the day and at dusk we joined the 'hell run' – the road into Beira – and began our drunken dodging of pedestrians and potholes, the latter assuming enormous proportions. Part of the problem was that our headlights illuminated the rim of pothole craters, but we couldn't judge exactly how deep they were. Avoidance was the best option, but in many cases the road looked like it had been strafed and the holes were packed so close that our speed had to be reduced to a crawl. As if this were not enough, big Zimbabwe-bound trucks bowled out of the darkness, snorting and honking and scalding us with their brights. At times we'd veer off the tar to escape the 18-wheel steamships, which were largely responsible for gouging up the road.

This got Mike onto the subject of truckers. 'I hate the mid-afternoon, graveyard sessions when lorry drivers are low on reactions and high on doziness, having knocked back a few *cervejas* or tontontos with lunch. The fuckers come straight at you, mesmerised. Like their internal computer has locked onto you. Even hooting and flashing your lights don't always work and you have to scoot into the ditch. When they pass you sometimes glimpse their eyes staring vacantly at the road ahead. It's as though they never saw you!'

It was already 20h00 when we reached the outskirts of Beira and found the turnoff for Rio Savane, a resort to the north of the city and our overnight stop. Thank goodness we were almost there, I thought. The troops were exhausted from the tension of the Beira run and we all needed sleep. However, within minutes we realised our travails were not over. The last stretch was an appalling sand road through marshland. To add to the sombre mood in the two cabins it began to rain, reducing visibility. We'd swapped vehicles and Tank was driving ours while Rob and I scanned for obstacles. For once, back-seat driving was proving beneficial. Tank followed the TDi at a respectful distance lest we be called on to pull them out.

A few kays down the track we came across a desperate scene: a modern, African version of Delacroix's *Wreck of the Medusa*. A bakkie was stuck in glutinous mud while a huddle of drenched figures dug, hauled and shouted in the darkness. They were covered from brow to toe in black mud. Framed by our headlamps the scene looked Purgatorial. Judging by their condition and the holes they'd dug around the wheels, the men had been there many hours, maybe all day. How the bakkie, which didn't have reverse gear or brakes or lights, had got that far down the Rio Savane road was a mystery.

The driver waded through water and showed Mike and Dave, who were in the leading Rover, a solid patch of ground which they could use to get round the worst of the mud. Dave hit the mousse at speed and catapulted through in a shower of spray. The Purgatorials quickly attached a tow rope to the TDi before it could fly away and their vessel was dragged 'midst much cheering to dry land. As we drove off, I glimpsed them in the rear-view mirror, bathed in red from our tail lights: scarlet figures scrambling aboard their raft.

We blundered on into the marsh, shrouded by our humid breaths which fogged the windscreen. After another hour of rocking and rolling the TDi stopped beside a hut and we heard Mike talking to a villager. Our guide was lost. The light was on in the other cabin and a map was being waved about. Heated voices. The three of us agreed we'd rather not be in the lead vehicle at this point. The villager climbed in and Dave ground the gears, spinning the wheels as he swung the vehicle round. We back-tracked along the road we had just painstakingly traversed.

Time lost its meaning in the limbo of rewind and our disconsolance. After an eternity we came to a hardly discernible fork. The stranger climbed out of the other cab and pointed the way. Meticais were handed through the window and he melted into the drizzle. Finally we arrived at a deserted parking lot to find that the resort was on the far side of a river. It was after 23h00 and there was no ferry to take us across. Both Dave and Mike were fuming. Bad navigation, bad planning, very bad moods. Mike had been chirping at David about his driving and I could see there was no love lost between them.

Dave honked the hooter, flashed the lights, but all remained silent on the other bank. Tank considered swimming, but it was more than 100 metres across and the current would probably have dragged him out of the mouth and into the ocean which was munching the shore on our right. Besides, there were probably crocodiles, maybe hippos, even sharks. Mike hooted some more.

Eventually we heard the sound of a generator starting up. Lights came on amid distant palms and figures appeared on the beach. Then there was the welcoming drone of an outboard engine and we discerned a motor dhow making towards us. Three sleepy boatmen helped us load our stuff and we motored back under a sky studded with more stars than I'd ever remembered seeing before. The night sky sometimes does that to you. Catches you unawares and proves that you never looked properly before. The boat creased a great triangle in the stillness, parting the stars' reflections. So real was the virtual sky that I looked up to see whether the stars themselves had parted. I glanced at my watch: it was almost midnight. So this was the real Mozambique.

Chapter 5

The dhow sank its nose into a sandbank some distance from our destination – the river was obviously tidal. We hoisted bags onto shoulders and began wading towards the lights.

'Hello there you lot, welcome to Rio Savane,' said an icy voice from the darkness. 'You were expected hours ago. What on earth happened?' Oh dear, I thought, we're in trouble again.

James was not in good humour. His words were thick – we'd clearly woken him. I hung back and, in what was becoming a set piece, let Dave take the flack. 'I'm terribly sorry ... we've come all the way from Vilankulo and didn't judge the time or the distance right. We're really awfully sorry. I don't know what to say.'

Unplacated, James listed the cost of our unpunctuality. 'We had a sundowner cruise and a dinner prepared for you. But the chef's gone to bed and we've put the food back in the freezer. Now the prawns are probably like rubber anyway.'

'Please don't worry about preparing dinner. Just some soup or bread would be wonderful,' Dave soldiered on, with just a hint of rebellion in his voice. Yesterday the Dane's lunch date, today Mike grumbling about his driving, and now this little man about punctuality. Dave was clenching his teeth between sentences and The Muscle was twitching in his jaw, warning signs to those who know him well. When David's jaw is in diff lock things can give way quite suddenly.

But I had reason to be proud of my friend and over soup he was able to mollify our host with charm. James' wife, fresh out of bed, appeared bearing a plate loaded with prawns, then one with crayfish. The food worked its own charm. We warmed to them, and they to us.

'We have thousands of hectares of wilderness here,' explained James. 'In the bad old days guys from Beira used to come and poach. At night you'd see spotlights across the river and hear the rifle shots. But we've put a stop to that. I deliberately allowed that first stretch of road to go to pot and we do the odd patrol across the river. It discourages people from venturing down here.'

'But surely that discourages tourists too – isn't it bad for business?' said Hayley.

'Yes and no,' replied James. 'The kind of people who come to Rio Savane are generally your nature-loving Zimbabweans wanting to get away from it all. They have their own 4x4s and enjoy the adventure element of getting here. Not being able to get their cars to the lodge adds to the allure and keeps things very peaceful. When you park your vehicle and cross the river, you leave your troubles behind.'

While James worked on Savane's PR, the rest of us worked on the shellfish. 'You can go 70 kilometres up the coast from here and you'll see no-one. Not even villagers. There are a few nomadic fishermen who come ashore to dry their fish on the beach, but that's all. You can see buffalo and antelope; we've even spotted lions and elephants on the beach near the lighthouse. Sometimes hippos come out of the river and graze right here in camp.'

It was surprising to hear there was game so near Mozambique's second largest city. This was thanks to flooding, impenetrable forests, landmines and horrendous roads … and in no small part, it appeared, to James's efforts. The *muzungos* (white people) sometimes, just sometimes, got it right.

We were exhausted and, apart from Dave, remained largely silent through the meal. Rob's head was coming perilously close to resting on the crayfish in front of him. One by one we excused ourselves and retired to the chalets. I borrowed the Iridium phone and stole down to the beach. Keeping an eye out for hippos, I found a palm log to sit on and dialled an attic flat in Covent Garden. Which felt a bit absurd. The satellites weren't conspiring in my favour and behind me the generator spluttered to a halt, the light petering out among the palms and thatch umbrellas (or what was left of them, after a recent cyclone). I couldn't get London, so I phoned home instead and woke my mother.

'Hello.' Groggily.

'Hi Mom! This costs a fortune so I can't talk – I'm sitting under a palm tree on a deserted tropical beach with hippos wandering about – we're near Beira, so you can follow us on the map – I'm missing you all – lots of love.' I hit the hang-up button.

Next morning James laid on the 'sundowner' cruise. Our host seemed to hold no grudges about our late arrival and was not, after all, going to set his hippos onto us. We launched a little late for the tide and headed upstream in a brightly painted motor-dhow. It was a breathless day as we creased a wake into the mangroves. It felt like Conrad territory: *Heart of Darkness* to be precise, but a jolly, musical version (I suppose every English lit graduate is cursed with carrying seminal images from Conrad – particularly Third World students fed on *Heart of Jim*, *Lord Narcissus* and *Nigger of the Darkness*). Round each bend I expected to see a paddle boat with Captain Marlow waving, a Gilbert and Sullivan ditty on his lips. The light danced between the mangroves, leaving strange shadows in the shallows.

As we headed further upstream the banks began pressing in. A fish eagle regarded us with open contempt from his perch on a dead branch. 'Piss off, foreigners,' he said. Dave asked the boatman to cut the engine and let the dhow glide up to the tree. As we drew level the bird launched himself into the air with such grace that we were awed, cameras forgotten.

Further upstream we came upon a nomadic fishermen's camp hacked out of the foliage. A cooking fire was smoking and a pair of fishermen clothed in rags watched us with dull eyes. They didn't respond to our waves. We passed one of their party paddling a canoe and bearing home a meagre catch, his dugout stacked with basket nets. Any Portuguese explorer venturing this way 500 years ago would have come upon an identical scene.

James stood on a thwart with his hands behind his back and his ginger moustache catching the early sun which dyed the tips red. He looked like an English lord, perhaps a colonial colonel surveying his domain. 'It's best that we have no good roads round here, or all this pristine nature would be a thing of memory,' he reiterated as a three-metre crocodile slid into the stream. 'All we have to contend with these days is the odd mangrove thief – nice wood for building – guys who arrive here at night in their 4x4s and hack out a chunk of forest, load it up and head back to Beira.'

The vegetation began changing from mangrove to deciduous forest. Rio Savane's banks were loud with birdsong and there was the occasional flash of coloured wings between trees and stag-horn ferns. Pied kingfishers were giving the minnows a hard time while their rarer cousin, the mangrove kingfisher, granted us a coy audience in the tree line. A pair of giant kingfishers swooped ahead of the boat to find a perch a short distance upstream. As we approached they'd proceed further, as if leading us deeper into the forest. 'Follow us and all will be revealed,' they called.

The incoming tide began to assert itself and already our journey home was going to be a slow one, so the dhow was put through a three-point turn, punctuated by the barking of a samango monkey which crashed about in the trees. Then we fought the tide all the way back. Nearing camp we passed an elderly Zimbabwean couple on a Hobie cat tacking across the flood. The bright sail and hulls seemed entirely out of place, too festive and summer gay for Mozambique's primeval mangroves.

Our dhow anchored beside the lodge and the gang waded ashore. We had a quick breakfast, packed our bags and gathered on the concrete platform above the beach to say good bye to James. I stepped down onto the sand and turned to tell Rob, Tank and Dave to hurry up – just in time to see them disappear into the ground. Swallowed. Gone. The earth had opened and devoured them. Surely this sort of thing only happened in fairy tales?

James peered into the crater. 'You all right?' he said in a tone you'd use for someone who had sneezed. I scrambled up the bank just as the three were handing up their bags and climbing out the hole. They were obviously shaken.

'The river's been flooding and has undercut the platform,' said James. 'I've tried to put sandbags along the bank to stop the rot. Look here, the water has completely eroded the foundations. Hell, I'm glad you guys are OK.'

Big slabs of concrete had fallen on either side of them. Was it a good omen? It could just as easily be a bad one. James looked relieved to see the back of us; we certainly felt we'd caused enough trouble in his Eden.

Bouncing along the road to Beira. By daylight it seemed in much better nick. Egrets scavenged the flood plains and deserted huts stood window-frame deep in water. Children ran beside the vehicles with cupped hands shouting '*dinheiro, dinheiro*!' We overtook cyclists bearing huge bags of charcoal on their panniers, bound for Beira markets to earn a few meticais – enough to buy basic provisions – before tackling the long ride back to their huts on the mosquito-filled plains.

At last we reached velvet tar, courtesy of an Italian road-building company, and threaded past behemoth Coca-Cola signs into Beira's outskirts. Driving through the slums I ran through the early history of the place in my mind. Beira sits on the north bank of the Púngoè River mouth and for a millennium this region has been the gateway to Mozambique's interior. It's the modern descendent of the legendary town of Sofala, Beira's predecessor 40 kilometres to the south, a settlement that has long since been swallowed by the ocean.

Sofala was home to Fort São Caetano, one of the earliest European structures in the southern hemisphere. The building was erected in the first decade of the 16th century to control the flow of gold from the Monomotapa Empire (in today's Zimbabwe). The Portuguese also planned to use the fort as a base to chip away at Muslim supremacy in the region. Arabs had lived and traded along the east coast of Africa since the time of Mohammed, sailing southwards on the summer monsoons and returning in the winter months with the southerly Kusi wind. There had been a Muslim settlement at Sofala from the ninth century where beads and cloth were bartered for gold, iron, copper, ivory and slaves. The town was a vital link between the gold mines of Karangaland and the wealthy trading sultanate at Kilwa (in Tanzania). From there the goods were shipped to all corners of the Indian Ocean.

It took the Portuguese seven years to complete the fort, with its rounded bastions, tower, residency and chapel. São Caetano was situated away from the Muslim settlement on an isolated sand spit. Masons from Portugal set up their workshops here and stone from Lisbon, shipped as ballast in the holds of outward-bound caravels, was supplemented by local quarries and stone from Kilwa. But this outpost of empire never lived up to King Manuel's dreams and the trickle of gold somehow made its way to India rather than into royal coffers. Lisbon was, after all, a long way away and the captains found they could make a quick buck in this lawless corner of the empire.

When the administrative centre was shifted to the safer, healthier Ilha de Moçambique in the mid-16th century, Sofala dwindled to a lonely outpost. Rioting vegetation encroached on the settlement from one side while sea gnawed away at the other. Hyenas dug up corpses in the graveyard and sometimes there were no soldiers at all in residence, the captain living alone in the fort, keeping his log book neat and pining for Lisbon. By the middle of the 18th century sea water lapped at São Caetano's battlements and Sofala's fate was sealed.

The Indian Ocean forts and settlements were intended as miniature Portugals, run with military discipline. But they were hot and unhealthy places, women were scarce, food supplies and wages irregular. The forts were also often governed by avaricious captains seeking to line their own pockets using the commercial monopoly granted them by the crown during their short terms of office. It was thus not surprising that a steady stream of deserters and adventurers left the confines of these outposts to try their luck in the interior, trading arms, fighting in local wars, converting to Islam or marrying into local clans. In this way a half-caste community grew up on the fringes of colonial control. The lifestyle of these Afro-Portuguese, known locally as *mestiços*, was often more African than Portuguese. In appearance they were often almost indistinguishable from their black kin, leading curious double lives with a townhouse in one of the Portuguese settlements, but living as African chiefs in the rural areas. Although nominally Catholic, they consulted witch doctors and were revered as spirit mediums after their deaths.

Ironically, although they were fiercely independent and resented interference from Lisbon, it was due to this hybrid, adaptable, 'cross-over' class of renegades that Portugal managed to stay an imperial power for so long. It allowed deserters, gold-diggers, prostitutes or runaway slaves to climb the ranks and attain undreamed-of positions of power. The warlords retained the loyalty of their followers by supplying a steady flow of plundered goods, slave girls, imported luxuries and land. They acquired a reputation for cruelty and for barbarous 'justice'.

In order to exert some influence over the Zambezi Valley, the king of Portugal instituted the prazo system, vast 'estates of the crown' given to private citizens who were instructed to bring the land under cultivation and maintain law and order. The prazo holder had to be a Portuguese woman and she was compelled to pass the estate on to her female heirs. Considerable power was vested in these 'Zambezi donas' who employed an entourage of servants and could raise private armies of slaves. In their heyday Mozambican prazos encompassed a greater area than Portugal and the prazo-owning families became a feudal aristocracy ruling the land with an erratic fist. There was often extreme factionalism between the dynasties. Indeed, one squabble between the wives of two of the Sena settlers resulted in the town being burnt to the ground. When I read this, images of an eccentric Lusitanian matriarchy blurred across time and I was reminded of an incident I witnessed in Lisbon. On entering a praça in the Alfama disctict I came upon two fishwives laying into each other with big cods, whirling them by their tail fins like ball and chain.

These 'half-caste' families were the conduits whereby Portuguese language and culture were transmitted though the country, but, as the historian Newitt points out in *A History of Mozambique*, they were also, paradoxically, at the heart of the nationalist movement that strove to end colonial rule in the mid-20th century.

One tale has survived Sofala's stormy history and captures the drama of personal relations in this part of Africa during the 16th century. Newitt recounts the story behind a certain document, which is addressed to the Portuguese king. It's an outpouring of resentment written in 1547 by João Velho, the king's Sofala factor in charge of the warehouses which stored cloth and beads used to buy ivory and gold from African trading caravans. Velho lived in a tower of the fort with Victoria, a white slave woman who cleaned and cooked for him. When the captain of Sofala was absent, Velho was left in charge and dealt with local traders and chiefs.

In 1544 an unscrupulous captain, Dom Jorge de Meneses, arrived with his henchman, Francisco Ribeiro, to take over the fort. At that time, trade in the area was dominated by a Muslim, Mohammed Dao, who was one of Dom Jorge de Meneses's principal creditors. The new captain summoned Dao to Sofala and instructed his henchman to murder him, with the result that 'one morning he was found all cut to pieces'. Dao's wife, Zara, was captured and put in chains. Dom Jorge intended to hand her over, probably as a slave, to his mistress and the captive was paddled out to his ship. Not far from the shore the dugout capsized and, weighed down by chains, Zara clung to her escort. Both were drowned.

Velho's document is an account of continued murder, intrigue and deception. He confides with indignation how goods from the crown warehouse were used by the captain to broker deals, buy allegiance and conduct illegal trade. 'God sees evil deeds and punishes them,' wrote Velho, 'but, in this world, the just sometimes suffer for the sinners.'

When the royal trading ship from Goa anchored in the bay, the loyal factor witnessed the king's ivory being thrown overboard to make room for Dom Jorge's ill-gotten tusks. He notes ruefully that in his fourth year as factor 'there was only one tooth [tusk] for Your Highness and the factory was left empty and without cloth.'

After an attempt on Velho's life following his efforts to stop Dom Jorge, the factor went into hiding, finally taking refuge in the church. From here he witnessed the kidnapping of Victoria, and watched helplessly as she was passed from hand to hand by Dom Jorge's retainers. In a dismal final note after the captain had left Sofala, Velho wrote to his king, 'I am keeping everything for Your Highness ... but woe to those who show any desire to serve you, for their life is empty.'

When Beira – 40 kilometres across the bay from Sofala – emerged as the port of the Manica and Sofala hinterland, the old fortress was finally abandoned to the tide. By that stage the Buzi River had long since ceased to flow into the bay, Sofala's harbour had silted up … and Velho had been dead for three centuries. In 1903 Sofala's protecting mangrove trees were cut down and builders began to remove the fort's remaining stonework to use in the construction of Beira's cathedral. Save for a few stone blocks and shards of china or pottery washed up on the sand, nothing remains.

Douglas Alexander's *Holiday in Mozambique* is enthusiastic about Beira's tourist potential, calling it Rhodesia-by-the-sea. 'Not many years ago people scoffed at the idea of a holiday in Beira. It was considered too hot, too inaccessible, had few tourist amenities and still bore the stigma of being a dreaded malarial swamp.' But now, 1971 that is, he describes it as a Continental-style playground.

The young city is the same age as Johannesburg and, like the gold metropolis, its early development was scarred by acrimony between Britain and the colonists. Cecil John Rhodes had demanded a sea outlet for his Rhodesian gold fields using the Púngoè River. The ensuing war of words culminated in a skirmish between Chartered Company mercenaries and Portuguese troops at Manica. Gentlemen that they were, the Portuguese officers allegedly doffed their hats to the enemy during the advance and retreat. The defenders lost 40 men, while the only Company casualties were two men who, in celebrating the victory, drank themselves to death on *vinho tinto* (red wine) plundered in Manica.

'Take all you can get and ask me afterwards,' said Rhodes, urging his column to advance on Beira. Meanwhile there was gunboat action on the Púngoè during which a British force consisting of the tug *Agnes* and launch *Shark*, under command of the fiery Sir John Willoughby, tried to force their way into the estuary, but were turned away by fire from three Portuguese gunboats.

Things in south-east Africa were getting out of hand and eventually a diplomatic solution was found in the shape of the Anglo-Portuguese Treaty of 1891 which defined the boundaries of modern Mozambique and its neighbours. According to its terms, the Portuguese undertook to build a railway from the Púngoè mouth to Rhodesia's Umtali Heights. Rhodes' friend Dr Starr Jameson (of later Jameson Raid infamy) and Major Frank Johnson, leader of the Company troops, immediately began exploring the Púngoè Valley for a suitable railway route.

We were driving into Beira with Rhodes' railway – so controversial a century ago – cutting through flatlands on our right. Until recently this strategic line was guarded by thousands of Zimbabwean troops intent on keeping open their country's lifeline to the coast. The Zim railway, and its branch line up to Sena, were constantly sabotaged by Renamo. How history trudges in circles: in the old days it had been Rhodesian troops who helped the Portuguese to guard the line against Frelimo attacks.

The railway's construction was a feat of engineering, and folly. On its short journey to Zimbabwe the line had to cross swamps and flood plains, traverse mountain ranges and ascend 2 500 metres to Mutare. It was estimated that during the building of certain sections, one man died for every sleeper laid. Beira's importance and growth were due almost solely to the long iron snake that linked Rhodesia to the sea. Other than a railhead plugging into a safe anchorage there was little else to recommend the fever-ridden mangrove swamps at the mouth of the Púngoè.

The young Kingsley Fairbridge describes travelling the Umtali line just before its completion in 1898:

> This was one of England's gifts to the world. Scores of Englishmen and hundreds of coolies and Kafirs had died in the building of it. It ran through a hundred miles of low-veldt, where dysentery, malaria, and wild beasts had swept off the contractors and their men as the August fires sweep off the long grass ... We travelled first, so we had a tarpaulin over our truck, and deck chairs ... Our train did not run off the rails but most trains did, and then the passengers had to get out and push them back again.

Engineer George Pauling concurred, 'We lost by death 60 per cent of our whites, including all the teetotallers. According to my experience teetotallers do not stand a fever country as well as experienced drinkers.'

Construction gangs were terrorised by big cats and on one occasion there were 32 lions blocking the track. 'In one month,' wrote Pauling, 'the lions scoffed two of our white employees, a yard foreman and a Frenchman.' The engineer comes up with other nuggets about the building of the railway. Like the severity of the heat which saw three members of the construction team drink 300 bottles of beer between them during a 48-hour trip up the line.

It was not until 1898 that the narrow, two-foot-gauge track reached Umtali (now Mutare). Two years later the track carried Australian, Canadian and New Zealand troops to the relief of Mafeking during the Anglo-Boer war. Rhodes's line thus served a purpose he had not, one assumes, intended.

The building of the country's three iron arteries – the Beira, Lourenço Marques and Nacala lines – transformed Mozambique in the first part of the 20th century. The tsetse fly curtain, fatal to horse column and ox-wagon train, had finally been overcome so that goods could now flow freely to the coast from the highlands of the Witwatersrand, the Rhodesias and Nyasaland.

Browsing through Mike's guidebook as we drove towards the centre past *favelas* crammed with shanties, I came across this warning: 'Many attractive, well-dressed Beira women (red hair dye is popular) are prostitutes who may mistake male tourists for sailors.' Even the straight-laced Alexander offers a word of warning concerning the freelancers of the night. I scanned the pavements as we drove, but saw no dusky redheads.

'The town is built on swampland,' said Mike as we slowed for suburban potholes. 'Many of the old corrugated-iron houses sit on stilts driven into the ground to stop them subsiding into the marsh. It was a white man's graveyard.'

The death rate from malaria and black-water fever was uncommonly high, but this didn't stop the influx of foreigners, mostly adventurers hoping to make their millions on the expected Manica gold rush. During the 1890s it was thought that once the railway to Umtali was completed, Manica gold would pour into Beira. Governor-General Ennes describes the scene:

> No sooner was it put about that there was gold in Manica, and that a railway would be constructed to transport it, than pounds sterling appeared by the ten thousand – opening stores, establishing steamship lines, starting industries, selling liquor, attempting to exploit in a thousand ways not so much the gold, as the future exploiters of the gold. What fantastic and bold schemes this inrush of sterling promoted! Even before a road was made into the interior, there were already at Mapanda fine mail-coaches, varnished like bridal carriages, bearing gold-lettered signs: 'River Púngoè to Manica.' At Mapanda, in the midst of swamps, two

> enterprising fellows set up a comfortable hotel, with polished metal beds clothed with diaphanous mosquito nets, where one could eat buffalo steaks and loin of zebra baked with spices.

The rapid transformation of Beira shocked conservative old Ennes: 'A few square inches of sand fetched as much as if it were mixed with gold-dust.' Wood-and-iron houses spread out along the beachfront and even the most rudimentary box cost 'rivers of money'. Ennes was incredulous: 'Ten or twelve pounds a month was paid in order to live baked by slow heat between the sheets of galvanised iron.'

It was like a Conrad novel: an outpost of empire where decadence and degeneration overcame the greedy adventurers (both men were writing about their experience of colonial Africa at the same time). When the *Agnes* began ferrying prospectors upstream, it ran aground on the Púngoè sands and crocodiles took to sunning themselves on its bridge. Shades of a boat on the Congo and a bunch of reprobate ivory seekers from Belgium.

Ennes continues in pure Conradese – it could have been straight from the pages of the not yet written *Nostromo* – exhibiting a keen understanding of the dark marriage of venture capitalism and imperialism:

> The buildings of Beira spread themselves day by day over the sand. Nothing is solid and firm, not even the ground one treads. Everyone knows that over the whole area hangs a doubt – of life or death of fortune or ruin, a formidable 'to be or not to be' – whether or not payable gold exists. Nevertheless, upon the shifting sands and with a question mark for the future, are already established innumerable businesses whose shares are quoted on the *bourses*. Funds press themselves on the company that directs this land of adventure and mirage, either for direct investment, or for ... any business that might recommend itself to the credulity of shareholders!

But the railway was interminably delayed and when the vast deposits of gold didn't materialise, Ennes took a certain 'I told you so' pleasure in noting the shattered hopes of the foreigners:

> In the evenings a visitor to the taverns of Beira could hear veritable concerts of curses and blasphemies from the disillusioned,

calling down fire from Heaven upon those who had deceived them with false hopes of wealth. The innkeepers, however, were ordering more liquor with which to stupefy the despair of more and yet more obstinate victims of the same hopes.

Despite the dearth of gold, Beira eventually prospered as Rhodesia's main outlet to the sea.

We drove on through the Maquinino *bairro* and into the centre past run-down, communist-style blocks. Many were half-finished 1970s apartments and offices, abandoned when the settlers evacuated. No-one had applied a lick of paint in 25 years and now the hulks weren't worth completing. The streaked concrete appeared to be melting in the humid air. I was on the lookout for Alexander's 'gaily painted villas' and the 'quaint blend of the East, the Mediterranean and tropical Africa,' but was disappointed by the bleak scene. As far as I could see there was nothing gay or quaint or cosmopolitan about the place. Indeed, it ranked only a notch or two above dirty, wretched Dar es Salaam – the most god-awful city in Africa.

As in contemporary South Africa, there was strict segregation in Mozambican cities. Whites resided in the 'cement city', a modern, exclusive equivalent of the Swahili 'stone town', while black people lived in the surrounding 'reed city'. Only since 1975 has the cement city been open to all Mozambicans and it is perhaps partly for this reason, along with poverty, that one gets the sense locals are camping in shells left by the colonists. In many cases families are confined to small spaces and replicate a reed-city existence complete with open fires and bucket ablutions within the fabric of a 'modern' apartment block.

In Beira our plan was to link up with Roberto Zolho, chief warden of Gorongoza National Park, who would accompany us on a tour of the reserve. We'd arranged over satellite phone with Henrique, our contact man in Nacala, to meet Zolho at Bique's Restaurant on the beachfront some time between 11h00 and 12h00. As always, we were running late.

We stopped on the coffee bar and palm lined town square, the Praça do Município, to take a few compulsory shots. There were vendors everywhere. If you hang around here long enough you'll be offered skins of endangered animals, ivory or even rhino horn. The square is flanked by colonial edifices, tea rooms and government buildings. I wasn't overly impressed, but then again I was getting the sinking Dar feeling. The street children were also very interested in our vehicles and I feared for the side-mirrors, lamp perspex and other urchin delicacies. Unofficial guides were making a good job of the diversion. '*Ó* senhor, I show you the *cidade*. Very beautiful city. Why don't you come with me?' Yeah right! I didn't know how to say 'I wasn't born yesterday' in Portuguese so I just chanted, '*Obrigado, mas não é preciso*!' (thanks, but it's not necessary), until we were all back in the vehicles and grumbling down Avenida 24 de Julho.

We arrived at Biques at 12h20 – as good as on time for us – but there was no sign of Zolho. Dave tried the warden's office from a pay phone. No answer. We asked the waiters if he'd left a message. Nope. Mike tried the proprietress, but she was rude to him. 'What's her problem?' asked Hayley.

She did have a problem, apparently, and for once it was not related to our time-keeping.

'I arranged for us to stay at Biques initially, but cancelled in favour of Rio Savane,' explained Mike. 'You just can't be sure of security around here. It's too close to downtown Beira.'

Lunch at Biques was pleasant enough. The restaurant is situated above the beach and the fish, calamari and chips were tasty. Although it was sweltering, none of us felt tempted to take a dip. The water was chocolate brown and the Púngoè seemed to be disgorging an awful lot of unsavoury stuff into the Indian.

'Now what?' asked Dave. 'We've made the detour down to Rio Savane and Beira just to pick up this guy. I was hoping to write a separate story on Gorongoza. Without a guide or at least some guidance, we won't know what we're looking for. It's a very big park.'

There was no option but to push on and see whether Zolho, or perhaps some delegated ranger, was waiting for us at the reserve. Leaving town we came upon two shipwrecks below the Macúti Beach lighthouse. It didn't seem like a good advertisement for either the efficacy of the light, or the expertise of the two captains. The vessels, reputedly the *Macúti* and the *Willem Eggers*, appeared to have embraced in their dying moments and now their metal ribs were intertwined and their paint work rusted – carcasses whose bones were crumbling together in brown flakes. The deserted sand, dirty water, stranded giants and confident red and white lighthouse made an incongruous combination. A sort of weird performance piece whose meaning remained elusive.

We learnt later that the *Willem Eggers* was an iron square-rigger which took part in the Australia to Britain grain races of the late 19th century. The ship was later used to transport mangrove wood from Mozambique to the United States, but was declared unseaworthy in about 1916 and beached in front of the lighthouse to act as a breakwater.

'The lure which draws Beira's 80 000 visitors each year is picturesque Macúti Beach with its attractive backdrop of shady trees and smart, brightly coloured Continental-style homes, holiday flats and hotels,' Alexander's guidebook prattled on. 'Because the sea is seldom unruly, water-skiers and powerboats skim the surface just beyond the breakers, while brightly rigged yachts and sailboats virtually mingle with the crowded bathers frolicking in the gentle surf. This is truly Rhodesia-by-the-sea where office worker, civil servant, tobacco farmer and their families play in the surf, or bask under coloured sun-umbrellas.'

Good grief, I thought, Macúti is not even a shadow of its former self. It isn't its former self! Apart from the lighthouse and the wreck I could find no point of contact with Alexander's text.

We split the city, taking a swing past the golf course which had last seen a decent birdie when the UN were in town after the war, but was sporting Marxist weeds again. The Hotel Grande was also overgrown: trees sprouted from balconies, squatters packed into the rooms and goats roamed the lobby. After refuelling in the outskirts Mike shouted, '*Então*, let's blow this paddy!' in his best *Apocalypse Now* impersonation and we rocketed out of BP leaving some bemused petrol attendants.

It was already mid-afternoon and we were stuck on the hell run with a long way to go before nightfall. Squatters had made their homes in swampland on either side of the road. Drawn to the supposed prosperity and relative safety provided by patrolling Zimbabwean troops, peasants had settled along the Beira Corridor during the war. But the huts were sinking, the rice crop had been washed away and maize doesn't grow in a swamp. Beggars lined the verges. They were starving and dying of cholera and malaria just like the builders of the railway a century ago. History, like a stalking leopard, silenced its footfalls by placing hind paws exactly in the prints of its forepaws.

The Land Rovers turned north onto the Gorongoza road and pulled off at a wayside market for provisions. Mike didn't figure there'd be any food to be bought in the park and Rob and Hayley (who'd graciously accepted the joint title of heirs apparent to the catering throne, a position Mike had not made his own) were concerned at the empty nature of the Slater provisions boxes. We were a long way from the nearest Pick 'n Pay.

Boys with bunches of bananas gathered around the vehicle's open windows. Hayley haggled with fruit sellers while Rob went shopping among the makeshift cafés adorned with hand-painted advertisement boards. A bus had stopped and people were piling on and off, vendors passing cold drinks and biscuits up to the passengers.

It was late afternoon by the time we'd done our shopping and Mike suggested we push hard to reach the bridge over the Púngoè River for sunset shots. We did, and were close as the sun was going down. 'It's wonderful the way the land begins to hunch its shoulders as you approach a major river,' observed Mike as we descended into the Púngoè's tributary gorges. I considered this flight of poetry with some admiration. Mozambique clearly has a bewitching effect on even the most hardened pragmatist.

The 12-arch bridge granted us a voyeuristic view of the rural scene below. A man fished from a bark boat and a naked Adam lathered himself, then poured a bucket of water over his head, the light catching shard-like droplets as they sparked off his skin. It was as though he was in a forge of water and light. A group of half-naked women were bathing directly beneath us, but when they became aware of our presence, grew self-conscious and moved under the bridge to escape prying muzungo eyes. A young man asked to have his picture taken and struck karate poses learnt from the Kung Fu movies that are rural Africa's entertainment staple.

The far side of the bridge had been sabotaged during the war and we carefully crossed the reconstructed, army-engineer section that replaced a span lost to Renamo explosives. I was at the wheel and chasing the light, hoping to reach Gorongoza gates before dark. It necessitated driving on the wrong side of the road for long stretches. (Inexplicably, the road is always less potholed on the side of oncoming traffic.) But I noticed Rob watching the road with hawk eyes and Mike's hand gripped the seat at my shoulder so I eased off the gas, returned to the right (left) side of the road and champed at the accelerator bit to Nota where we turned into the reserve.

Parque Nacional de Gorongoza was the showpiece national park of colonial Mozambique – 'probably the finest game reserve in Africa,' gushed Alexander, who claimed that lion sightings were guaranteed and elephant herds were bigger than anywhere else on the continent. Comprising 5 300 square kilometres of game-rich flood plains, hardwood forests, swampland and savannah between the Púngoè and Urema rivers, it had a formidable reputation. But during the civil war Gorongoza had been a Renamo base and wildlife became a casualty in the conflict. Apart from animals providing food and target practice, vast amounts of ivory and rhino horn were exported to South Africa in exchange for weapons.

'The camp we're staying at tonight, Chitengo, was once the Renamo HQ. You can just imagine how the hungry rebels cleaned out that area for bush meat,' said Mike. 'But in 1996 they did an aerial survey of the park and found that you could still find most species. Albeit in bloody small numbers.'

The actual entrance to the park lay some kilometres down the track and by the time we reached the gates it was dark. We hooted for the guards and while paying, Dave asked after Zolho and Paul Dutton, a South African environmental consultant who'd been passionately involved in conservation thereabouts for 30 years. The guards hadn't seen the two men in ages. Great, that's going to make Dave's Gorongoza story a real challenge.

The route to Chitengo led through lovely miombo woodland and trees closed overhead, blotting out the stars. We surprised banded mongooses and porcupines in the road and had to brake while they regained their composure after a headlight dazzling. I thought of the soldiers and wondered what braaied porcupine tasted like, but guessed the quill-plucking operation would be a pain.

Chitengo comprised a large, treed campsite with a few scattered buildings. There was only one other tent in evidence, but no accompanying vehicle, which was strange, given how far off the beaten track we were. We asked the guarda about the other campers: '*Duas raparigas*,' he said enigmatically. Two young girls, here, alone, with no vehicle. We *were* intrigued.

Tank and Rob manoeuvred the 4x4s so that the brights shone onto a patch of grass beneath an umbrella of branches. It was our first night of camping and we hadn't yet sorted out the tents, sleeping bags and cooking equipment. It was a pity that on the first occasion it had to be done in the dark. Mattresses, gas stoves, chairs, tables, cutlery and crockery spilled out the back of each vehicle. We picked through the chaos.

In no time it looked as though Frelimo had strafed the place. Mike discovered that his newly purchased poles were too long for his dome tent and set about modifications with a bow-saw. Mine was new and I hadn't used it before. After tying myself in knots and distributing tent pegs over the ground in the darkness I gave up and asked Tank for help. He and Rob had long since set up camp and looked like a married couple: their tent was pitched, mattresses and sleeping bags rolled out, flashlights strapped to their heads making them look like efficient Cyclopses. They were lounging in fold-out chairs sipping cold beers beside a fire with amused expressions on their faces. It took Tank two minutes to erect my tent. Meanwhile Dave and Hayley had sorted out their rooftop contraption and were banging about in the sky.

'It's mosquito time everyone,' Hayley suddenly got into caretaker mode. 'So cake yourself with Tabard, Peaceful Sleep, mozzie wipes ... whatever you've got.'

'*Porra*, these things are useless,' grumbled Tank, holding up one of the wipes. 'I can never stop a mosquito long enough to wipe it, and as for Tabard mosquito sticks, I can't ever get mozzies to stick to them.' It must've been the doxycyclin (Tank's preferred prophylactic) talking.

'And these bloody anti-malaria tablets don't work either,' he complained. 'Even if you grind them down to powder and feed them to the mosquitoes on a plate with garnish, the buggers simply refuse to eat the stuff.'

It had been a long day and we were looking forward to a hearty meal from Chef Mike and an early night. Unfortunately, our guide was not firing on all cylinders due to what we'd taken to calling his 'prawn chest'. It was a condition he'd picked up in recent days and the symptoms were a choking cough accompanied by much beating of the chest. We thought it was indigestion, although Mike described it as feeling like a piece of prawn had got stuck somewhere in his system. His condition aside, we noted with dismay that the provisions he had brought from South Africa – now that they were fully unpacked – were even more inadequate than we'd feared. A pity, since there was plenty of room in the back of the vehicles and a more than adequate budget.

Mike had packed the kind of frugal, survival rations he supplied to students and backpackers who accompanied him on his overland adventures. The types who enjoyed living on Provita, marijuana and the milk of human kindness. In short, the Alisons of the world. But we were not the wing and a prayer brigade; there were deadlines and vast distances to cover. Scrounging for food and recuperating from the effects of bad meals and a lousy diet couldn't be factored into our itinerary.

A stony silence greeted chunks of stale bread and noodle soup served into our coffee mugs by Mike. Perhaps sensing that some repair work was called for, he announced he was going over to invite the *raparigas* for a drink. We saw him talking to a tent which glowed from within. A few moments later two figures emerged and came over to our fire.

Lily was Chinese and Francesca German; both belonged to a Danish-funded aid programme. Hayley, also a teacher, engaged them in conversation. 'What subjects do you offer?' she wanted to know.

'English and mathematics at a school in Maputo,' said Lily. 'But at the moment we're on vacation, hitching around the country.'

There were the dreadlocks, capulanas, headscarves and a hunger to see the good in Mother Africa, to be at one with the continent. It was Alison all over again. They were perfectly nice women who expressed a genuine concern for the plight of the poor. It's just that there was something too proselytising in the way they went about their do-gooding.

'We're visiting villages, you know, meeting the people,' said Francesca. 'We've done a bit of reading on farming methods and we try to advise them on this and that.'

I found something empty about a year-long stint in Africa, teaching a spot of maths and English, showing the locals how stupid they were. Look Sambo, young foreign women with English as a second language and no teacher training does better, and knows better, than your Mozambican teachers. Was it their First World (in Lily's case, Second) patronage that irked me? Was I being too tough on them? Probably.

Francesca and Lily had been dropped at Chitengo by the gate guards and had set up camp all alone in the wilderness. They were, if nothing else, enterprising and brave. The two were hungry and we offered them stale bread. Hayley made them some tea for which they were overly thankful; then we offered beer which they sipped delicately. I warmed to them: rural Mozambique is quite a thing to tackle if you're on a tight budget, without transport, from the North … and women alone. We started exchanging Larium and doxycyclin stories, which is always a sign that the ice has broken. Mike offered more beer, but the teachers were tired and, thanking us, slipped into the darkness.

After the others had gone to bed I took the Iridium satellite phone to the far side of the campsite where no-one could hear my voice. I dialled Jennifer's cell-phone and suddenly her voice was there, inside my ear, clear as a mountain stream and slightly more English than I remembered it. 'Hello sweetie!' she said. It exploded in my head, triggering a torrent of emotion. 'Hi Jen,' I said, 'We're half way through Mozambique and, God, I'm thinking of you every damn minute. Where are you?'

'I'm at a sidewalk restaurant in Soho with a group of friends. It's a balmy mid-summer evening – still broad daylight. I miss you too darling.'

I imagined her full dark lips, offering these words. Her small and delicate ear, pressed to the cell-phone, receiving mine. 'How's pre-production on the movie going?'

'Oh it's OK, I guess ... Tell me about Mozambique.'

The few minutes of conversion went by like an emotional tornado. Then: 'Listen we shouldn't really talk much longer on your satellite phone. It must be costing a fortune ... '

Within moments she was gone again, the celestial bodies having parted us. My face was wet with tears – the bloody Larium, with Iridium as chaser, I thought as I stumbled back to my tent in the darkness, my head still haunting the streets of Soho.

This aspect of the trip was harder than I'd imagined it would be. I resolved not to embark on something like this again when I was in the full flowering of new love, not that it was ever necessarily going to happen again. Perhaps I had reached a destination of sorts? Perhaps this travelling was bringing me into harbour? It certainly felt that way as I curled up in my sleeping bag. Night noises crowded round the tent, trapping my loneliness, but not my thoughts which arced through the night sky to far Londonium.

Breakfast didn't help Mike's culinary cause much: a tablespoon of scrambled eggs to set us right for an 11-hour drive. There was grumbling in the ranks. One of Chitengo's guards came over and introduced himself. João offered to be our guide for the morning, but warned that both our proposed routes to the east were impassable. The road to Muanza on the main drag between Beira and Caia was flooded and the ferry wasn't operating. To make matters worse, the bridge over the Urema River to the north-east of Gorongoza town (which would get us to Inhaminga) had been washed away. I could see the consternation on Mike's face, which meant the situation must be serious, given that our guide thrived on adversity.

Mike called Dave over and spread a map of south-east Africa on the bonnet. 'Look, the national road, in effect the EN1, from Dondo to

Caia is really kak. It's been chewed into oblivion by trucks and is often completely under water. At times it can take days to cover a hundred kays – I'm not joking. An option would be to strike west and then north, do the Tete Corridor, go through Malawi and cut back down to Quelimane,' he said with a grim look in his eyes.

Here was our Camel-man guide, an African overlander of note, suggesting a thousand-kilometre detour to avoid a hundred-kilometre stretch of national road, the surrogate EN1 north, to boot! The oesophagus prawn must have been getting to him. That and the doxycyclin. Thank goodness I was on Larium which only messed with my balance, emotions, nerves, sleep, dreams and mood. The larries amongst us clearly had it lucky.

Dave said he thought that kind of a detour was excessive, but agreed to drive north after leaving the park to have a look at the bridge. Perhaps makeshift repairs had been effected by now. News sometimes travelled slowly in that part of the world. It was, nevertheless, a troubling situation and Mike was being evasive about why he wanted the Malawian chicken run so badly.

We paid the guard our camping fees, but predictably he didn't have any change and would have to 'go and fetch some'. It was a story we knew well. After half an hour he hadn't returned – must have been turning his room upside down looking for that damn *troco*.

Surprisingly, he wasn't. I found him sitting under a tree hoping the rich *muzungo* had given up and headed out. What he didn't know was that the not so wealthy tourist had to produce receipts for a threatening *muzungo* in Cape Town and account for every missing metical.

Walking back to the vehicles slightly less out of pocket I noticed that the two *raparigas* were having similar difficulties with their guide. It seemed that the quoted price for a morning's tour had doubled overnight. Photo: two haggling tourists and guard with shrugging shoulders. Caption: 'What to do? Inflation be rampant.'

The sun was already high when we headed east and deeper into the park. Renamo had surrounded their base with minefields so I was wary of letting our tyres stray from the tracks, but João insisted that a full mine-clearing operation had been conducted in the reserve. He said the rehabilitation of the park was being instituted with the help of a grant from the International Monetary Fund.

We drove through an enchanting landscape, soft and lush with ilala palms spreading their fans against the sky and glades of fever trees, so named because it was thought you would catch the fever – malaria – if you slept under one. There was dew on the grass and impala tripped along the tree line. Baboons barked a warning and a pair of marabou storks took flight, hammering their great wings overhead to gain altitude.

We halted beside a river overgrown with lilies and reeds in every shade of green. A jacana – or Jesus bird, as they're affectionately known – was striding purposefully across the pads, obviously late for an appointment. Then Rob nearly tripped over Eden's serpent and shouted, 'Guys, snake!' We rushed over to identify the species, but the grey-green thing didn't look like a snake any of us knew. We called João and he said without any hesitation, 'Cobramamba, very dangerous.' This had us flummoxed. No such snake existed. He was cheating: you couldn't just double-barrel two different species. Perhaps all snakes in Mozambique were called 'cobramamba-very-dangerous'. Maybe it's what locals told their children in order to strike the fear of God into them. Children and tourists.

We came to the Urema flood plain, studded with palm-topped islands formed by termite mounds. A hippo cow and her calf were out of the water, grazing on the bank beside a herd of waterbuck. A binocular scan of the marsh revealed a scene that would have given even the most jaded birder a flutter. There were more waterfowl gathered on the section of wetland closest to us than I'd ever seen before: every shape and colour of kingfisher, heron, egret, stork, duck … and a delegation of crowned cranes up close.

The place was hardly being overgrazed and the grass stood tall, green and succulent. Had I been a grazer I would have had a hard-on. Gorongoza was crying out to be restocked with game so that it could again stand alongside the Kruger, Hwange, Moremi and Etosha as one of southern Africa's great parks. Already the terrain, vegetation and bird life would give any of those parks a run for their money. Better infrastructure and a big injection of mammals and capital would do the rest.

Further on we came to the Casa dos Leões, the House of the Lions, original site of the visitor's camp before it was moved to Chitengo. It was a magnificent spot, but the mosquitoes must have been unbearable in the rainy season and flooding of the plain would have made access difficult.

'True to its name,' João said whimsically, 'the house was taken over by lions after humans abandoned it. We used to see the cubs clambering over the framework and broken walls.'

Back in camp we took a look round. Until recently many of the buildings were booby-trapped and by daylight we could now see evidence of the fighting.

'Chitengo is named after the son of Gungunhana, king of the Gaza and Shaka of Mozambique,' said João. So this was another link in our chain of Gungunhana encounters, begun in Maputo, continued in Zongoene. I find it fascinating when you keep crossing the paths of characters from history while travelling, spinning a personal web of connections. In those moments the past seems palpable and, in this particular case, recent strife became more comprehensible. Renamo's resistance to the authority of the centre was matched a hundred years ago by Gungunhana & Son's resistance to colonial overlordship. Both considered Gorongoza a fine place to hide. South Africa's equivalent bolthole was the Drakensberg-Maluti mountain range into which first San, then Basotho retreated from invaders.

Chitengo's buildings had been patched up, but you could still get a pretty good idea of where the bombs had fallen and which structures had been strafed. Some roofs were still missing and there was political graffiti on the walls. As I picked my way through the ruins I imagined the chaos that reigned as Frelimo Migs screamed overhead ... men running everywhere in terror, not bothering to grab weapons, as death was administered from the sky.

I also had Alexander's contending description of the camp in my head as I wandered around its ruins: here were the foundations of guest rondavels, a swimming pool for the post-game-drive dip, the remains of a cocktail bar once decorated with hides and horns. The ghosts were everywhere, speaking Portuguese and eating ice-cream.

We came upon an abandoned Volkswagen Kombi, probably dating back to before 1975. The rusted thing had no wheels, just a few bullet holes and a national-park logo on the door. What sights it must have witnessed in the intervening 25 years: rich Portuguese families with their children frolicking in the pool and silent, attentive black staff bearing trays of drinks; then tough Russian and South African big-game hunters during a time of virtual anarchy; Renamo child-bandits carrying AK47s as big as themselves (the Kombi was standing in what would have been the parade ground – that is, if they were organised enough to have drill instruction); Frelimo forces on mopping up expeditions; next, as the fighting died down, came a handful of nervous Tanzanian honeymooners and Russian military advisers, then UN mine clearing teams, and now a trickle of tourists: history coming full circle. Almost. If only the old Volksie could talk.

One thing we did know about was the near-legendary relationship

Paul Dutton and Roberto Zolho had with the park. Chief game warden Zolho was sent back to Chitengo straight after Frelimo had retaken it and posted a battalion around the perimeter. However, the Frelimo soldiers grew less and less vigilant … began stealing mattresses from camp bungalows to sleep more comfortably in their trenches. Then in the dead of night a great Renamo force materialised out of the floodplain like a tidal wave, driving the befuddled soldiers from their path. The spirit of Gungunhana seemed to be with the rebels. Zolho woke to the cough of mortars and fled into the bush with a few of his rangers. They kept running for 125 kilometres to the coast and safety.

South African environmental consultant Dutton returned to Gorongoza after the war, driving a Land Rover up a narrow cycle path, expecting at any moment to be blown sky-high by an anti-tank mine. Camping in the bush on his first night back he was shocked by the silence. 'The only sound we heard was a nightjar,' said Dutton some months later. 'Nothing else, not a hippo's snort nor the roar of hunting lions. I sat beside the fire and cried.'

Dutton conducted the first post-war aerial survey and noted that of the 20 000 waterbuck in pre-war Gorongoza about 950 remained; of the 18 000 buffaloes, he could find 13; of 7 000 elephants only 19; of 5 000 hippos ten remained. After days of searching he could not find a single rhino. It was indeed something to cry about.

I'd read about Dutton and Zolho's crusade to save the park. They set about rebuilding bungalows, and fresh water now runs in the pipes. Poaching and illegal logging was also being brought under control. In order to entice visitors back, they'd recently started small with birding safaris (an estimated 500 species occur in the park) until the herds had been rejuvenated.

But it was a huge task. Sometimes poaching is the only means by which villagers can feed their families and logging is a scourge. In the 1960s this part of Mozambique boasted huge hardwood forests; now much of the land is denuded. Currently loggers have their eyes on the last ancient forests within the park's boundaries. Behind Chitengo's main buildings I found a pile of maybe a hundred kiaat logs, felled giants confiscated from illegal loggers operating in Gorongoza itself.

Chain saws are nibbling round the edges and corrupt officials have sold off concessions in the park. What the loggers don't understand, or don't care to understand, is that when you chop down the matriarchs and patriarchs of the plant kingdom, the two- and three-hundred-year-old hardwoods, you're decimating the genetic stock. It's botanical genocide.

Chapter 6

Out of the park we headed north on the Púngoè road to inspect the damaged bridge, but after stopping a trucker and hearing the bad news, turned round. Mike looked despondent and beat his chest in a storm of baboon-like barking – in truth, it looked as though he was in a lot of pain. I wondered whether the thought of the Dondo to Caia road wasn't exacerbating his 'prawn' condition.

Back on the hell run into Beira for the third time. Me at the wheel. We'd done the night run to Rio Savane, the day drive back to Gorongoza and were now returning to Beira, heading for the Dondo turnoff. This time I learnt the trick of tucking behind local drivers. They inevitably knew the best route through the potholes and as long as I could keep up with them, and trust their instincts, I could use them to get me through.

Everyone should do the Beira hell run once in their lifetime, as a sort of *rite de passage*. Twice would be labouring the point, but three times is excessive. We all felt the weight of that excess as we swerved and thumped towards the port town dodging children, chasms, chickens and thundering trucks. Typical African buses – piled high with baggage, passengers hanging on the side and disgorging black diesel fumes – would yaw out of the dust. They're an institution, and every now and again one of them goes careening off the road killing half the occupants.

Like the nearby railway, this route was once patrolled by Zimbabwean troops. There were curfews and vehicles were sniped at. Locals were Frelimo by day, Renamo at night. 'Most of the countryside around here covertly supported the rebels,' said Mike. 'You still can't get anything done in these parts without the sanction of the Renamo chiefs.'

The *Sempre Coca-Cola* signs and swish BP garages began reappearing, indicating that we were nearing the peri-civilisation (or should I say peri-peri civilisation) of Beira. Not far from the city we took the Dondo turnoff.

So this was it: the dreaded Dondo to Caia. Initially the road was fine and seemed to have been recently graded. The sun was westering and we were making good time. Of course it didn't last. After a few kilometres gnarly conditions slowed us to a crawl. I was still driving with Rob beside me and Hayley held on as best she could in the back as we bucked and bronco'd our way northward. There were places where we had to climb out and wade through water to gauge depth, then get up as much speed as possible to clear the donga. I hit the water features at pace in second gear, spraying black, stinky mud over the bonnet, engine and windscreen wipers screaming in unison. I was having great fun, but my two passengers looked shaken. When we eventually pulled off at a rural, trucker's siding I leapt out saying, 'Yes please, more of that!' It had been a thrilling two hours of tense, but none too taxing, driving, boasting almost every genre of sand, mud and water obstacle. I was elated.

'Don't worry buddy,' said Mike, 'there'll be plenty more tomorrow. Just you wait.'

The sun was scarlet and melted as soon as it touched the horizon. Our rest stop was a primitive motel: just a few scattered huts in a roadside village. The owner showed us the ablutions, which comprised a bucket of water in one reed shelter and a pit latrine in another. Dave whipped open the roof-top tent and handed down the trommels, tables and chairs while the rest of us pitched tents inside the wooden lattice structure of an unfinished hut. Setting up camp proved much more efficient in daylight. In 20 minutes beers were cracked and water was boiling on the gas.

Village children watched our antics. When we set up our fold-out table and chair contraption, which fits snugly in its own suitcase, the kids broke into wild laughter. Tinny Zulu traditional music issued from a radio somewhere in the dusk and soon the stars materialised. A mother came to shoo the children off to bed and drumming started beyond the tree line. Bats wove erratically through the beams of our unfinished roof. We ate our tuna and rice mess from tin plates and then sat in silence listening to the hiss of the stars. When we turned in, the drummers were still at it.

Tank giggled inside his tent: 'Cobramamba, my arse!' Rob was already snoring. I lay reading *Short Stories from Mozambique* by torchlight for a while: tales of racism, street children, liberation and civil war. The overriding theme was one of pain, of a country ravaged by senseless cruelty and killing. I read a short prose piece, 'The Little Girl Who Never Learned to Dream' by Lina Magaia, which was particularly harrowing. It was about 'bandits', which I knew to be a thinly disguised reference to Renamo. As we had been staying in a former

Renamo base the previous night, the tale held added significance. It was the story of countless similar attacks.

Bandits swoop down on a village at night. They steal and plunder, then force the villagers into a long march, carrying their loot for them. Those who can go no further are disembowelled or beheaded with bayonets. At dawn they halt and the bandits select those who may return home and those who must carry on. The young boys are retained, destined to be 'reprogrammed' – to become murderers. Girls between ten and 14 are also retained, soon to be raped and turned into sex-slaves. As a final warning to those being released, the bandit chief picks out an eight-year-old girl to tame in front of everyone. He finds her vagina too small, so opens her with his pocket-knife. She does not live long.

I woke several times during the night, frightened by my own nightmares or the sound of approaching trucks. Our camp was just a few metres from the road and the noise of engines grew to a crescendo until it seemed the vehicles would plunge through our tents, crushing us under a dozen tyres. As the noise died away and I slipped back into slumber the nearby drumming took over like a pulse. I surfaced from a dream in which I was trying to scoop Mike out of a bowl of cereal with my spoon. He was drowning in the milk and holding on desperately to a piece of muesli.

We broke camp quickly. The drummers were still at it. Their beating hands hadn't stopped once during the night. Now they were building for Sunday's church service: climax, I presumed, to the hypnotic night.

I hunkered over the 'toilet' with flies swarming round my nethers. A group of girls heading for the fields passed the front of the breezy ablution block. I felt self-conscious and embarrassed in my squatting position, but they smiled sweetly and seemed to think nothing of it.

Then we knuckled down to the business of the Caia road. In retrospect, the whole experience is murky … like we were in a storm at sea for days and emerged into calm again as if surprised to be alive. The road was surreal. It wasn't as though there was any section that was impassable – in fact, we hardly got stuck at all. It was more the attrition of being thrown around a cabin for hours. Land Rovers are hardy 4x4s, but they're not built for comfort. Your bones get knocked about and eventually the nerve ends begin to fray. The cabin of a 4x4 is a mighty confined space and we'd been living out of each others' pockets for ten days, which didn't help matters.

Dave was in the back: 'Can't you go a bit slower … and is it *really* necessary to *hurl* the vehicle into every ditch and over every bump?' he said sarcastically.

Fuck off, Dave. Mr bloody 4x4 bloody expert. Just wait till you have to drive this road. 'Sure, no problem,' I said, slowing us down to five kilometres an hour.

We were making heavy weather, the vessels lurching from crest to trough and taking spray over the bows through the water obstacles. Our movement had none of the rhythm of a boat negotiating swells. The rocks and jolts were unpredictable. The moment you took your eye off the road, or released your grip, you'd be thrown off balance or bruised against some sharp object specially designed by Land Rover for the purpose of keeping you alert: the elbow bruiser, knee-cap bludgeoner, ear smacker.

The sky was dark and spitting. Our moods had taken a turn for the worse and words were few as we blundered along. The road was straight for long stretches: a ruler line drawn through tropical forest with vegetation pressing in on both sides. Classic ambush territory. Evidence of fighting was everywhere apparent. There were burnt out and bullet-holed trucks, rusting armoured cars, an abandoned Russian tank. The trans-Zambezia Railway line, built in the 1920s and running from Beira to the southern bank of the Zambezi, sat on raised ground parallel to the road, but had not been in operation for many years. We came upon derailed engines lying on their sides, carriages and goods trucks festooned with vegetation. Even an armoured train had been shot up and abandoned. In places the tracks themselves were contorted, twisted into improbable shapes like spaghetti. The effect was ghostly and disturbing. Here was the pride of Mozambican rail: carriage after carriage derailed, burnt, overgrown. Politics had set the process in motion and nature's anarchy had seen to the rest.

There are plans for a new main road to the west of Gorongoza on high ground, away from flooding where there's gravel and rock to give some purchase. The track we were on was never meant to be the national highway north. The area's loose, sandy soil is unsuitable for road building and parts are under water during the rainy season. The road is consequently a mess. But when the bridges inland are down (like now) it becomes the main south-north artery, and trucks have to come this way to get to cities such as Quelimane, Nampula, Nacala and Pemba. Otherwise they must do the long Tete Corridor and Malawi detour, which had also been our alternative route.

When six-axle lorries plough along this sandy road, often needing considerable speed to punch through the obstacles, they leave chaos in their wakes. At the spots where these monsters had got stuck and been towed or dug out, the road looked like it had been dynamited. The ruts were so deep that even a Land Rover in first gear, four-low, had little chance of getting through. In some instances truckers had hacked alternative 'chicken-run' routes through the bush, linking up with the road further on. In the bad old days, coming this way must have been a nightmare. What better place to set an ambush, than at one of the impassable sections? It would have taken days to cut a path through the forest and all that time a growing queue of vehicles would have presented themselves as sitting targets.

For today's truckers it is, relatively speaking, a doddle: no landmines and no teenagers with RPG rocket launchers merry on tontonto. Just a bit of a shake-up and a fairly good chance of getting stuck or breaking down. This was luxury trucking!

To avoid stodgy sections we took the chicken runs whenever they offered themselves. However, the detours presented their own hazards and you had to watch out for inadequately hacked tree stumps or sharp roots which could puncture a tyre wall like a bayonet.

Every now and then we'd come across broken-down trucks. Some of the stranded drivers dozed beneath their vehicles (no doubt so they didn't have to go far to tinker with the engine). Others had set up camp, fatalism being the better part of valour. A message would have been sent to the nearest village to get a message to the boss to ask for the spare part. Maybe it would come; maybe it wouldn't. But the driver had to stay with the truck, like the captain of a stricken ship. It might take days, even months. We passed one guy who'd made himself comfortable with a make-shift tent. He even had a woman with him doing his cooking and washing. Maybe she was being paid for her services or perhaps he'd sent word for his wife to come and sit it out with him. His vehicle looked to be disintegrating and grass was growing up around the wheels.

Later we passed a field demarcated with red-and-white plastic tape. 'Why's that area cordoned off?' I asked Mike.

'Oh, it's an uncleared minefield,' he answered nonchalantly. 'Just keep to the road.'

I kept to the road.

Eventually the Landies mumbled into Muanza, the one-horse town we would have reached the previous morning had the bridge not been down. We disembarked on decidedly shaky pins. The world was rocking, like being back on land after a voyage. Hayley bought Cokes and we drank them on the porch of a burnt-out building. There was drumming and singing coming from both sides of the road – church services in full swing. I guessed this lot had also been at it all night.

'It's a long, long way to go before Quelimane,' warned Mike. Tank suggested we try to aim for a body-surfing session on the beach at Quelimane at dusk. A sort of incentive. Rob and I heartily agreed: a sunset swim would be the carrot. Mike didn't say a word.

Alerted, I browsed through his guidebook in the cab: 'Dondo to Muanza is usually fine but the next 65 kilometres to Inhaminga takes two hours at best and two weeks at worst.' If the road we had been on since dawn was, in Mike's terms, 'fine', then we had a hell of day ahead of us. I didn't tell the others, but I could hardly have felt more miserable.

Back on the slow-motion roller-coaster ride we passed men on bicycles bearing chickens and even the occasional goat tied to the panniers. We weren't going much faster than our two-wheeled 'compatriots of the road'. The hours passed and we remained stationary as the road swell seemed to surge beneath us. I examined the map, checked the odometer, looked for landmarks with which to pin our co-ordinates, but Inhaminga refused to materialise. The vehicles were averaging less than 15 kilometres an hour and the troops were griping. If this ride had come in the first few days of the journey we wouldn't have felt it so badly, but everyone was exhausted.

Dave was driving and I attempted to doze in the back. I packed mattresses and pillows around me, trying to lodge my body so as to make sleep a possibility. But each time I began to nod off, the vehicle jolted me from the gates of slumber, banging my head against the window or depositing me on the floor. It was my turn to berate Dave, and I made a meal of it. The odd groan for potholes also served the purpose. I'd like to blame my petulance entirely on Larium, but weariness, depression and my own little mean streak must shoulder some of it.

Every now and then I'd sit up and stare at the map. Surely we had travelled further than the odometer suggested? The vessels ploughed on, like two warships sailing line astern in foul weather and trying desperately to keep to their battle stations as wind and waves dragged them from their course.

Eventually, hours later (I don't know how many, because we lost track of time and the sun was absent behind clouds) we reached Inhaminga and the road began to improve. Once we'd passed nearby Inhamitanga it was a stroll in the park up to the Zambezi floodplain. Indeed, we were flooring it and reaching speeds of up to 25 kilometres an hour. Body surfing by nightfall after all!

North of Inhamitanga we passed the turnoffs to Chupanga Mission (where Mary Moffat Livingstone, wife of the intrepid explorer, was buried in 1862) and Marromeu, which lay on the edge of the Zambezi delta – a place of derelict sugar mills. Mike also pointed out the overgrown road to Lacerdonia, a town which he told us was booby trapped and forgotten. There's nothing like the statement 'booby trapped and forgotten' to get the imagination working. Was anyone still living there? Were there burnt-out armoured cars and mass graves? What atrocities had forced the locals to flee?

We raced across the Zambezi flood plain past Caia towards the southern bank of the mighty river. 'Let's just hope the ferry is running because the alternative is too awful to contemplate,' said Mike.

'What's the alternative?' asked Dave, trying not to sound alarmed.

'Well bru, about 60 kilometres upstream at Vila de Sena there's a railway bridge that's been converted for road traffic. It's nearly four kilometres long and was – in its day – one of the engineering wonders of the world. Only problemo is the road to Sena is often flooded for weeks at a time. It makes Dondo to Caia look like an eight-lane Autobahn. Believe me, you don't want to do it.'

It was mid-afternoon by the time we reached the ferry slipway on Zambezi's southern shore and I had my first view of its dark, brown waters. One of the world's great rivers, it is also one of it's most capricious as the stream follows an unpredictable course through a shifting landscape of islands, sandbanks and shallows. In the rainy, summer months when the central African plateau disgorges its water down the escarpment, the Zambezi bursts its banks and sprawls across a vast flood plain. Any habitation within kilometres is at risk. Six months after our journey, the flooding of the Zambezi filled television screens around the globe as the river wrought destruction on central Mozambique leaving many dead, thousands homeless and hapless victims waiting days in the tops of trees for rescue by helicopter.

Not surprisingly it's a difficult river to navigate, as the course of the main stream changes from year to year. This is why mariners preferred to enter the Zambezi by way of the more predictable and less boisterous Qua-Qua River on which the town of Quelimane was built. Anything rather than facing the violent floodwaters of the Zambezi's many mouths.

This river has played an integral part in the history of Mozambique, having an inordinate share in its more colourful episodes. With Quelimane as its port and the trading towns of Sena, Tete and Zumbo along its course, the Zambezi basin became the chief artery into the interior of Portuguese East Africa.

One event in its long history had grabbed my imagination when 'Uncle' Pancho first told me about it: the Silveira expedition and the ill-fated crusades it spawned.

'In 1560 a Jesuit mission led by Father Gonçalo da Silveira set out to convert the most powerful monarch in subequatorial Africa, the holder of the title Monomotapa,' said Pancho. 'Incidentally, did you know, Silveira was a relation on my grandmother's side?' he would always add.

'Yes, Uncle Pancho, you've told me before.'

'Oh, he was a hot-headed character, one of the "heroic school" of missionaries,' Pancho continued, getting into his stride. 'To be honest, he was more interested in winning fame for taking the gospel to the far corners of the globe than getting down to the nitty-gritty of building missions that would be of some long-term benefit. Martyrdom was just the sort of thing he was looking for … '

Silveira travelled up the Zambezi Valley, converting furiously as he went. A bell would be rung to collect villagers, followed by a recitation of the Lord's Prayer, the creed and a few Hail Marys. An interpreter would then rattle off an approximate translation and the heathens were lined up for baptism. At Sena the good father was shocked to find the Portuguese consorting with African concubines and being corrupted by what he called the 'infernal sect of Mohammed.' He tried to restore some semblance of propriety by holding marriage ceremonies for the white traders and their black mistresses. Children and slaves were baptised by the hundred. Then he headed deeper into the interior, past the last Portuguese outposts.

On New Year's Day 1561 he reached the Monomotapa. The priest entered court wearing his religious robes, and aristocratic bearing, which made an immediate impact on the 'black emperor', as did his refusal to accept gifts of gold, women and cattle. So impressed was the Monomotapa that the priest was excused the ritual of approaching him crawling over ground spread with fresh cow dung. Silveira was allocated a hut and, after several discussions, the king became interested in being baptised. Alas, this can be attributed less to Christian piety than the fact that the Monomotapa had become obsessed with Silveira's effigy of the Virgin Mary and had begun having dreams about her. What kind of dreams? It's not recorded.

'The Muslims at court were naturally alarmed at the power Silveira had over the king,' Pancho recounted. 'They plotted his demise, spreading a rumour that the priest was both a wizard and a spy for a mighty Portuguese army. A Christian trader warned Silveira of the plot, but the man of God accepted his impending martyrdom. He gave away all his possessions and waited for the executioners who came to strangle him. His body was thrown to the crocodiles.'

The murder of Silveira had momentous consequences in Portugal and there were calls for revenge. A crusade was initiated, the gold mines of the Monomotapa serving as added incentive to the conquistadors. The fiery Francisco Barreto, former captain of the royal galleys and viceroy of the *Estado da India*, was to lead the expedition of a thousand soldiers. Only vaguely aware of the problems of campaigning over great distances in south-east Africa (we could have given him a few tips) he resolved to use river transport initially and provide his men with oxen, carts and camels for the overland section. Cannons and a contingent of cavalry were also shipped to Mozambique, along with 100 Moroccan grooms to look after the Arab steeds which would carry the Portuguese knights into battle. This was the stuff of medieval legend. Little did they know that sword, arquebuse and armour would provide scant defence against the guerilla tactics of mosquito and tsetse fly.

Barreto's force travelled up the Zambezi in November 1571. Theirs was a longer and riskier route than necessary, but one insisted on by the Jesuits in the party who wanted to symbolically follow in the martyr's footsteps. At Sena, fever struck both men and horses. Not understanding the cause, Barreto blamed local Muslims for the deaths and ordered them to be massacred. One priest recorded the fate of the heathen swine:

> Some were impaled alive, others tied to trees in the extreme branches thereof, the branches being forcibly brought together then released, the victim being thus rent asunder. Others were cut up with axes from the back, others with bombards.

So much for loving thy neighbour.

Barreto's depleted force pressed on into the interior, fighting off guerrilla-style skirmishers as they went. Upstream from Sena there's a narrow gorge in the Lupata Mountains where the column was ambushed by Mongas warriors who inflicted heavy casualties and continued to harry the Portuguese as they struggled westward. Eventually, at the height of the rainy season, the force ground to a halt and the commander decided to abandon the campaign.

Barreto died from malaria in Sena before he had even engaged the main enemy and his successor, a far better military commander, withdrew the soldiers from the fever-ridden river and struck inland from Sofala, conducting a successful 400-kilometre march into the Manica highlands where the army captured and burnt the capital of the Kiteve people. But the gold fields were puny by comparison with what their Spanish cousins had found in the Americas and the Portuguese retired to the coast. After another short campaign up the Zambezi this same army was overwhelmed and massacred.

These early expeditions set the tone for centuries of futile Portuguese attempts to enforce a grip on the 'overseas province'. Lack of resources, bumbling and feudal administration, unhealthy conditions and geographical obstacles made campaigning in south-east Africa a nightmare for any European force. Small, mobile bands of raiders or renegades could bring a whole army to its knees. Things hadn't changed much 400 years later when first Frelimo, then Renamo managed to keep control of the countryside using time-honoured bandit tactics.

As elsewhere in Mozambique, the social fabric of the Zambezi was prone to shredding by ecological disasters and the culture of banditry. Neither Portuguese nor Africans were able to create the conditions necessary for stability and the growth of trade. The footprints of one generation were easily erased by the next. Drought, flood and famine turned peasants into bandits resulting in the collapse of the agricultural economy into another cycle of chaos. Perhaps most damaging of all was the slave trade which decimated communities, emptied farmland and encouraged rule-of-law by thuggery. There was nothing like a Great Zimbabwe citadel or a Basotho mountain kingdom to hold back the dystopian tide. Like the plains of Eastern Europe over which warring Turks, Mongols, Russians and Germans poured, the lowlands and flood plains of Mozambique were the ungovernable flatlands of the subcontinent.

Banditry along the ancient trade routes was endemic. It was carried out by escaped slaves or dissident chiefs who built themselves strongholds from where they could raid the trading caravans or villages of the Zambezi prazos. These fortified stockades, known in the 19th century as *aringas*, were almost permanent fixtures in the history of the Zambezi, allowing renegades to exert a powerful influence over the region. In 1858 Richard Thornton, geologist to Livingstone's Zambezi expedition, described the recently captured *aringa* at Shamo, Mozambique's version of a castle on the Rhine. The fort was situated a little way upstream from where we were awaiting our ferry at Caia. The outer stockade was more than a kilometre in circumference, three metres high and

> of poles about the thickness of one's leg & thicker. At the bottom a clay wall about 3 feet high was built up to shelter the musket man. Facing the river were brick earthworks.

Aringa fortifications were often of green timber which would take root, forming a strong wall of living trees which was difficult to breach, even with artillery. There was an inner enclosure comprising the chief's house and other important buildings, often an Africanised version of Portuguese design. In peacetime, these bandit strongholds were places of trade where slaves were brought and goods stockpiled in warehouses. In times of strife, they were the focus of battles and long sieges. As such, they formed part of the Zambezi Valley engine room and defined the nature of the settlements along its banks, for all the world like fiefdoms in medieval Europe struggling to maintain independence from the central monarchy.

The more powerful Afro-Portuguese families also had their own *chicunda* (slave) war bands, often filled with fighters who had a reputation for cannibalism, and although the areas they controlled nominally fell under the crown, the lawlessness and continual factional warfare were not conducive to permanent settlement or development. The Zambezi was a region governed by rebellion and the diplomacy of vendetta. As such, baronial warlords had as much of a destabilising effect as the raiders. Indeed, they were glorified *banditos* themselves.

Against the chaos of the countryside were posited the few towns, the prazos (at least in theory) and the *feiras*. The latter were outposts of trade, a place where adventurers and wild men congregated. A typical feira would consist of a captain, lieutenant and a dozen or so

African soldiers stationed in a square fort built of stone and clay with straw-covered walls. There'd be a mast to raise the tattered flag and within the walls a tiny church. The feira was a place where foreign traders could do business with chiefs in a relatively controlled environment and where tax could be levied on imports.

But neither the towns, prazos nor feiras could prevent the waves of chaos and destruction that would sweep through the region in times of drought or flood, war or famine, when the earth would be scraped clean to make way for a new set of footprints, a society built from nought again.

In the second half of the 19th century a series of imperial expeditions were dispatched to finally bring the warlords to heel. Newitt notes that the first four expeditions were military disasters almost without parallel in the history of European campaigning in Africa. The riverside Massangano stockade was adorned for decades with the whitening skulls of Portuguese soldiers, a sobering sight for passing traders and travellers heading upstream. Shades of Mr Kurtz. Newitt goes on to describe António da Cruz, the apotheosis of the Zambezia warlord, as a three-headed monster: the prazo-owning head wore a Portuguese military hat, another wore the insignia of an African chief, while the last was decorated with the trophies of banditry. You had a bunch of upstanding Jeckyls in Sena or Tete turning to murderous Hydes in the countryside.

Perched as I was on the bank of the Zambezi I thought too about Livingstone chugging upstream on the leaky *Ma Robert* back in 1858, perhaps stopping to gather wood at the very spot I was sitting. He would have been only dimly aware of prazo politics and the great faction-fighting barons on either bank. And what indeed would *they* have made of the little steamer with its bunch of mad-hatter, diary-writing, proselytising Brits? Catholic, Afro-Portuguese warlordism of a feudal cast meets a Scot bearing notions of Calvinism, industrial capitalism and a set of ethics half a millennium away from theirs. No wonder they failed to find common ground.

The Caia ferry remained tethered to the far bank, reminiscent of Rio Savane. As it was a Sunday, perhaps the ferryman had knocked off early? Maybe he was a member of the church choir on an outing to Quelimane? Or was he sleeping off Saturday night's revelry in a tontonto stupor? We hooted and flashed our lights. No response. All we could do was wait.

'God, it's so darn complicated trying to traverse the length of this country,' complained Rob.

With nothing more pressing to occupy our minds, we fell to speculating why this should be.

'Northern Mozambique is like an island,' Hayley mused, 'cut off by this terrible highway and erratic ferry service.'

'Maybe there's some premeditation in this. You know, antagonism between north and south,' suggested Mike. 'There's certainly no burning desire to be efficiently linked. Isn't it weird that it's easier to get to the north by making a long detour through a neighbouring country? This keeps the north cocooned, free of basic infrastructure, but also free of tourists, which is pretty cool.'

There was still no action on the far side, so I hauled out a Frisbee and we started giggling and running around wildly. We were all a touch 'cab happy'. Tank was throwing the saucer with a lot of aggression and somehow I knew that if it landed in the crocodile-infested water, he wasn't going to follow it in. Rob set up the gas stove and began to boil water while Hayley scanned the other bank with her binoculars reporting on ferry developments.

'There's someone coming!' she shouted eventually. 'A guy in a white shirt is approaching the jetty with a very determined stride,' she reported. 'It's got to be the ferryman.'

Soon the throb of an engine was heard across the water and the vessel swung away from the far shore. It was grabbed by the current, obviously much stronger than it looked, and the driver upped the revs. 'Boys? Boys! Get with it!' called Hayley. 'The ferry's almost here.'

We gulped a few mouthfuls of Rob's tea and rusks. Then the Landies shuddered onto the loose planks of the Caia ferry. The sky was pocked with strange, tortoise-shell clouds and Mike stood on the roof rack of the TDi looking like a panzer commander. A couple of teenagers boarded with their dogs. The animals had wire around their necks in place of collars and were all mangy skin and bone: war victims. When the ferry crunched into the sand on the far side, one lad started pulling the most miserable of hounds off the boat. It dug in its claws and wailed as the boy alternately kicked and dragged the traumatised animal.

'I'd better just look the other way,' said Tank, 'or I'll kick the living daylights out of that prick.'

The scene reminded me of 'We Killed Mangy-Dog', a tale by Luis Honwana I'd read in my bed-time *Short Stories from Mozambique*. In it the sacrifice of an old dog – 'bones all sticking out of his thin body, and his old skin full of white hairs, scars and lots of sores' – symbolised Mozambique's plight. The ill-treatment of an animal seemed emblematic of society's brutalisation by war. I couldn't but see the scrawny boy and his terrified dog on the ferry in the light of Honwana's tale.

Our road arced to the east. The surface was fine while the light held and we could make out the ruts. I found that a good indication of potholes or trenches up ahead was patches of sand on the verges, marking where vehicles had swerved off the tar, killing the vegetation. But after dusk the telltales were harder to spot and driving became a trial: each time you picked up momentum, either a careless pedestrian or a cluster of unavoidable potholes would force a sharp reduction of speed, or worse, a jarring crunch as the Landy's wheels disappeared into a hole.

There were other niggles related to night driving. Although in Mozambique it's compulsory for vehicles to carry red warning triangles, and failure to produce them an obvious contravention for cops to capitalise on, locals seldom have such luxuries. The Mozambican 'triangle' is a couple of branches placed in the road in front of and behind a broken-down vehicle. Similarly, potholes under repair are often indicated by placing a branch in the hole. So when coursing along at night, every stray piece of foliage requires a judgement call.

In each vehicle three pairs of eyes stayed glued to the pool of light cast by the headlamps. This was another of the irritations of night driving in tricky terrain. Your two passengers became mesmerised by the road and felt themselves victims of your driving more acutely than during the day when sightseeing was possible and dangers fewer. The situation became exhausting for driver and passengers alike and fuses were short. I noticed in my rear-view mirror that Rob was driving slower and slower, not keeping up with me, even when I was being especially cautious. Later he confided that Mike had been on his shoulder, a bundle of talkative nerves, guiding him through the potholes.

'It sucked,' said Rob irritably. 'The only way to shut him up was to drive ridiculously slowly.'

We reached Quelimane's bairros at 21h00 and took a slalom ride through the streets. Although nominally tarred, the avenidas were almost as bad as the road from Dondo to Caia. How two-wheel drive vehicles survived here was a miracle. I wouldn't want to be a car in Mozambique. The bairros were busy, but the lack of street lights leant a sinister atmosphere to the town. I could make out some fine colonial architecture in the darkness, but there was no time to look around as the troops were grumpy and ravenous.

We passed a local night-club, the Clube de Desportos Estrela Vermelha Zambézia, and Mike piped up, 'We should'a been here last night. This place kicks on Saturdays: samba, salsa, lambada, rumba, macarena!' I imagined the exhausted mess of humanity we represented and wondered how we'd have fared in a night-club. That's if the bouncer – who would have had to be blind, philanthropic or bribed – let us through the door.

Mike directed us to a restaurant in the city centre opposite an 'upmarket' hotel. It was blissfully air-conditioned and we slumped at a table ordering a half dozen frosty *cervejas*. Heck, this was one beer we deserved after our road ordeal. The waiter politely refused, pointing to a fridge packed with cold drinks.

'Sorry, guys. This is a Muslim restaurant. No alcohol served.' Mike might as well have announced a death, such were the looks of despair. I could smell the whiff of mutiny. Why had Mike brought us to a restaurant where we couldn't have beer? Tonight of all nights. When Rob suggested we go to one of the eateries round the corner that *did* serve alcohol, Mike failed to read the signs. No, he insisted, this restaurant had the best – and safest – food in town and he, for one, was going nowhere. So we stayed.

Fortunately there was a high-tech phone booth across the street, so each of us excused ourselves to phone home. The calls gave us a chance to let off steam. Curiously, Mozambique is blessed with one of the most up to date phone systems in the world. An Australian company installed the network (still in its experimental phase) which runs surprisingly smoothly. All over the north we came upon little cabins where operators could connect you to anywhere on the globe in a matter of seconds and your bill popped up on a computer screen.

Dave got his mom, Rob his partner in New York, Hayley her sister and Tank his girlfriend. I looked at the expensive rates for London and toyed for a while. Five minutes before closing time I took the plunge. The operator, a delightful elderly gentleman, tried all Jennifer's numbers and simply got '*as máquinas*' which I took to mean answering machines. I felt pretty downhearted, specially when I saw how rejuvenated the others were by their calls. Tank had had a particularly good conversation with girlfriend Emma and wore a Cheshire beam, all thoughts of beer deprivation forgotten.

The lights were garish neon and the beef looked dodgy and smelt rancid, but it was food. Conversation turned to bed. Mike was being very relaxed about the 'beach house' we were to stay in that night. It was late and he hadn't yet contacted the person with the keys. Eventually he went outside to make some Iridium calls, but couldn't track down 'our guy', so he called a local man of God. In theory, making contact with the Almighty through his intermediaries in Mozambique wasn't a bad idea. During his travels as a backpacker extraordinaire, Mike had met and befriended many of the missionaries working in out of the way places, particularly up north. These men, Mike assured us, were invaluable in a crisis. When in doubt, send for the missionaries, was one of Mike's mottoes.

True enough, a man of the cloth arrived a few minutes later in a Toyota Land Cruiser. He drew up with squealing tyres and, without so much as a proper greeting, told us to follow him. He was a big, brusque Portuguese fellow who seemed the antithesis of my conception of a missionary. We jumped into the Landies and hurtled down the main avenue, trying to keep up with his disappearing tail lights.

The priest's home was surrounded by a high wall and barbed wire. Two rottweilers kept guard (maybe it's my imagination that supplies the slavering curs, I can't be sure anymore). An iron gate was opened a crack to allow us in. The missionary told us to take a seat in his living room, appointed with ugly 50s furniture in matching shades of brown. We were exhausted and dropped into the chairs, hardly able to make even the idlest banter. I buried my head in a scuba-diving magazine and eluded the laboured conversation. It slowly became clear that:

1. the gentleman with the keys to the guesthouse was probably not going to materialise; and
2. the missionary wasn't going to be a good Samaritan and invite us to stay the night.

It was now 23h00 and we had no place to go. All we really needed was a small patch of his lawn on which to pitch our tents, but the padre wasn't prepared to take us in. I started to wonder whether he was a man of God after all. The way he drilled his 4x4, his determined gait, his not offering us anything to eat or drink, let alone a place to stay ... I decided finally that he was a drug dealer using the church as a front.

Mike continued to make phone calls and eventually managed to ascertain the whereabouts of Mr Keys. Apparently he was knocking back a line of Manicas with the boys at a local shebeen. The missionary pointed us in the direction of the haunt and waved us good riddance. May you rot in your warm bed, I cursed, as we drove away.

Almost immediately I felt a glimmer of remorse. After all, none of us would like to be hauled out late on the Sabbath by a posse of dirty South African overlanders demanding assistance. Moreover, we looked like a disreputable bunch and heaven knows how badly we smelt as we hadn't showered in three days. I too would have pointed uninvited guests in the direction of the nearest drinking hole and unchained the rottweilers, lest they come crawling back.

It was midnight by the time we'd found the shebeen and Mike had dragged Mr Keys away from his beer. Tank and Dave helped him into the lead vehicle and we headed out of town on Avenida Julius Nyerere, lined with ghostly palms. The streets were thronged with villagers, which we found strange at such a late hour on a Sunday night. It was also apparent that the locals were unused to tourists, and they were hostile. In one village a stone struck the side of the TD5 and we accelerated away.

It was a short drive to Praia de Zalala, the beach resort of Quelimane. A line of decrepit beach houses was set well back from the water's edge. We drove to Kass-Kass Complex, which consisted of a restaurant and a few villas for hire. The 4x4s drew up at the appointed house, but now it became apparent that Mr Keys was not, after all, Mr Keys. He was more like Mr Go-Between, or Mr Charlatan.

Mr Go-Between still had to find the real Mr Chaves (Keys). We parked in a stand of casuarinas which whispered conspiratorially in the breeze and watched as our newly made friend tried to rouse Mr Chaves, who was evidently the owner of Kass-Kass. He started by knocking firmly on the back door. No answer.

One has to be philosophical in moments like these: this is just how things work in Mozambique. Of course Complexo Turistico Kass-Kass had been faxed with the date of our arrival and all the details, and of course – it turned out later – they had never heard of us or Mike Slater or *Getaway*. But it's hard to be philosophical when you've been on the road for 17 hours and been shaken like a martini, when hot water or soft pillows have become distant memories.

Our friend began shouting for the real Mr Chaves, then hammering on the door. Our silent and menacing presence in the shadows was having an unexpected but desirable effect. After glancing again at the unshaven bandits, he began kicking the door. At least he could say, when we had the noose around his neck, the loose end slung over a casuarina branch and attached to the bull bar of the TDi, that he had done his best. 'Senhores,' he would cry with pleading eyes and a quivering voice, 'I did my very best for you. What more can you ask of me?'

'No Senhor Keys,' I would say in a slow drawl while revving the engine. 'Your best is unfortunately not enough.' Then I'd accelerate away in a mud-slinging wheel spin.

My dark reverie was cut short when lights were switched on. Someone opened the door, words were murmured, keys exchanged and Mr Keys led us to the entrance. Our dream beach house did not turn out to be as luxurious as we'd hoped. Not by a long shot. Mosquitoes flew in squadrons that appeared to have some order to them, like geese flying in a V – a cunning enemy in the battle ahead. I went straight to the vehicle and hauled out my army-green mozzie net.

The bathroom boasted a toilet that did not flush and a shower comprising a bucket of cold, dirty water. At least there were beds, although the cement floor may have proved more comfortable. Less lumpy. A nice touch was a packet of Jeito condoms on each pillow – very considerate in a country ravaged by Aids, but you had to wonder what sort of clientele they'd been expecting. Tank, Rob and I shared a room and we each had a triple-pack so the possibilities would have been endless had we not been so shagged out. We didn't even have enough energy to crack the obvious jokes.

Before we'd managed to unload our bags, Mike had already rolled out a mat in the lounge, thrown a net over himself and fallen soundly asleep. The rest of us fought with our nets, trying to find something on the wall or ceiling to attach them to. I was standing on my bed attempting to tie the string to a gaudy reproduction of an English country scene when the electricity was cut and we were left to blunder about in the dark. Just when I'd finally managed to find my pillow and lever myself under the net, deranged cocks (not to be confused with their silent, edible, free-range wives) started crowing. For the next four hours they kept warning us of the impending sunrise until, when the dawn did indeed become bloody fingered, they fell strangely silent. War trauma, perhaps.

As my sleeping bag is one of those tapering affairs moulded to snugly fit the body for a chilly night on Everest, in the tropics I conduct a night-long wrestling match with it. Add to this the cocks and a mosquito net that falls on you at intervals and you end up with a frustrating set of mini slumbers, punctuated by Larium-fuelled nightmares.

We heard Dave getting up for sunrise, but none of us stirred, leaving him to bag some great shots of fishermen launching boats. Tank and I were the last up and headed through the trees, hoping to emerge onto a tropical beach adorned with a pealing break for a spot of body surfing to blow the cobwebs. Alexander had revved my hopes with a description of great swimming, fishing and sunbathing at Zalala Beach.

Wrong again. Praia de Zalala was wide, long, flat and hard enough to drive a T54 on (I learnt later that world landspeed record-breaker Sir Malcolm Campbell had seriously considered this beach instead of Daytona for his record bids in *Bluebird*). It was also a mustard colour matched by an ocean that appeared yellow. We'd just begun advancing into the Van Gogh seascape when my foot sank into something soft and warm. I had heard that people use the beach as a toilet in parts of Mozambique, but the oozing between my toes did come as a surprise. Closer examination revealed that the sand was littered with these 'landmines' and we picked our way gingerly to the water's edge. The foam from the onshore slop (not surfable, even with a jetski) was brown, and bath warm. Neither Tank nor I wanted to do it, but it might have been many days before we saw a shower. So we waded in, turning up our noses at each oncoming wave. It felt like swimming in a sewer and I kept examining the water around me for human sea mines.

Although we roundly cursed the locals for their sanitation measures, Father António Gomes, wrecked on this coast in the early 17th century saw the inhabitants and their ocean in a more pleasant light. His impression was favourable despite noting how the women wore scarcely 'two fingers' width of cloth' while others were stark naked. One wonders how the priests back in Coimbra Jesuit school had prepared him for this sort of encounter with the Noble Savage. But his affection for the locals shines through:

> There came an old man with parched skin and grey beard who must have dated back to Afonso de Albuquerque's days; I started to complain about the sea that had done us so much wrong and he gave me the answer which I considered very wise. 'Master, if you know the sea is crazy and has no brain, why do you venture upon it.' ... He had come to meet us, as he had had word that we were on his beach, so that no-one would touch anything of ours and this his elders had done many times.

No mention of the human landmines. Maybe Father Gomes was wrecked at high tide? He goes on to display a fascination for the people of this coast. They had tattooed faces and bodies, and were 'pretty as characters out of hell' with filed teeth 'as sharp as a dog's'. Some had leopard- or lion's-claw crowns and the women wore lip rings, which the good father seemed rather to fancy: 'Those who stretch the lower lip the most are the prettiest.' He also notes that the locals lived by fishing in the lagoons and by hunting. 'They all get together and surround a big piece of land and then set it alight; as the animals get out, they spear them.'

Entering a nearby village Father Gomes's picture of the peace-loving savages took a bit of a knock. The stockade surrounding the huts was decorated with a dozen or so skulls, including 'three heads recently cut off'. The castaways were invited for a meal, an act of hospitality that was much appreciated. That is, until one of the Portuguese found a human finger in his soup. It was probably only the digit of a baboon, as cannibalism in Africa is far rarer than chroniclers would have us believe, but a conversation stopper nonetheless.

Back at our beach house I couldn't get the idea of sewage out of my head, so I braved the dirty water in the bathroom, splashing myself down while my run-off seeped across the floor into the lounge. Breakfast was next door at Complexo Kass-Kass. We ordered eggs and chips for six from the proprietor who was also in charge of renting out the delightful accommodation we were currently occupying.

While we ate our paraffin smelling omelettes (thankfully no baboon digits), a blind man played a tune on his guitar. His retarded and squint minder tapped the rhythm on the side of the instrument and joined in the mournful choruses. We were the only customers and these two had been rustled up to entertain us. One of the songs was about a girl who'd drowned in a river. I thought of Jennifer, her sister on the *Marchioness*, Father Gomes being cast away and the shipwreck that was this trip, and felt miserable.

'Not all the music from this area is so sad,' piped Mike. 'There's a band called Thulrúka that often does gigs here. *Thulrúkas* are reed flutes played to summon the forest and ocean spirits to ensure bountiful harvests and full nets. One of the band's favourite songs is called 'Ciao Quelimane'. It's a happy number that celebrates once again being able to say good-bye to Quelimane after years of isolation when bandits and ambushes prevented travel between towns.'

I sympathised with the band's sentiments.

We returned to Quelimane along the beautiful, palm-lined avenue we'd driven the night before. Marshy clearings on either side revealed plantations stretching for kilometres in every direction. Quelimane is the coconut capital of Mozambique – the trees thrive in salty soil and sea breeze conditions of which they had plenty thereabouts. Locals don't necessarily own the land, but rather individual trees, which serve as a vital form of income. When early Portuguese empire builders wanted to bring recalcitrant towns on the East African seaboard to heel, they sometimes cut down the palms, an act that was tantamount to a death sentence.

Capital of Zambezia Province, Quelimane is set among mangrove swamps on the north bank of the Qua-Qua. This tidal river is navigable for more than 50 kilometres and further upstream it joins the Zambezi. Its mouth is protected by a treacherous sandbar and, for ocean-going craft, access to the port requires local knowledge and steel nerves. In the past, vessels would often trans-ship their cargoes for passage upriver.

Quelimane harbour marked the end of David Livingstone's trans-Africa trek from the Atlantic to the shores of the Indian, which he reached in 1856. 'The bar of Quelimane is so bad that every vessel which enters is in danger of shipwreck,' wrote the missionary-explorer. 'My joy on reaching the east coast was sadly embittered by the news that Commander MacLune, of HM brigantine *Dart*, on coming in to Quelimane to pick me up, had, [with six men] been lost on the bar. I never felt more poignant sorrow.'

In his epic Renaissance poem, *Os Lusíadas*, Luis Vaz de Camões describes Vasco da Gama's arrival here. When the navigator landed in 1499 he named Quelimane's waterway the Rio dos Bons Sinais (River of Good Omens). For the Portuguese mariners, evidence of trade with the East was a sign that they were on the right track in their quest for spices. Indeed, the locals 'had dealings with some more civilised race, and in their speech an occasional word of Arabic was recognisable. They wore turbans of fine cotton weave, and a loincloth of the same, dyed blue.'

The sailors were overjoyed and erected a stone pillar on the river bank to celebrate the good news. They also took the opportunity to careen ship, scraping the keels of the 'slime and shells and molluscs they pick up in the deep ... The natives meanwhile played friendly hosts to us, hanging about and showing signs of merriment and delight. They were people wholly without guile.'

However, not all the omens were good. After so long at sea some of the sailors began to succumb to scurvy (and, no doubt, malaria). Camões's poem notes how disease

> attacked first the mouth and gums, leaving them all swollen and distorted, and as the flesh swelled it rotted, in a way that no-one who had not seen it would believe. The stench of putrefaction poisoned the air all around.

With no doctors on board, the sailors took to 'cutting away the poisoned flesh' with their knives, but even this did not prevent Da Gama leaving a number of his men buried on the river bank. The mariners were finding that south-east Africa was not a healthy place for Europeans. But these early fatalities would not discourage half a millennium of persistence.

In the early years of Portuguese occupation, Quelimane consisted of a kind of fort known as a *chuambo* – similar to an *aringa* and comprising a wooden palisade of stakes with a trench around it – and a few wattle and daub houses surrounded by groves of palm, orange, lemon and mango trees. Traveller António Pinto Miranda, fresh out from Lisbon, visited the settlement in 1766 and was not impressed:

> The town of Quilimane which is totally a wasteland where tigers [sic] ... and hippopotamuses roam, is full of native concubines who serve some Portuguese scattered in the town, the men who have deserted from the garrison to the moors, and heathens who come in the ships from Mozambique as well as their European owners.

The 'moors' who operated from here and other ancient settlements like Sofala, Sena, Tete, Angoche and Ilha were linked by marriage to Muslim lineages, which controlled the Indian Ocean trade, and to the chiefs through whose land their caravans had to pass. These external links resulted in a hybrid society, often run by Islamic brotherhoods, which had the benefit of new foods and technologies from all corners of the ocean. The coastal trading class brought a range of innovations which were adopted and then adapted to the African environment: outrigger canoes, looms, square houses; as well as the introduction of foreign crops like rice, bananas and cotton. Most fascinating was the influence on architecture: Persian Gulf and Arabian designs customised for tropical Africa. In Mozambique's far north the presence of coral reefs allowed for construction using more permanent materials, whereas further south, building was with wattle and daub – and consequently little evidence remains.

It was trade in slaves, particularly illegal commerce after abolition, that brought great prosperity to the town in the mid-19th century. Lieutenant Barnard, serving aboard a British anti-slave-trade ship describes how, during visits to Quelimane, he gradually became aware of the extent of the continuing trade. He mixed socially with the Portuguese slavers in order to glean information, and the stories he heard bear witness to the horrors of the clandestine commerce. Barnard records some of the atrocities: '300 slaves burnt alive in a baracoon; 700 drowned when a slaver drove on to the reef of the Bassas da India; hundreds dead of disease before being loaded, half the consignment dying on board and the slaver returning to port with the remainder past help.' In a strange twist the lieutenant records an incident in which liberated slaves from a captured ship raided the spirit kegs and in the orgy that followed many suffered agonising deaths from alcohol poisoning.

As cities go, the river port of Quelimane feels utterly remote, cut off by years of war, atrocious roads and the Zambezi. It has the aura of a forgotten or besieged city and isolation serves to keep the place trapped in a former era. Prior to the civil war, the port was a point of export for Zambezia's crops of cashew nuts, coconuts, citrus fruit, tea and sugar. The harbour is becoming important again, but it will be many years before the province's agriculture is back on a decent footing. However, rich deposits of titanium, asbestos, granite and precious stones have been found which will speed up development of the region. For better or worse will depend on how carefully the authorities monitor unscrupulous developers who are a dime a dozen in towns like Quelimane.

For now, it's still a frontier town, a refuge for some of the muzungo world's detritus. Human flotsam and jetsam wash ashore here. Disreputables, chancers and criminals always gravitate to places where the rule of law is a thing of patches and opportunities for underhand deals are rife. Post-war northern Mozambican towns are just the place for starting a profitable career in black-marketeering, drug trafficking or trading in sex-slaves. And during our brief visit we sniffed its stench.

We heard about two young Australian guys who'd been living in the town's best hotel for months, spending bundles of meticais on girls who they kept for days at a time in their room. Mike told us the men had worked their way systematically through the teenage population of Quelimane. 'Drugs,' he said, tapping the side of his nose.

Over lunch we met an American couple high on cocaine and polishing off a bottle of whisky. They enthused in a breathless flow of words about all the incredible 'opportunities' Quelimane offered. We looked around at the sleepy town and said, 'Yeah, right.' One of the 'opportunities' came from an unexpected quarter. Notwithstanding the fact that her husband was sitting beside her, the woman casually leaned over to Mike and, in a hushed voice, offered to give him a blowjob under the table.

Despite it being a pavement restaurant I decided I needed some air and went walkabout. I was keen to photograph the town's architecture and the river-front wharf Alexander had enthused about: 'a bustling scene with ships discharging and loading, small narrow-gauge trains puffing up and down, and African dockers swarming over the quayside.' As expected, the wharf was a ghost land, though I did come upon some fine colonial buildings. The riverfront cathedral (built in the 1770s, twin spires, tiled roofs, gothic windows) was crumbling away – a tragedy, given that it's one of the loveliest churches in Mozambique. In the yard I met an old woman who told me she'd been living in the church. She was wizened and dirty and obviously a squatter. When I looked hesitant about entering, she took my arm and pushed open a side door. There, under a high roof between columns of light was a single bed in the middle of a cavernous room. A boy in torn shorts and T-shirt sat in the corner. It was Pedro, her ten-year-old grandson and she asked him to show us around the church precinct. He had a sweet, open face and intelligent eyes, but my Portuguese wasn't good enough to get much out of him.

Dave asked Pedro to pose next to the tall wooden doors and he sat on the steps staring with doleful eyes, making for a wonderful picture. I also wanted to take the shot, but saw that Dave was getting irritated with me muscling in on his set-ups, so resisted. Besides, I was running low on film and needed to rein myself in. Dave gave Pedro a few coins and he was overly grateful. When his grandmother came to thank us as well it became embarrassing.

Back at the restaurant, lunch was turning into an interminable affair. Besides, the troops had scattered to change money and see the sights. I ate my *feijoada* (bean stew) and rued the slipping away of the day. The meal was delicious, but eating was made difficult by the presence of beggars at every table. Ours was graced by a blind woman, foul smelling and in rags, led by a boy who held out her cupped hand. It felt like a macabre puppet show, the child working the strings of a broken marionette. He stood mute and open mouthed watching us shovel soup and bread into our mouths. It had the desired effect. I coughed up a guilty mess of meticais and the double act moved to the next table.

Hayley arrived back from the bank where it had taken an hour's heated exchange to change a few dollars.

'The guy behind the counter was either a complete moron or very clever,' she complained. 'I'm sure he was trying to drive me into accepting his rate out of sheer exasperation. He was slower than a snail and, even though he had a calculator, he managed to get every sum wrong in his favour. Eventually I grabbed the thing from him, did the sums and reached over the desk to count the money myself. He didn't seem fazed, as though this were normal procedure. Heaven help you if you want to take out a home loan. You'd have to bring a sleeping bag and provisions!'

It was now mid-afternoon. Rob and I, the impatient ones, were anxious to get going. Our next destination, a town called Alto Molócuè, looked a long way on the map. Although Mike assured us there would be hotel accommodation and hot baths waiting at the other end, we didn't want to have to play dodgems in the dark again. After the body surfing by sunset miscalculation, I didn't hold out much hope for our ability to cover distances in the time allotted by our guide.

We drove out of town past the *mercado central* (central market) which Mike described as having 'pineapples the size of beach balls, papaya as sweet as strawberries and enough coconuts to float an ocean liner', but we weren't going to stop and verify his claims. The Landies were hammering towards Namacurra, trying to make up time lost. Soon we'd eased back into driving rhythm and rural Mozambique spooled by like an unending road movie.

We passed people carrying *mandioca* (cassava) branches bound for the pot. *Mukwa de mandioca* is a traditional dish in these parts, a staple of the Chuabo people. It's cheap and easy to make: you strip cassava leaves from their stalks, crush them with garlic and peri-peri, boil them for an hour, add grated coconut along with its water and milk (squeezed from the flesh of the nut) to a pan and cook them sizzling with prawns for ten minutes. It's delicious and inexpensive.

The gang whiled away the slow hours talking about nothing in particular and reworking the tired jokes about our cleanliness, larry versus doxy symptoms and other favourites. The day drained away and we yearned for respite from our vehicles' drone. The 4x4s trundled through a military settlement whose walls were adorned with patriotic Frelimo art and graffiti. We kept passing overloaded bicycles: a father with two children on the pannier; then a man bearing his wife, breast-feeding baby and luggage. What balance and what a great advertisement for the work-horse African bicycle!

Darkness fell and we were an eternity from anywhere. The Land Rovers slowed to a crawl and all eyes again became mesmerised by the headlamp beams and the startled creatures they snared. Why, oh why, had we left so late, I grumbled, making myself unpopular. Dave should have insisted on an early departure. Leaving after lunch had just got us back into the demoralising cycle of nocturnes.

I was reading by torchlight and flipping through Mike's guidebook to see what he said about this part of the country. Concerning the road we were traversing I read: 'Varies from excellent tarmac to diabolical deviations ... Pot-holes and old trenches remain a hazard – keep looking well ahead!'

Not so easy in the dead of night, I fumed quietly to myself. Then I read, 'WARNING: Between Mocuba and Molócuè there are three unmarked deviations off the tarmac road to the old bridges. Where new bridges should be, there is a gaping hole.' Oh that's just delightful, I ranted inwardly. If we'd known this, and Mike most certainly did (seeing he'd written these very words and was looking a little pale each time we came to a dip), then why on earth had we sauntered out of Quelimane after a morning of abject leisure?

Riveted by the thrilling read I devoured Mike's prose. 'There have been isolated incidents involving "ninjas" or bandits in this area.' Now there's a useful titbit of info that might have come in handy before sundown. I *was* having fun. But the pièce de résistance came at the bottom of the page. Printed in large bold capitals I read: 'DRIVE SLOWLY AND CAREFULLY AND NEVER AT NIGHT.' The man who penned those words was hunched over the wheel with a creased brow staring into the darkness beyond our weak headlights, looking for what exactly? A band of Mozambican Samurai dressed for the latest tropical spoof of a Kurosawa movie? Or a dark hole in the road that would swallow us, like mariners sailing off the edge of the world?

Oh joy, oh rapture! Oh bring on Alto bloody Molócuè ...

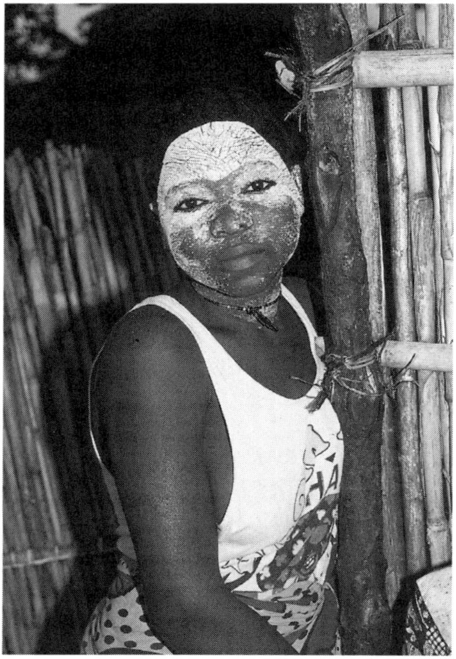

O NORTE

Chapter 7

Alto Molócuè was jiving and dance music issued from makeshift bars on the town square. Alas, our moods were not in tune with that of the 'Alto Malucos' (*maluco* means mad in Portuguese, so we dubbed them the people of 'high madness').

'There's a pretty decent hotel here,' said Mike. 'We'll have rooms with private balconies, fans 'n fridges.' He parked and ran into Pensão Santo António to get the keys.

After a long while he emerged looking perplexed. 'Um, sorry guys, the hotel seems to be, um, fully booked.'

'How's that possible? Didn't you make a reservation?' said Rob, his New York twang edgy.

'Er, actually, I didn't. This place is always empty. Apparently a bunch of bridge-building Murray and Roberts engineers from South Africa have taken over the hotel.'

This posed a problem as Alto Molócuè is not a metropolis graced with more than one passable establishment. There was only one alternative. On the pulsing main square stood Pensão Fambe Uone, to which we wended our weary way. By this stage the town's electricity had failed and cooking fires provided the only light on the praça. The scene didn't look promising, unless you were in the most festive of frames.

Members of a Muslim woman's organisation were encamped on the veranda of the 'hotel'. They were bound for Maputo on a bus, but at this point appeared royally drunk. The letter of Islamic law seemed to be malleable in this part of Mozambique. Or perhaps it was just a matter of interpretation.

Mike negotiated three rooms out of a gruff, elderly woman who didn't take kindly to being disturbed by the nuisance of guests after 21h00. He ordered some food while a minion showed us the rooms. By candle-light we trooped up the open-air stairwell, past an odorous toilet, to inspect our quarters, and were not encouraged. An imaginative thread of memory has created a scenario in which the room was shrouded in cobwebs, and rats had taken up residence in the mattresses. This was not quite the case, but close enough to the spirit of the truth. Hayley sat down on one of the beds and it sagged, hammock-style. The room was filthy and without mosquito nets, the sheets were soiled and noise poured through the window from the street.

'Maybe we could pitch our tents in the room?' suggested Dave. But the proprietor's lackey didn't think that would go down well with management. Besides, what would the other guests think?

We decided to mull over the problem during dinner. The band filed down to the restaurant, which proved to be a table tucked behind a curtain in the bar. We carried in chairs ourselves and laid places from the cutlery and crockery dumped by the surly patroness. The electricity was back on and we settled down to a beer. Moments later food thudded onto the table: a mound of rice and a pile of chicken bits. But before we had a chance to examine our dinner, the lights were peremptorily doused and the vixen appeared with a single candle.

This ruse didn't fool us. The food was cold and the chicken, if that's what it was, looked half eaten. My romping imagination suggests that the bird was crawling with maggots. Before our hostess managed to slip away Mike picked up the dish and handed it back to her saying there was no way we could be expected to eat it. She looked furious, but took the fowl back to the kitchen, banging the door behind her.

Now what?

The rooms were not an option and there were no other hotels or guesthouses in Molócuè. 'Why don't we push on to Nampula?' I suggested. 'It's a big town, capital of the province, and will have plenty of places to stay.'

'Nah, it's way too far,' said Mike. 'But maybe we could head out of town a way and pitch camp by the roadside.'

This didn't appeal to us either. We could end up sleeping in a mine field. Then Mike had a sharp idea. 'Why don't we doss on the roof? Come on, let's go check it out,' he said, leading us up the stairs to the third story of the Fambe Uone. The roof looked a touch Spartan, but Mike was adamant.

'Hey, it'll be fine. Let's just pitch our tents, have a quick bite and get some shut eye. We'll be gone first thing anyway, so aesthetics don't matter.'

We sighed. Our guide was right. Mike made an arrangement with Mrs Surly and she agreed that we could pay camping fees – not cheap, I might add – to stay on her roof. Dave and Hayley were to sleep in their rooftop tent where they could keep watch over the two vehicles in the hotel's back yard (our arrival had drawn interested eyes which tracked every move from neighbouring roofs). We pitched tents and soon rice and soup were simmering on the gas burner. Then rain began to sift down. We laughed. Slowly at first, then hysterically. What else could you do?

But the shower didn't last long and we salvaged the plain, but filling, supper. Our Manicas were frosty and the stars came out flaming bright. The soft Algerian strains of Cheb Khaled drifted up to our perch. The night in Alto Molócuè – snatched, as it were, from the jaws of a tourist nightmare – was going to be OK after all. Locals were dancing in the street and the Muslim Association women were snug under blankets on the veranda below us, packed like cigarettes and snoring contentedly.

Mike was talking about the civil war. This part of the country had been staunch Renamo territory and towns like Alto Molócuè had remained islands of Frelimo support in an enemy-controlled sea.

'Hell, we had some adventures on northern Mozambican roads in the old days,' he said. 'Worst were the Tete Corridor runs when snipers were still taking pot-shots at convoys. Vehicles used to gather at the border and, when a convoy had formed, Zimbabwean armoured cars used to escort us via Tete to Zimbabwe. It was a helluva drive. Sometimes there were as many as 150 vehicles in a convoy and everyone was trying to go as fast as possible. I was in my old Kombi and these giant, Mad-Max truckers – some stoned, some fortified for the death run by a swig from the hip flask – came racing past, riding me right off the road. I used to pull off and let 'em chuck, taking my luck at the back of the convoy.' Mike scratched the stubble on his head, then drank a mouthful of soup from his tin mug.

'The Renamo boys would shoot from the hills,' he continued. 'Fortunately most of the bullets went high. They also used to plant landmines in potholes, so vehicles would be like slewing all over the road trying to avoid them – difficult if you're driving a pantechnicon. The bandits were just trigger happy kids ... didn't want to risk coming too close, seeing as the armoured cars returned fire with heavy-calibre machine guns. It was hectic.

'I hitched a ride in the back of a truck with a bunch of young Frelimo soldiers once. We came under fire and they were so petrified they just started shooting wildly, not aiming at all. Some of the guys didn't even point their rifles over the side of the truck and bullets were ricocheting everywhere.'

'Bloody hell,' said Tank. 'That must've been entertaining.'

'What about when you were on your own? How did you handle roadblocks and that sort of thing?' asked Hayley.

'You know, I used to carry a soccer ball in the Kombi to defuse situations with police or border guards. Whenever there was a hassle I'd haul out the ball ... start kicking it around ... challenge the police to a pick-up game and suddenly we were all mates.

'Once we didn't feel like waiting for the convoy to reassemble in Tete for the last leg to the border. So a buddy and I decided to make the run on our own. It was foolish, I know. We were heading along this narrow road with tall grass on both sides – classic ambush territory. Suddenly two ous with semi-automatic rifles slung over their shoulders stepped into the road in front of us. I kakked myself and thought of flooring it when I noticed the incline ahead. My old Kombi didn't have enough speed and would have crawled up the hill, giving the guys plenty time to unsling their weapons, stub out their cigarettes, find comfortable positions and turn the back of the vehicle into a colander.

'So I stopped and greeted them as if they were lifelong *vriende* ... or comrades. At that stage I didn't know whether they were Renamo (South African origins helpful, even life-saving) or Frelimo (South African connections unhelpful, but not life-threatening). Their uniforms weren't obviously one or the other.

'It turned out they were Frelimo guys, but it wasn't easy convincing them we weren't spies, bandits or hijackers. That's when the ball came in handy. We challenged them to a game: Wits United pair versus Tete Maxaquene pair. It felt fully weird playing soccer on a road in the middle of rebel and landmine territory. Then it started to rain and they piled into the Kombi with us. By the time the convoy bowled through we were best amigos. It just so happens that those two could have saved our lives, 'cause sniper alley was just ahead and a lone, sluggish Volksy with no Zimbabwean covering fire would have been like a cut-out in a shooting gallery.'

Despite Mike's organisational lapses I had to recognise that he was an excellent guy to have along and his raconteur skills filled many of the dead night hours. His knowledge of Mozambique, although not always accurate when it came to the refinements of itineraries, was indispensable. Even the mishaps, when viewed in the rosiness of retrospect, were humorous and provided better anecdotes than any luxury lodge hopping could.

It was getting late and conversation became more sporadic. Hayley and Dave slipped off to bed and although the night sky held us enthralled, there was another long day of driving ahead. We zipped ourselves in and listened to the pulse of late-night blasters echoing through the alleys of Alto Molócuè.

It was a grey dawn beyond our rooftop penthouse and I crawled from my tent to photograph the passing fray from the parapet while Dave and Rob went marauding through the market with their semi-automatic Nikons, flashes fixed and no prisoners taken. I contemplated having a wash, but perusing the bucket shower, decided there was no harm in remaining one of the great unwashed.

The road to Nampula snaked through lovely undulating terrain of deciduous miombo woodland. The road surface had also improved. There were cashews everywhere and rocky outcrops stood up blue out of the landscape. Villages dotted the valleys. The local Makua hut design was quite different to that of the south. Here dwellings were rectangular instead of round, spaced further apart and the thatch had overhanging eaves supported by wooden pillars. The materials were also different, a lack of palm trees being the most obvious missing ingredient.

We came upon an old Portuguese prison beside the road. The white-washed structure looked like a fort with its crenellated turrets. I stopped to photograph it, but as I crouched down, focusing my 20-millimetre lens, a policeman materialised. '*Atenção senhor!*' he shouted. 'You can't take pictures of a government installation. This prison is still in use.'

This I found hard to believe, but put the Nikon back in my bag. Then Mike stepped in, explaining our mission, exchanging pleasantries and stories, and soon we had permission to snap away.

A bit further on we stopped at Murrupula Cathedral. Its presence in this remote part of Mozambique was incongruous, particularly given the predominance of Islam in the region. The edifice was being renovated by a group of Italians and there was a bustle of activity around the structure. It had a wooden, barrel-vaulted ceiling, but was as yet without windows, allowing a breeze to eddy through the space. For a moment it reminded me of the ruined Cistercian abbey of Tintern on a bend of the Wye River in Wales.

The priest was doing sterling work: women tended communal fields and children were being schooled, continuing a tradition of Catholic education established by Portuguese missions over the centuries.

Beaming girls and boys crowded round, wanting to show us their school books. Rob found a bench in the shade and began helping a young boy with his maths. They had no language with which to communicate, but multiplication and long division proved a passable common tongue.

Young women were peeling strips of beans on the cathedral steps. One thin teenager caught my attention. She couldn't have been much older than 15 and was breast-feeding a sick-looking baby. Both Madonna and child had a bereft look, their eyes glazed. Aids? Probably. Some villages in this region had been all but wiped out by the modern plague. The pair cast a shadow over what was otherwise a scene of hope.

The road eastward was lined with increasingly surreal outcrops: breasts, phalluses, a granite hand holding a ball. They were unlike anything we'd ever encountered and I quoted a lapel pin I'd once seen: 'I'm experiencing a *voujà dé*: that strange feeling of never having been here before.'

Lilliputian hamlets were scattered among boulders, some of the poorest rural communities in Mozambique. 'As long as whites don't start sticking their noses in, these folk will be OK,' said Mike. 'You see, muzungos inadvertently disempower the locals through their supposed omnipotence. They come along and show that they can supposedly fix anything, do anything. Then suddenly they're gone. Left to their own devices, the peasants often fare much better.'

Mike swerved to miss a goat. 'I tell you, the villagers round here are the most hospitable people on earth,' he continued. 'Whenever I camp in these parts I find a church and pitch my tent next to it. That way I'm sure to be near a village and safe from landmines. Locals invariably receive me with open arms. Poor they may be, but nothing is too much trouble for these people.

'I remember one occasion. It was five o' clock in the morning and I woke to a soft voice outside my tent: "*Dá licença, senhor,*"' Mike mimicked the apologetic tone of the intruder.

'I remember thinking it was a beggar: "Oh fuck off, I'm fast asleep," I wanted to shout. In fact it was this ou with a bucket of warm water for me to wash. Warm water! D'you know what that means? The guy had to walk bloody miles to draw it, then light a fire to heat it. I'd never met the man before and he certainly didn't want anything in return. It was such a humbling experience.'

We reached Nampula, a modern town with a white, domed cathedral – nicknamed Gina Lollobrigida because of its mammary-like cupolas – etched against an indigo sky. Once a sleepy trading centre, Nampula was jolted into life when it was made the capital of the north, the Portuguese having decided to establish a military base here to counter Frelimo activities. They'd also come to realise that tiny Moçambique Island could no longer house the brigade of civil servants, nor was it central enough.

Mike directed us to Clube de Ténis restaurant which he said served great food. It was quite a happening place with Euro-disco pumping beneath thatched umbrellas and spreading jacarandas. Dave and I climbed onto the restaurant roof to get better satellite reception and again tried Henrique, our travel contact 'up north'. First we reached his Nacala office and were told he was in Maputo. The Maputo people were on lunch. When we got them they said no, he was in the north. Finally we ascertained he was probably at home and left a message saying we'd be arriving in Nacala at 18h00 and would meet him at his soon to be completed guesthouse on the main drag. The port town was only two hours' drive away and it was lunch time, so we could do things at a slower pace than the usual scramble. Or so we thought.

I was sitting waiting for our food with Hayley, Tank and Rob who were griping (again) (justifiably) about our lack of provisions. 'Here we are in a major town with supermarkets and instead of buying food, we're sitting in a restaurant waiting endlessly for *frango zambeziano*,' said Rob. 'The planning is all haywire. This business of buying a few tins of tuna and a bag of chips at each stop is ridiculous. Why should we be on short rations?"

'Stop worrying about damn provisions,' said Mike. 'We're sorted for the next two nights. Besides, the supermarket is on the other side of town.'

Tempers bubbled and a two-hour wait for chicken didn't help the situation. The sun was already starting to wester when we finally headed out of town. I suggested we cut down on the photo calls in order to make our appointment with Henrique. But one picture opportunity none of us could resist was the Cathedral of Santuário de S M Mãe do Redentor. It was a classic Catholic precinct at the end of a long, tree-lined avenue. The light was softening and girls in capulanas moved silently about the place. The spire was decorated with a large *azulejo* (traditional Portuguese tiles) image of the Virgin and Child, complete with floating pink cherubs, which reminded me of the mother and baby I had seen earlier in the day at Murrupula Cathedral.

Here the presence of Portugal still lingered, a faint colonial footprint.

Further along the road was yet another stop to admire capulanas at a market during which Mike disappeared into the village to check out a dingy, backpacker's lodge he was going to recommend to the lambs who'd buy the next edition of his guidebook. Before we knew it, the sun had set, 18h00 had come and gone and Henrique had been left high and dry at the allotted meeting point. We were going to be in trouble again.

After some time-consuming wrong turnings we found the guesthouse, a construction site, on a hill overlooking the port of Nacala. Of course Henrique wasn't there, but after a few tries on the satellite phone we managed to raise him at home. In a matter of minutes a swish, new Pajero pulled up in the drive and Henrique stepped out. He was a big man with moustache, beer gut and loud gold jewellery. He spoke in a big voice with a Portuguese accent, '*É pá*! I was-e waiting for you 'ere, but a man-e can wait only so long-e. What 'appened to you?'

'*So* sorry,' said Dave. 'We got held up along the way taking photos. It's a very long journey; we're exhausted and we often slip behind schedule.'

'*Não faz mal*, no worries; just follow me to your rooms,' he replied matter of factly. 'Have a 'ot shower and den you must-e join me in my 'ome for dinner.'

Hot showers? A home-cooked meal? Were we hearing correctly? I'd begun to doubt such things existed. We piled in and squealed off after Henrique's disappearing tail lights. The accommodation he'd arranged was in a high-walled enclosure and comprised a cluster of upmarket family homes with toilets that actually flushed, telephones and air-conditioning. After Alto Molócuè this was as good as the Polana.

'De compound was-e built for Finnish engineers constructing Nacala's cargo terminal,' explained Henrique. 'When dey left, de town took it over for use as-e guest accommodation.' (For 'town' read 'mayor', in one of those dodgy arrangements that smack of corruption.)

We plunged into showers, lathering and scrubbing ourselves until we were pink. Tank emerged from his room with a can of bug spray called Flysquito. 'Have you guys seen any of these around?' he said, pointing to the picture on the can. It showed a ravenous flying insect-thing with huge eyes and bloody mandibles. Like the cobramamba, it was a composite creature. 'Better watch out for the dreaded flysquito tonight,' he said, laughing.

We arrived at Henrique's lavish home like kids on an outing: self-consciously clean, with washed-combed-and-parted hair and dressed in our last moderately unsoiled clothing, dredged from the bottom of our packs. Rob, as always, was neatest of the boys in clean white shirt with button-down collar and Hayley looked lovely in a short summer dress. We filed in and sat awkwardly on the lounge furniture, unused to soft seats.

Henrique's wife, Maria, a young Colombian woman who spoke no English, and very little Portuguese, fussed over us, hauling tray after tray of hors d' oeuvres and ready-mixed drinks. Henrique sat with his hands on his knees pontificating about tourism, his guesthouses, and the 'great potential' in this part of Mozambique. He had big plans.

Our host made no attempt to hide his self-importance. Henrique had grown up in Mozambique, studied in South Africa, then Europe. He'd worked in the catering industry in Los Angeles (which accounted for some of the self-promotion) and then spent a long time managing in a hotel in Colombia, where he'd met Maria.

Now he'd returned to Mozambique and all that 'potential' needed to be milked. 'Just give-e me some of Mozambique's 3 000-kilometre coastline and I'll turn it into tourist 'eaven: 'otels, resorts, casinos – der's enough space for everysing ... for your wildest dreams!' he enthused.

Conversation went on in this vein over dinner. Maria never sat down. She and the servants kept ferrying platters of chicken, fish, prawns and crayfish. When she did eventually eat, it was on her own in the lounge. Henrique obviously ran a traditional ship: his woman knowing her place and the servants on tip-toe.

I wondered how he'd made all his money? And how had he managed to acquire land, property, tourist concessions and thread his way through the spaghetti of Marxist bureaucracy? Sure, he had friends in high places ('I was just-e talking to de minister of tourism de other day ...' pregnant pause so that we all registered), but I felt sure he was a shady one. Were his grand guesthouses a front for money laundering? Was he into drugs, arms, smuggling? Who was being blackmailed, who bribed, who was getting a cut? Was he part of the Portuguese Mafia? Or maybe I was just maligning a fatcat for being a fatcat in such a poverty stricken place.

Henrique saw himself as the *grande senhor*. 'No problem. Just-e leave it to me. I can organise anysing in dis town ...' There's something awfully sinister and implicitly corrupt in being able to 'organise *anysing*'. Then again, when we pressed him, it was often hot air – a rhetorical flourish designed to impress the visitor.

'De road from Nampula to Cuamba is *horrível*,' cautioned Henrique. 'It's impossible. I 'ave friends in 'igh places who know about de road. But leave it to me. I can-e organise dat your vehicles are put-e on de train from Nampula to Malawi.' Nonsense. There was no train transport laid on, and his experts got it wrong about the condition of the road.

Just before I dozed off that night I thought about our luxurious accommodation. If this compound had been taken over by Nacala's mayor as part of his fiefdom, how had Henrique organised us free accommodation? Or was it one of those I'll scratch your back you scratch mine arrangements?

Henrique collected us early the next morning. Hayley was so tired she couldn't make it out of bed so we left her asleep. I also felt shattered and a comfortable bed was such a luxury ... but the light was good and beaches beckoned. First we took a look round the unremarkable town of Nacala. 'Dis is de finest natural, deep-water 'arbour in de world – a deps of 300 metres!' boasted Henrique as though he were responsible for dredging the bay himself. 'With its fantastic railway link to de interior, it's become de major port for Malawi and Zambia.' True enough, Nacala's natural harbour could accommodate the world's biggest super tankers. Only problem was, they had no reason to stop here.

Next we visited the beaches at nearby Fernão Veloso, dotted with colourful dhows. But Relanzapo Beach was the jewel: a long stretch of powder sand with a handful of reed *barracas* serving as bathing huts. The sea was a pale, milky blue and dhow sails flecked the ocean beyond the reef. We dragged off our clothing and ran naked into the shore break. The water was as warm as the air and we splashed about like seals.

It had been almost 2 000 kilometres and over a week since we'd disported ourselves on Mozambique's famous beaches. For an expedition that was supposed to be following the coastline, we weren't doing very well. In our defence there are vast tracts of coast without road access and all the arteries stretch far inland, parallel to the region's rivers. How many perfect beaches must there be between Vilankulo and Nacala that are only accessible to sailors or 4x4 adventurers with plenty of time on their hands?

'I come 'ere on Sundays with my *familia*,' said Henrique. 'We buy fish off de boats and get de boys to cook dem over a fire. It's paradise ... no-one knows about dis place. Just imagine a resort right 'ere. Big reception area among de trees; maybe 'undred chalets along de beach. It would make a fortune, I tell you. We just 'ave to sort out 'ow to pipe in fresh water. But I tell you, come back in ten years and dis will all be developed.'

My heart sank. I prayed that the fresh water problem would be insurmountable. This beach, this haven, this heaven must not be spoilt. But how to keep the likes of Henrique in check? With corrupt officials, all it took was a little grease to the right palm and building could begin tomorrow.

We collected Hayley and sped south to Ilha trying to keep pace with Henrique's Pajero. Now and then we'd pass a blackened stretch of tar, evidence of a skirmish in which a truck had probably been brought to a halt, the contents looted, driver shot and vehicle torched. Henrique must have assumed we were trans-Africa rally drivers and wanted to impress us with his flashy vehicle, or maybe it was just his Lusitanian exuberance, but we found it hard keeping him in sight. I flattened the accelerator to overtake a truck which tore along with goats on its roof. So confident was the driver in the sure-footedness of his cargo that the animals weren't tethered.

We took the turnoff to Mossuril and blasted through villages at an unhealthy lick. Soon Henrique had vanished and at each crossroad we checked the direction of his tyre tracks. In one hamlet we saw the results of his passing. The body of a white duck lay in the middle of the main street, its head crushed by Henrique's tyres. The earth and scattered white feathers were stained scarlet. Sullen looks, angry shouts from the villagers.

Finally we caught up at Praia das Chocas, yet another comely stretch of peninsula sand. Out to sea dhows lay becalmed, standing over their reflections, while to the south-east lay legendary Ilha de Moçambique.

'Dis promontory is de perfect place for a 'otel, don't you think? Guests would just-e roll out of bed onto de sand,' said Henrique, smoothing his facial hair, forefinger and thumb gliding from nostrils to moustache ends. 'In de meantime, when my inn on Ilha is ready – just a couple of weeks – I'll ferry my guests across to 'ere. It's only an hour by boat. No-one wants to swim at Ilha's disgusting beaches.'

We arrived at the bridge which connects the famous island to the mainland and paid the toll. I was terribly excited: Ilha was a place I'd longed to visit ever since I'd researched the aborted dhow documentary and become intrigued by the melting of cultures that had produced the Swahili people and by the Persian, Arab and early Portuguese exploits in East Africa.

Ilha de Moçambique: the tiny island – a mere 600 by 2 500 metres – that gave it's name to the province, then the country. At the time of Da Gama the place was the stronghold of Sultan Moussa Ben Mbiki (or perhaps he was the founder of the Muslim community there – no-one really knows) and the Portuguese corrupted his name to Moç-am-bique. It's a palm and coral-fringed gem crammed with 500 years of European history, and a far longer Arab and African heritage. It was the capital of Portugal's overseas province until 1886 when the isle lost out to LM. A place of pirates, slaves, gold and ivory; an island haunted by the legacy of Jesuit priests, Arabian merchants and Dutch invaders; site of sea battles and sieges, intrigue and passion. For centuries it had been the symbol of Portuguese presence in the Indian Ocean, one of the few bastions able to withstand concerted attack. On paper at least, it was everything I expected of an East African isle.

We crossed the three-kilometre causeway. Children played on the mud flats below. A dhow packed to the gunwales sailed towards us, then tacked neatly beneath our vehicle in a flurry of flogging rope and canvas, just metres from the pylons. It was crowded with islanders in colourful garb, women with matching capulanas used as skirt, wrap and head scarf – worn Muslim-style. In 1517 the Portuguese chronicler Duarte Barbosa described the locals in very different terms: they went about 'naked smeared with red clay ... their lips bored with three holes and in these they place bones with little stones and other little pendants.'

As we crossed over to the island Mike regaled us with its past. The settlement came about as a result of the isle providing refuge from strife on the mainland, because of its safe anchorage and strategic position on a trade route dictated by monsoon winds. It was a haven for traders and became known as the *ponto de encontro de civilizações* (meeting point of civilisations).

We drove through '*makuti* town' and into stone town passing a beach where boat builders practised a craft conducted here since long before the Portuguese dropped anchor. As the light was beginning to soften, we made straight for the castle, Fortaleza São Sebastião – a legendary stronghold built in the 16th century which dominates the isle. As our vehicles drew up beside the bastions we were surrounded by urchins in rags offering everything from car protection to 'old Portuguese coins' and hand-made necklaces. Mixed in with glass and plastic baubles were a few porcelain Missinga beads, used by Arabs as currency. During the trade war of the early 16th century the Portuguese sank many Arab vessels in the roadstead and 500 years later their bead cargo is still being washed ashore.

Henrique didn't seem much interested in the historical significance of São Sebastião. 'It would make a great tourist 'otel, don't you think?' he suggested. 'Just-e imagine what you could charge people for staying in a Renaissance Portuguese castle!' With this flourish he knew he had really impressed us and decided to make an exit. We thanked him for his help and in a cloud of dust he was gone, bulleting down the narrow Ilha lanes.

The fort is massive and my unofficial guide, a disreputable-looking character who it took some time to shake off, told me in broken English that it was, for centuries, the biggest human-made edifice in the southern hemisphere. The sprawling structure had in its foundations granite quoins shipped from Portugal as ballast in the caravels, naus, galleons and carracks plying their trade with the East. The casements and quarters could accommodate a garrison of up to 2 000 soldiers and a huge courtyard cistern assured them of enough water to withstand lengthy sieges.

Fortifications were begun in 1508 and it was almost a century before the last great bulwark was completed. The objective: to guard the sea route from Lisbon to Asia. With 12-metre high battlements and a 750-metre perimeter studded with 400 guns, this motionless battleship constitutes one of the great engineering feats of the subcontinent. Given the isolation in this corner of the Indian Ocean you might think it was overkill on the part of the Portuguese, but history proved the architects and strategists right. In the 17th-century Portugal was to lose most of its Indian Ocean possessions and forts. The initial test came soon after the completion of São Sebastião, and probably constituted the first battles between European powers on African soil. The aggressors were the Dutch; after them came the English, French and Arabs.

Long before they finally chose the Cape of Good Hope as a replenishment station, the Dutch had set their hearts on seizing Ilha as the westernmost pivot for their proposed Indian Ocean empire. In 1607 eight Dutch ships under Van Caerden anchored in the road and entrenched 1 500 men ashore. After a determined, but unsuccessful six-week siege by a force severely depleted by malaria, Van Caerden withdrew. This despite the fact that the defence was conducted largely by civilians and women.

The next year was Admiral Verhoeven's turn. He arrived with 13 ships and nearly 2 000 men, but still the tiny São Sebastião garrison held firm. Again the Dutch were defeated by the high morale of the defenders and the massive strength of the battlements which they were unable to breach, even with a siege train. Had the Dutch taken the fort, the history of the subcontinent would certainly have been different. Their occupation of the Cape in 1652 may not have occurred and the Afrikaner nation never been born.

The Portuguese hung onto their patch of coral for nearly 500 years. Whenever their imperial chips were down, they'd retreat to Ilha. Hounded from most of their possessions in India and the Gulf, chased from their bases in Malindi, Mombasa and Zanzibar, only Ilha held out.

I took the stairs to the ramparts from where I had a commanding view of the island, mainland and, in the foreground, battlements defended with heavy-calibre cannon. Fellow travel journalist, Jackie Nel, had told me that when she visited Ilha islanders had offered her 16th-century cannon balls from the fort at one dollar a piece! In the courtyard I could see the cisterns designed to provide the besieged with an ample water supply. They remain the only source of permanent fresh water on the island.

I sat on a cannon and looked to sea where I could make out Goa and Das Cobras (snakes) islands. The latter got its name from a myth involving strange serpents with fat breasts and dark-framed spectacles which inhabited the isle. Below me was the tiny Capela de Nossa Senhora do Baluarte, the Chapel of Our Lady of the Bulwark, built at the beginning of the 16th century on a coral promontory just metres from the sea. Not only was this the first church built in southern Africa, it was also the first building erected by Europeans in the southern hemisphere. I noticed that the Manueline style in which it was built, popular in Portugal during the Age of Discovery, looked quite Islamic – a hint of things to come.

I imagined I could see Persian and Arab dhows approaching from the north, those pioneers of the Indian Ocean trade routes (Greeks and Romans *had* ventured down the African coast before them, but did not set up such a complex network). They'd pull into the anchorage to exchange beads, spices and cloth for slaves, ivory and gold. Soon they opened trading houses on the island. Later came the Indians and, from the south, the dreaded Portuguese to wreak havoc on the ancient commerce.

I imagined Vasco da Gama's fleet nosing into the bay on 2 March 1498 and coasting up to an anchorage full of Arab dhows laden with riches. He must have been thrilled to see all this evidence of trade: the grail was at hand. Assuming the strangers were of his own faith, the local sheikh was at first welcoming to the dishevelled sailors from the deep, cold south – from that 'other' ocean. Gifts of yellow jackets, brass tankards and hats were exchanged for jars of Arab sweetmeats and the sheikh's personal *masbaha* (religious beads). Alas Da Gama could not produce his copy of the Koran: he'd 'left it at home'.

But then suspicions arose, a story that would become commonplace as Europeans butted heads with Indian Ocean cultures. Someone saw Da Gama's crew preparing to hold a religious service and recognised them as Christians. Insults, a foiled kidnapping, a scuffle at a watering place, and the cannons roared out from the Portuguese ships. Gunboat diplomacy had arrived in south-east Africa. The stage was set for a long struggle.

Armed with crossbows, swords and lances and wearing half-armour in the hottest tropical climes the Portuguese buccaneers outclassed all Indian Ocean communities who tried to resist them. Their enemies had a slim chance when contesting the *fidalgos* on land, but on water, the Portuguese were invincible. The ubiquitous Arab *mtepe* – a dhow whose planks were sewn, not nailed, together – stood no chance against a Portuguese broadside. Their sturdy vessels could survive Atlantic gales and venture far into the ocean without needing regular replenishment stops. Navigational innovations such as the astrolabe allowed captains to make fairly accurate landfalls after weeks at sea. But most important was the firepower these vessels housed between their decks. Heavy cannons of the 15th century were clumsy and immobile on land, but mounted on a ship's gun deck, they were easily brought to bear on coastal settlements refusing to trade or pay tribute. Once bombarded, towns could be occupied and Portuguese factories and forts built. In the first decades of the 15th century a number of these stations grew up round the Indian Ocean rim.

The more easily protected Ilha soon replaced Sofala as administrative centre on the coast. It was the compulsory port of call for ships rounding Africa, each vessel leaving its complement of sick at the island's royal hospital. The town became a Renaissance hub thronged with soldiers bound for military expeditions, slaves being amassed in the market place, survivors of shipwrecks straggling in, passengers awaiting ships and missionaries on their way to bring light to darkest corners – or to become martyrs. Carracks hammered by storm or battle limped into Ilha for repairs, spawning a class of boat builders, carpenters, rope-makers and ship chandlers.

Dave, Rob and I made a quick dash along the west side of the island, grabbing shots as a low sun illuminated the flaking coral of warehouses, homes, and fortress walls. Some dhows lay becalmed in the channel, others were being rowed like drunk, flailing insects into the anchorage below us. I climbed down a sea wall and stood on a ribbon of sand beside an ancient warehouse, now empty. Once the stone edifice was crammed with goods bound for India or Lisbon: ambergris, the finest cloth, spices, beads for bartering and ivory tusks.

The golden age of trade was over, but there was also thankfully no more black ivory, for Ilha was a major slaving centre. A large portion of the more than a million slaves shipped out of Mozambique's ports during the 19th century left from Ilha. The isle has its share of horrific accounts. One of the more gruesome is by a Dominican friar, João dos Santos, who tells of an event that took place in 1586, the year he arrived on the island. Whether true or apocryphal, it stands as a symbol of the consequences of famine and destabilisation in the region. Two locals brought a girl for sale to a Portuguese woman, but the senhora found their price of ten pieces of cloth too expensive and offered them half. 'No,' said one of the men, 'we'd rather eat the negress than sell her so cheaply.' As no other buyer came forward, the men 'proceeded to a thicket that was close by and killed the negress, and remained there three or four days eating her flesh boiled and roasted.' The captain of Moçambique laid part of the blame on the woman who'd refused to buy the slave, and punished her along with a number of 'heathen kaffirs who resided in these palm groves as he learnt that they had assisted in eating the said negress.'

Slaves collected at Ilha were bound for ports all over the Indian Ocean and beyond, some ending up as far away as North America. One of the major markets was India, more precisely the Portuguese stronghold of Goa. Many travellers have recorded the cruelty, idleness and lustfulness of the Portuguese in India. One Neapolitan chronicler noted that most men in Goa kept an entourage of female slaves, known as 'mosses'. These women were allegedly kept busy all day 'caressing and massaging' their masters. Their collective name referred not only to their duties as slaves, but the home they would never see again: Mossambique.

Long after the slave trade had been abolished, Ilha's anchorage remained a place of intrigue full of rumours about the sale of lives. William Devereux entered Ilha harbour in July 1861 and noted

> two or three dhows, miniature junks, alias slave-coffins, and a French barque ready for their living freight; also a Portuguese schooner of war (which will do a stroke of illegal traffic at a pinch).

When the light had finally gone, we made for our guesthouse, a restored building with high ceilings, on the eastern side of the Museum Quarter, just metres from where waves stroked the coral.

'The storey you are occupying is a mere 300 years old,' said the dona who ran the establishment. She threw open the windows offering an uninterrupted view of ocean. The voices of two lovers sitting beneath a palm reached us faintly. Then she led us down some stairs into an older space with low ceilings supported by chunky, mangrove beams. 'This part of the house is nearly 500 years old,' she said proudly.

After a quick bucket shower I wove through cobbled alleys to join the others at Restaurante Âncora d' Ouro (the golden anchor) on a praça opposite a Renaissance church. We downed a few Dois Ms by candlelight. Dave told me he was moved by the seductiveness of the place; that it was playing tricks with his mind. Confirmed old bachelor that he was, there were 'unimaginable stirrings' between Hayley and himself. I, too, could not get Jennifer out of my head. Were we losing it, I wondered?

When we emerged it was dark and the street was lit with paraffin lamps. From inside the church came the murmur of voices and glow of candles. I mounted the steps and found a priest leading a group of islanders in prayer. Ilha was once the centre for the Christian faith in Africa, seat of rival Jesuit and Dominican houses. They'd divided the coast among themselves for the saving of souls and priests had led war bands into the interior in pursuit of their orders' political objectives. Today only a handful of Christians are left on what is a Muslim island, an Islamic coast.

We dined in nearby Relíquias Restaurant, a more upmarket – and trendy – establishment than you'd expect in a place where tourism has not yet arrived. By the time we'd finished eating, a bunch of young locals had gathered at the bar, but, lacking the stamina for a night of revelry, we moseyed back to our guesthouse through streets too narrow for traffic. Children played in the dark. Candles cast erratic light from doorways. The night was windless and balmy, and the sea hissed against the coral tidal wall at the end of our lane. I could smell the salty air and feel the centuries of history that hung like a vapour in the ancient alleys. We left Dave and Hayley, strolling arm in arm, far behind.

It was a night too freighted to resist a call to Covent Garden, so I grabbed the Iridium phone and found a nook on our praça overlooking the ocean to make the connection. Jennifer's mobile phone gave me a recorded message saying the number had been 'discontinued'. I was alarmed and quickly dialled her home number, from which I received the same news, delivered in a trite computer voice that made me want to hurl the handset into the sea.

I started to feel panicky. If she'd suddenly got cold feet about the relationship, I thought she might just be decisive enough to have her numbers changed – give herself time to compose a suitable retraction. My mind was racing: could she be having an affair, or was this her way of terminating things?

I gave it ten minutes then tried again. Then half an hour. Same story about being discontinued, a disconnection I could feel in my stomach. In desperation I phoned my parents and left an only vaguely coherent SOS message on their answering machine about the sky falling on my head and could they please call Jen and ask her to get in touch with them ... tell them what was what ... and then call me. I walked the shores of Ilha – most bloody romantic of locales – in a tizzy of love-sickness bordering on nausea.

The trade wind played sibilantly in the fronds and the ocean sighed along the sea wall. I walked and walked, trying to still my fears. I was a slave to the emotions that assaulted me from all sides. Eventually I crawled into bed, but couldn't find sleep. A noisy child in the next room was talking at the top of his voice to his mother. When the odd bout of slumber finally overtook me, it was infested with paranoid Larium dreams of relationship fall-out which shocked me awake.

Next thing I knew, it was light outside and the photographers were stirring for the dawn patrol. I downed two cups of disgusting powdered coffee and joined the others at the base of the statue of Luis

Vaz de Camões, the Shakespeare of Portugal, commemorating his two years on Ilha in the late 16th century. I loved the poet's work and his presence, albeit in bronze, was somehow comforting. He'd been trapped on this island, waiting for a ship to bear him back to Lisbon, and I empathised with his loneliness and sense of isolation. In the east the sun fondled a horizon cloud, then lanced it with a shaft of red light.

Camões was born in about 1524 and attended university in Coimbra where he received a thorough grounding in Latin, history and mythology. His family were related by marriage to Vasco da Gama and his father was shipwrecked and drowned off the coast of Goa. The son's fate would also be inextricably linked to the empire. After becoming involved in an unfortunate love affair he was banished from Lisbon and served first as a common soldier in North Africa (and then did a stint in prison for brawling), before ending up on a ship bound for the East, there to seek his fortune. During his long sojourn in Macau and Goa he began working on *The Lusiads* and in 1567 decided to return home and see his poem, which was to become the national epic of Portugal, published. The return journey took him three arduous years. His ship took him only as far as Ilha, and he couldn't find a friendly captain to give him a berth for the homeward leg. Camões languished on the island in near penury, working on his poem and pining for Lisbon until a group of friends finally defrayed the cost of his passage home.

When it was eventually published *The Lusiads* received little acclaim. What's more, a broken-hearted Camões was forced to witness the beginning of the disintegration of his beloved empire when the boy-king Sebastião was killed, his army defeated in battle and the Spanish crown took over Portugal. On his deathbed Camões wrote: 'All will see that so dear to me was my country that I was content to die not only in it but with it.'

I'd first read *The Lusiads* during my voyage on the *Bartolomeu Dias* caravel. The Portuguese are mad about their history, particularly what they call the 'Age of Discoveries', and our whole crew was swept up in that fervour during the Lisbon summer of 1987 … less so during the three months of interminable tacking down the Atlantic into an obstinate south-easter.

Camões lived during that golden era and his epic poem celebrates not only the feats of Vasco da Gama, but also the Portuguese people whom he named the Lusitanians, or sons of Lusus – companion of

Bacchus in Greek mythology. Like Virgil's *Aeneid*, the tale recounts the exploits of a storm-tossed sailor (Da Gama) venturing into uncharted waters to lay the foundation of a new empire. As a romantic-spirited 20-year-old clad in medieval costume bobbing down the Atlantic in a replica caravel, I was naturally taken with Camões's heady prose, even in translation.

Upon re-reading the epic years later I was amazed to find how blind I'd been to its glorification of violence and conquest. The canto concerning Moçambique Island makes the point. The brave sons of Lusus step ashore in coats of armour and bearing shields, muskets, longbows, firebombs and mortars to be used on a defenceless population. The Muslims are described as vermin who plot to overthrow the Portuguese. Their treachery is avenged with 'killing and destruction; for the settlement had no walls or other defences, and under bombardment its dwellings collapsed and burst into flames.' When the inhabitants flee, the brave Portuguese show little mercy:

> Then, abandoning everything and turning their backs on the island, they made panic-stricken for the sea and struck out for the mainland but a short distance away. Those who could crowded into canoes, on which the Portuguese rained shot, smashing many to pieces. The rest swam, some only to be engulfed by the waves and perish, others, swallowing the sea-water, to be spewed back by the sea. Such was their punishment at the hands of the Portuguese for their malice.

Camões describes the Portuguese sailing into the sunset, flanked by 'an escort of nymphs' and laden with loot, well-satisfied with their Moçambican spoils. How did the barbarism elude me on the first read? Youth, perhaps, and my own uncritical vision of 'discovery', the 'glamour' of a Portuguese maritime empire based on a handful of courageous men in tiny ships criss-crossing the globe. But then again it's a colonial vision that has afflicted Europe – and, for that matter, the Americas, Africa and Australasia – for centuries.

We were walking along the corniche towards the fort and its superimposed church of Santo António. Soon we trailed a flotilla of children whispering 'amigo, amigo ...' I lagged behind with Hayley and told her my tale of lost love in chivalric terms borrowed from Camões.

'Don't overreact, Justin,' Hayley said, putting her arm around me.

'You have a tendency to melodramatise. Wait to hear from Jenny before plunging into self-pity. There might be a simple explanation.'

It was good advice, but I was already wallowing, taking in more woe than my pumps could handle. When the sun finally broke through to illuminate the chapel, beach and fishing boats, I managed to switch into photographic drive, which helped somewhat to take my mind off emotions. I picked my way between nets and children kicking a soccer ball. Fishermen manoeuvred their boats in the shallows, preparing for sea. F8, 125th of a second, click. Remember to bracket: open two thirds of a stop, click; close two thirds of a stop, click.

The beach was strewn with human faeces, and excrement was floating between the boats. Further down the beach squatting figures emptied the previous nights' dinner for all the world to see. There's something so undignified, base even, about humans hunkered down shitting en masse. Perhaps it's my Calvinistic upbringing. Certainly the locals didn't seem to see it that way, but I couldn't get my mind around this communal, open-air ablution performance. Alexander's guidebook is effusive about Ilha's white sands, claiming they are 'reminiscent of secluded coves in Greece. There are long stretches of beach and coral to explore for shells, which are beautiful, prolific and varied.' Sorry old man, shell hunting along the tide line is out these days; swimming too.

Rob and Dave are more dedicated photographers than I and waded between the *lanças* (fishing dhows) and *galawas* (dugout canoes) getting some great shots. I chickened out and headed for a food market in front of the church. It was a gay scene with bright capulanas complementing the light's texture. I would have been in my element, camera snapping happily, had it not been for the Jennifer cloud. We were reluctant to dish out coins to the boys who were tagging us, but if any of them did a little job – anything fairly arbitrary, like guarding a camera bag – I'd give him a tip. One lad with buck teeth had been following us around since the evening before at the fort.

'Senhor, I know the house where Camões stayed when he was here on Ilha,' he said in a high-pitched voice. 'You know the poet?'

'*Sim*,' I said. 'Hey, what's your name?'

'Rui. You want to see the house?'

'Sure, lead the way.'

I followed Rui through side streets and past the ruins of coral houses. 'Where you from?' asked Rui.

'*Do Cabo*, Cape Town.'

'Ah, Bafana Bafana, good side. Bit weak on defence, even if you got Radebe,' said the boy, referring to our national soccer team.

We came to a fairly ornate entrance and he told me to enter. I pushed open a wooden door studded with spikes and stepped into a run-down courtyard which had doorways leading off it – almost like a hermitage. 'Camões he slept in one of these cabins,' said my guide with authority.

If Rui could be believed the poet penned some of the immortal verses of *Os Lusíadas* by candlelight here. There was no commemorative plaque or museum, but then again, this was Mozambique and no-one would have been eager to retrace Camões's footsteps in the last 25 years. Maybe the kid was right.

Giving Rui some notes and the slip I went exploring the back streets of stone town. I passed the gabled gates of the port captain's villa guarded by cannons and flanked by massive anchors ... then a school where children queued silently for class, and the hospital built in a late-classical, Schinkel style, complete with sweeping staircase and crenellated portico. The hospital was second only to the fort in importance on the island. The arrival of a fleet to winter at Moçambique invariably filled the hospital with patients and often resulted in the outbreak of epidemics. Countless thousands of Portuguese lie buried in the sand and coral of Ilha.

Venturing into the alleys it seemed that nothing had changed much in hundreds of years. Heavily bolted doors, walled gardens and old villas ... hints of Arabia, touches of medieval Portugal, a Goan flourish, something of Madeira. Around every corner was another architectural delight and I felt I could keep on exploring all day. Ilha boasted the evocative elements unique to East African trading ports like Lamu, Mombasa and Zanzibar. Although the Muslim quarter had been largely destroyed during the two Dutch sieges, the town's atmosphere, layout and render-and-lime façades covered in colourful lichens, were reminiscent of those other African ports. The Portuguese elements were most apparent in the public buildings: forts, churches, hospital. The flat roofs – for rainwater collection – and courtyard-based designs of the houses were of Arabian origin while hints of Goa were evident in the building's ornamentation and in the carved, and often spiked, wooden doors reminiscent of Zanzibar.

Indeed Iberian, Islamic and Indian traditions were married in this place thick with cultural memorylines. For centuries the traders who operated from these towns linked themselves by marriage and commerce to Muslim lineages which controlled the trade between Ilha and the rest of the coast, as well as Arabia and India.

The island museum is housed in the Palace of São Paulo, built in the 17th century as a Jesuit college. It's a maroon coloured edifice with adjoining church and flanks the waterfront square on the west side of the Museum Quarter (declared a Unesco cultural heritage site). The praça – so reminiscent of Portugal – is laid with dizzying black-and-white mosaic cobbles. Today rope makers spread their coir hawsers on the spot where once a garrison of tall, ebony soldiers in white uniforms drilled before the bandstand and, in the evenings, town notables were brought in their palanquins to promenade.

For a frustrated sailor like myself, the lower storey of the palace offered a trove of model square riggers, dugout canoes and ships' cannons. Upstairs was the restored governor's residence, lavished with antiques from Goa, Portuguese paintings, Chinese porcelain vases, Indian tapestries and other artefacts purchased or plundered from possessions in the East.

My circuitous walk landed me back at Relíquias for our prearranged 08h00 breakfast. Paraffin-smelling eggs, white bread and kick-ass coffee were eventually served at 09h00, offering a frustrating hour of watching boat builders hammering away at the ribs of a soon to be launched craft and a young man taking an eternity over his defecation on the beach below us. No toilet paper, I reluctantly noticed, feeling grateful that our food did not arrive until he was done.

Back at the guesthouse we found Mike surrounded by a mêlée of miniature mechanics. His clothes were covered in oil and his face was hidden under the bonnet of the TDi where he was fiddling with the hooter which had died on us a few days previously. A hooter is indispensable in Mozambique, second only to brakes in the safety stakes. One of the kids was sitting in the driver's seat wearing a huge grin and honking the horn at Mike's command, and a few times extra for good measure. The thing sounded sick and out of key, but at least it was working and we would again be able to warn mentally challenged furry animals – and humans – of our approach.

Driving back towards the causeway we threaded through densely packed houses: clearly the population had outgrown the isle. In the early days, black people were not allowed to live here, but the abolition of the slave trade saw permanent settlement on the island by Africans (coinciding with more freedom of movement into the interior by white people). The influx of mainlanders increased during the civil war. With Renamo bandits wreaking havoc in the countryside, Mozambique's islands remained safe havens from attack, thereby fulfilling their age-old roles as fortresses. Today there are more than 15 000 people on the island and, if the sanitation and fresh-water arrangements are anything to go by, that's about 14 000 too many.

The Landies coursed northward through country dotted with *monte-ilhas* (island mountains), baobab and star chestnut trees. We were nearing Cabo Delgado Province, the northernmost reach of our trek and home to the Makonde people. Renowned for their fighting spirit and traditionalism, locals here still cut initiation scars into their foreheads and cheeks, while some leaders sport teeth filed into points, wear plugs in their noses and discs through their lips. Fiercely independent, the Makonde resisted Portuguese rule and in the early struggle years Frelimo drew its main support from Cabo Delgado. More so after the 1964 Mueda massacre – Mozambique's Sharpeville.

Through its long history of colonialism in south-east Africa the Portuguese came up against their independent spirit. By the late 1960s Frelimo had firmly established itself, with support from the rural population, in northern Cabo Delgado. The Portuguese responded with a huge resettlement programme, herding more than a quarter of a million peasants into new villages, or *aldeamentos*, circled with barbed wire.

Then in 1970 came Operation Gordian Knot, a veritable military invasion of the province by tens of thousands of Portuguese troops in an attempt to stamp out any remaining guerrilla enclaves. They used all the elements of modern warfare including artillery and aerial bombardments, but, as in Vietnam, they could not pin down an enemy that dissolved into the bush. The failure of Gordian Knot spelt the beginning of the end for Portugal in Africa.

We drew to a halt on the Lúrio River Bridge, marking the border between Nampula Province and Cabo Delgado, and got out to stretch our legs. An entire household of washing was laid out below us – sheets, shirts, shorts, trousers, capulanas – forming an abstract pattern on the sand. Naked children splashed in the shallows. Lunch on the far side of the bridge was the usual poultry affair.

'Which to eat first?' asked Tank. 'The chicken or the egg?' Having recently stocked up at a roadside market, we had more boiled eggs than we could manage. Tank offered some to passers-by who had stopped to warn us not leave the road as the spot was heavily mined.

I'd contemplated relieving myself in the derelict guard-post, now overgrown with wild fig, but settled on the verge.

Later, we came upon a de-mining operation and stopped to chat. The men and women were clad in blue flak jackets, helmets with visors and protective padding. The clothing was more to prevent injuries if someone near them stepped on a mine: padding wouldn't help the leg of the person doing the stepping.

'We've been trained in de-mining by the United Nations and our unit camps out here in the bush,' said one of the men. 'We work slowly-slowly through the areas marked by red poles.'

'Do you get scared?' asked Tank.

'*Sim senhor*, sometimes. But it's our job and it's good for our country.'

A woman was clearing a patch of long grass with a sickle. She stopped intermittently to brush her mine-detector over the place she was about to tread. Even at a distance you could feel her concentration – and the tension. What a day at the office.

We were witnessing just one of the success stories of Unomoz. Under the guidance of UN troops and advisers, Mozambique was helped back from the brink of a precipice over which Angola had leapt. Apart from initiating the large-scale removal of mines, they secured and revitalised the Beira and Tete corridors and assisted with the elections. It has been one of the most successful interventions in the history of the organisation.

We pushed on through lush countryside. Then, in my rear-view mirror, I saw a policeman step out behind us and hail the TDi, driven by Tank, to a stop. I pulled off the road and watched from a discreet distance. We were pretty far from civilisation and if the cops wanted to haul us back to the station it could be a lengthy process.

After a protracted discussion (strange that, as the two Portuguese speakers – Mike and I – were in the lead vehicle) I saw the headlights go on, then the hazards. The hooter blared – a sickening bleat, but at least it was working. They were being given a full going over and we suspected that Tank may well have to reach for his wallet to extricate himself.

Eventually the cop waved them on and the TDi drew up next to us. 'Hell, that bloke so badly wanted to nail us,' chuckled Tank. 'In his broken English he asked me to put on each indicator. I know one of them isn't working so I just put on the hazards and he didn't see anything amiss in that. In the end, the guy said we had to give him a Fanta or a Coke before he'd let us go. We said we didn't have any, so he demanded that we nip to the nearest town and buy him one. I began laughing and then he started laughing. He shook my hand and that was that – he let us drive on. Rather ineffectual extortion if you ask me. And a pretty decent bloke after all.'

We reached Pemba long after dark (sigh), took a right at a dilapidated army barracks and followed the coast past ghostly baobabs to Praia de Wimbe. Some of the giants were uprooted and lay like elephant carcasses beside the road. They appeared to have been planted in a straight line. The locals say this is because fruit were discarded by travellers following a path over the ages. I thought of the many walkers, maybe shackled slaves, heading to and from the interior – some having crossed the entire waist of the country. It was as though the footprints of an ancient trail had found organic manifestation here on the Indian shore.

Chapter 8

We halted at a cluster of thatched bungalows on Wimbe Beach. The gruff maître d' at Complexo Náutilus had, of course, never heard of us. This despite the faxes Mike handed across the counter to prove otherwise.

When Mike emerged looking dejected and beating his chest in prawn-tail anguish we couldn't muster much sympathy. Complexo Náutilus was full. His suggestion, 'Maybe we could drive a bit down the road and pitch our tents,' went down like a leaky carrack. Then Nic came to our rescue. Nic is a South African-Portuguese working as the watersport manager at Complexo Náutilus and knew how to talk his way through the bullshit at front desk. After a couple of phone calls and a heated discussion in the back room, keys and smiles were produced. Everything was going to be fine: just a small technical misunderstanding.

It was a balmy, windless evening and water licked the sand only metres from our barstools. I got chatting to a guy who ran a backpackers' haven nearby. When I told him I was a surfer he began enthusing about a local break I was soon itching to try.

'Bru, these classic, glassy walls loom out of the blue,' said my drinking buddy as he flicked bleached blonde hair out of his eyes. 'It's quite a mission to get to the spot though. You've got to take a boat a long way out to the reef, but the waves are absolute perfection. Sometimes I've been out there alone, just bodysurfing with fins and handgun. It's so kif!'

My *lulas grelhadas* (grilled calamari) was exceptional and the prawn eaters (bar Mike, who was doing his painful King Kong routine – minus pretty blonde in fist) tucked in contentedly. Conversation grew sparse and my head lolled towards England. It had been a long, Jennifer-filled day and I wanted to make another call – even on a hotel land line if necessary. Tonight was N-Night and I longed for, and dreaded, the voice I felt would decide things one way or another. The tension grew insupportable and an inane dinner conversation about provisions for the next leg only added to my frustration.

Eventually I could bear it no longer, excused myself and took the satellite phone for a walk along the beach. Down at the water's edge I phoned home and hurriedly asked my parents to call Jennifer and give her the number of my hotel. Then I ran back to the bungalow … and waited.

It's an eternity before the thing squeaks. I lift the receiver with my heart clattering. Behind the percussion I hear her sensual voice, clear as vodka. With assurances of love she reels me back in. My fears are Larium induced, she thinks, and my proclivity for creating mountain-size mole hills … but her even tone belies the fact that she knows I've been a tad derailed. I'm grateful for her perception. She says she asked my dad to tell me that she was completely committed, a brave thing under the circumstances. Alas, she's left a group of guests stranded at dinner table … hot food … social graces. London. She has to go. I hang on her words, finding trivial importances to delay. But she says good-bye and the phone goes quiet in my hand. Bloody London.

The room swam into focus and I heard the lads coming back from the bar. I knew I'd soon sleep the sleep of the dead, reach the deep cavern I can normally find only in her bed.

We headed into town at dawn to try and find a guy with a microlight who could take Dave up for some aerial shots of Pemba. The pilot was sleeping off a hangover and the wind was getting up, so we resorted to delicious *pasteis de nata*, melt in your mouth Portuguese milk tarts, and decent Bicafé coffee at a local *pastelaria* (confectionery). The pastries were expensive and Mike paled at the extravagance. He stood on the pavement mumbling in vain about a very cheap market nearby. But this was one of those times we had to overrule our guide's frugal instincts and let him suffer the indignity of watching us gorge ourselves on treats. Hell, we deserved it: we'd made it from Durban to Cabo Delgado Province in 18 days and bagged our stories … plus a couple of thousand images.

We drove to Pemba's traditional *bazar* in the Paquitequete bairro and spent an hour exploring lanes packed with stalls selling fruit, capulanas, spices, live animals, baskets and the like. It was bustling, noisy and colourful – as any good market should be – but this had a special quality and was on a scale I had not yet seen in Mozambique. Hayley and Rob set about buying provisions, Mike went walkabout with his notebook, Tank and Dave started taking photographs, which left me at a loose end as I'd forgotten my camera in the bungalow.

But I soon felt the liberation that comes with not carrying the infernal *máquina* and experienced the place without the nagging mediation of photographic vision, an affliction that can spoil things for a traveller overzealous in recording events for a dubious posterity. I came upon a tailor sewing children's outfits, and a man making rope from strips of car tyre (many reed walls and fences are held together by these black rubber thongs). Women sold grain, rice and flour by the cupful from white sacks. Others sat behind stalls packed with spices – peri-peri powders, nutmeg, cinnamon, cloves – and ubiquitous roasted cashew nuts.

Back at the beach I wanted a swim, but we'd run out of time again. We packed the vehicles while Mike tried to extract from management the money we'd been obliged to pay for the rooms. I watched a group of prostitutes weaving between the resort's palm umbrellas, trying to corner guests. They were chased away by security guards in a game of cat and mouse. Young shell vendors were more adept at eluding the guards, slipping the cordon to present their conch and lambris wares to recumbent tourists. Mike was failing at his cash retrieval, so we decided to chalk it up to experience and took to the saddle.

The Land Rovers steamed out of town past Pemba harbour. Mike told us the port was located at the entrance to the largest inland bay in the world, which was hard to believe (as so often with biggest-highest-longest-stupidest claims, this one all depends on your definition of 'inland'). Alexander writes that the bay could accommodate all the merchant fleets of the world with room to spare. Apparently German U-boats used to slip into the anchorage at night to recharge batteries and take on supplies provided by German sympathisers in the area.

On our left, a valley sprinkled with huts and stands of mature baobab trees led down to a beach lapped by pale water. We pulled off to take in the sight and a boy approached us carrying bunches of golden, gourd-like objects. Baobab fruit look like hairy ostrich eggs. Where so many other trees were felled for firewood and building materials, baobabs survived the civil war because the wood doesn't burn well and is powdery and soft, making it useless for structures. The fruit, however, is rich in Vitamin C. The boy offered us a bunch, which we bought, more as souvenirs than out of vitamin deficiency.

'There's a cemetery nearby with the epitaph "Sacrificed for monarchical ambition" on one of the headstones,' said Mike. 'About 120

Commonwealth soldiers are buried there, including a few South Africans, who fell during the First World War campaign against the Germans in Tanzania.' Another trail of colonial footprints running dead.

We drove inland towards Ancuabe, then north on the road to Moçimboa da Praia. Cabo Delgado saw some of the worst fighting during the civil war and the road we were on was a place of regular ambushes. Today the journey from Pemba to Moçimboa should last no longer than a day, but at the height of hostilities it could take the convoys up to a month to cover the distance.

The road wasn't nearly as bad as expected and we made good progress. For once we really would make our destination – Ibo Island – before nightfall. Ibo is one of 27 coral isles in the 250 kilometre long Quirimba Archipelago and, as we neared the embarkation point, Mike explained why he'd been keen for us to bypass the place and head north to Pangane instead. 'You see, last time I was in Moz a group of us took a dhow to Ibo and camped a night there – a night I'll never forget as long as I live. We'd intended to spend the weekend, but got the hell out the next morning.'

'What went wrong?' Hayley asked.

'Well, we landed there late afternoon and pitched our tents near the village. The place is pretty spooky, what with squatters living in the semi-derelict homes of the Portuguese ... gardens overgrown, thick mangrove swamps all around. I'm not superstitious or anything, I just didn't feel good about Ibo.

'Then drumming started. I decided to go take a look at what was happening. I came to a clearing and there was some kind of ceremony – unlike anything I'd ever seen. People were dancing around with plugs in their noses and ears – completely entranced, in a world of their own. But the really shocking thing was the audience: they were losing it, shrieking and going demented. Possessed!

'I was spell-bound and edged closer to ask the only compos mentis onlooker what was up. The only phrase he said that I could understand was *'procurar o diabo'*, which means they were calling up the devil. I went completely cold. I ran back to camp shit scared. It was too late to catch a dhow to the mainland so we had to spend the night on the island. The drumming kept going after sunset, and well into the night. Needless to say, none of us ventured out to see how the party was doing. Although I'm not in the slightest bit religious, I really sensed they were calling up the devil. I can't explain it, but the feeling in that clearing was palpable, unmistakable. It was evil, man.'

Hayley was in the passenger seat next to Mike and I could see she was disturbed by the story. She asked more questions and Mike went so far as to suggest that he might pitch his tent on the mainland and wait for us to return the following day. 'I vowed never to set foot on Ibo again,' he said. 'I'm still not sure I've got it in me.'

The road deteriorated and soon our vehicles were navigating mud-caked tracks, thudding through dongas and slipping sideways into culverts. 'Civilisation' seemed to have been left far behind – indeed, I'd read that this section of coast was still inhabited by fairly substantial numbers of game, including elephants and predators like leopards and hyenas. I was at the wheel of the lead vehicle and keeping a lookout for wildlife when we rounded a corner to encounter the kind of situation we'd feared all along. Bandits.

His clothes were filthy and torn and for all the world he looked like a homeless person. The only thing elevating him above vagrancy was the .303 rifle. This is it, I thought. To stop or to flatten the pedal and give the engine the kind of fuel injection that adrenaline was giving my body. We were travelling slowly, but I could probably be far enough away before he had aimed and fired. However, the sluggish TDi was trailing some way behind and would have no chance. The bandit smiled at me, touched his hat, and I returned the greeting. Then we passed. That was all.

At Quissanga we took a wrong turn and ended up bundu bashing down a coastal track so overgrown it seemed no vehicle had used it since before the war. We turned the Landies round and backtracked inland to find an easier route. Cruising down a narrow lane I surprised two guys on a bicycle from behind. The pannier passenger must have shouted something alarming in the cyclist's ear, because the bike left the road at speed, crashing and overturning. Two wide-eyed faces emerged from the long grass. We waved and they beamed back at us – obviously no bones broken. Their panicked reaction suggested some drivers in these parts – the Henrique school – behaved like they owned the road.

Tandanhangui. A pretty coastal village opposite Ibo where Mike knew a dhow captain who could ferry us across. It was mid-afternoon and we'd finally broken the cycle of arriving after dark. In no time Mike had found Sufu, a handsome befezzed gentleman, who joined us for the drive across sand flats to where dhows and outrigger canoes were moored at the head of a channel through the mangroves.

We parked under a baobab and Sufu disappeared among the trees to check on the tide. He returned a few minutes later shaking his head. No, the water was still too low and his dhow was sitting high and dry on the sand. We would have to wait for the boat to float on the flow. 'How long?' we wanted to know. 'Oh, quite a while. You'd better come back to my village. You'll be eaten by mosquitoes if you stay here,' he said in Portuguese. Frustrated and realising 'a while' in this part of the world could mean a considerable wait, we headed back to Sufu's house. For the record, it meant five hours. So much for racing to get to Ibo.

Tandanhangui is one of those paradisiacal African hamlets untouched by the ravages of Coca-Cola, television aerials and cars. It was almost a cliché – like an advert for what a perfect, self-sufficient village should look and feel like. The houses were neat wattle and daub structures with palm-frond roofs and ample courtyards where children played, chickens clucked and women pounded rice with pestle and mortar. Even the paths were swept.

We strolled through lanes basted in rosy light. The young women's faces were painted white as is the Makua custom and struck postcard poses in doorways.

'They smear their faces with powder ground from the bark of the nciro tree,' explained Sufu. 'When you mix it with water, it forms a paste. It's like a moisturiser or skin softener and it protects you from the sun.' Apparently a European cosmetic chain is interested in the bark's 'beautifying' properties.

A wizened woman washed her grandson in a zinc tub and beamed at us with pride. Others were shy of the camera, but not the village children who leaped in front of every aimed Nikon, clamouring to be snapped. Dave, the softy of our group when it came to kids, soon resembled the Pied Piper. They knew a sucker when they saw one.

Fires were being lit and spicy smells wafted between the huts. It was dusk and we wandered back to Sufu's place to prepare our own dinner. A table and chairs were set out in his courtyard and Dave's children were shooed away by the dhow captain. The sound of a muezzin calling the faithful to prayer hung in the stillness. Curious, I walked down the lane under a belt of stars, just emerging from a purple sky, and found pairs of shoes outside a door, the only clue that this was a mosque. The hut with its row of broken and holed shoes was strangely moving: the walkers come to rest. The spell of the moment was enhanced by the fact that the muezzin's voice was melodic and without amplification. In every Muslim quarter I'd ever visited from Cape Town to Cairo, the haunting call to Allah had been sullied by tinny megaphones or worn recordings. This was pure and unmediated and I felt the spirit of Muslim Africa as never before. '*Allahu Akbar*!' God is most great.

While we chopped onions and tomatoes and peeled potatoes, the murmur of prayers continued to reach us through thin mud walls. We kept our voices low so as not to disturb the worshippers and it was only the loud pop of Rob's bottle of Thelema Merlot that might have caused minimal offence. After a simple dinner of tuna and rice, Sufu and his two boatmen led us back across the sand flats to the inlet. There was no moon and we stumbled in the dark trying to sort our overnight packs, tents and sleeping bags.

Tank and I were winding Hayley up with stories of devil-raising ceremonies. Mike joined in and confided that it was on moonless Friday nights – just like tonight – that such rituals were performed. He was quite convincing. I came up with the contention that Sufu was spooked and wouldn't set foot on the island, sending us with the boatmen rather than venturing across the channel with his crazy muzungo charges. Hayley was clearly affected.

'I don't think I want to go to Ibo,' she said. 'Maybe I could camp here and wait for you guys to come back tomorrow.' Dave then took us aside and told us to quit our nonsense, which we were about to do anyway, as we'd started to scare ourselves.

It was 21h00 and the *barco a vela* was still not riding easily on the tide. Nevertheless we waded out to it through a mangrove swamp dotted with other grounded boats. I made out two pairs of eyes and two sets of white teeth on the prow of a motor dhow. '*Boa noite, tudo bem*?' the mouths called. Yes, everything was *bem*, we called back. 'Probably smugglers,' muttered Mike. 'Nice fast boat like that. No lights. Lying in a quiet mangrove inlet near the Tanzanian border. They're not your ordinary fishermen, that's for sure.'

With much huffing and heaving we dragged the dhow through knee-deep mud, out of the shallows and poled it away from Tandanhangui's mangroves, scanning for cat's paws. The dhow was well clear of the tree-line and still no wind. There was hardly a ripple and stars in their billion lay dead in the water.

When we felt the first warm breath on our cheeks, Sufu ordered his two crew to raise the *vela*. The yard was already half way up the mast when we realized the sail was badly torn along the luff. There were curses from all three. As it is, Mozambican sails are things of patches – bits of cloth and sacking inexpertly sown together – but these tears looked bad.

'I let some fishermen use my boat, and this is how they treat my equipment!' fumed Sufu in colourful Portuguese. 'Never mind, I'll repair the sail on Ibo. We'll get there a little slower tonight. As long as we sail her gently I don't think it will rip any further.'

I found myself a relatively comfortable nook among the bags near the prow and relaxed into the rhythm of creaking rope, worn wood and canvas quivering in the wind. It is an alchemy that never ceases to thrill me. The vessel – a *lança* – was smaller than the *jahazis* and *mashuas* I'd sailed in Kenya and Tanzania, those ocean-going dhows that ply the Indian from Somalia right down to Mozambique, but still a joy to sail. The basic elements remained the same: a triangle of lateen-rigged canvas, a bowsprit holding down the loose end of the foot, an open deck with salt-worn thwarts, an alert tillerman playing the breeze with instinctive skill. We had a gentle following wind and ran on a broad reach between mangrove islands, our steersman picking an intricate course through the shallows. Occasionally we lay becalmed in the lee of an isle, but it was invariably shallow enough for the crew to pole us on towards the wind and in the direction of the outer Quirimbas, which lay low and black on the horizon.

'Why don't we call 702 and get them to put us on air?' suggested Dave. 'It'd be quite a novelty to have us reporting from a dhow in this remote spot.' He hauled out the satellite phone and immediately got through to a talk-show producer. 'I know this isn't our usual slot, but could you tell us what's the topic of discussion?' asked Dave.

'We've got an expert talking about the mysteries of the pyramids,' said the producer in a sing-song kugal accent. 'Have you got anything to contribute?'

'No,' said Dave. 'But we're journalists sailing on a dhow towards a haunted island off the coast of Mozambique. We're on satellite phone. Wouldn't your host like to chat to us for a moment.'

'I don't think so,' she replied doubtfully. 'What's a dhow, anyway?'

'Well, it's a kind of boat … oh never mind, just forget it,' he said and hung up.

Hours passed and my fellow passengers lay sprawled on their bags, either asleep or in deep reflection. I lay back, sensing the mainsheet tug in the puffs, sag in the lulls; feeling our dhow's exquisite cleave and ride. It was a sumptuous night with the sky preternaturally bright as though some festive god had shaken up an expensive bottle of stars and popped the cork. The bow wave peeled a wash of phosphorescence and marine stars fizzed magically in our wake.

'Senhores, that's it!' said Sufu, pointing to a confusion of mangroves due east of us. Almost as he said it, I heard the drums. Just a low pulsing at first, easily confused with our own heartbeats, but growing imperceptibly as we neared the island. Everyone was wide awake now and all eyes trained at the silhouette – there was obviously no electricity on Ibo. The drumming was without tune or variation, just a steady rhythm like a musician keeping time, waiting for the inspiration of a riff that never came. I did not look at the others – anyway it was too dark to make out expressions – but it didn't take an astral navigator to know what they were thinking. Friday was *diabo* night. I must admit to a touch of nerves as we slipped under the lee of Ibo and into blackness.

'You know, I took some photos of the trance dancers and berserk spectators.' It was Mike again. 'But I've put the pictures away at the back of a drawer. I can't look at them. Just seeing them sends a feeling of desperation through me.'

Before the Portuguese conquest, the Muslim inhabitants of the Quirimba Archipelago had close ties with Kilwa, Zanzibar and Malindi and were involved in the medieval trade network that linked all East African ports. The islands were known for their cowries, turtleshells, ambergris and for a weaving industry that produced fine maluane cloth. When Sofala and Kilwa were taken over by the Portuguese, many displaced Muslim merchants settled among these islands. But when the Portuguese got wind of this, they sent a raiding party which looted the trading posts, destroyed houses and torched the ships at anchor.

Later, Portuguese senhores settled on the islands, establishing plantations of millet, rice, beans and palms. By the early 17th century there was a mission on Quirimba Island and a settlement on Ibo, fortified against attack from raiders. Some of the atolls became centres of cloth manufacture and a lively trade grew up with the mainland. Each island was a mini state with the senhor in charge of a household of slaves, king of all he surveyed.

Ibo became the capital of Cabo Delgado district and towards the end of the 18th century two forts were constructed as well as a church, warehouses and a customs house. In time, fine avenues of houses were built and public buildings erected around the main praça. The buying and selling of humans proved very good for business. Trading was brisk and all buyers were welcome at the Ibo slave market, including the French, who needed an increasing number of labourers for their sugar plantations on Indian Ocean possessions such as Île de France and Île de Bourbon.

Although slave trading on Ibo officially ceased in 1842, the volume of slaves passing through here (and the other two major ports, Ilha and Quelimane), increased during the two decades following abolition. In 1861 it was estimated that more than 3 000 slaves were still being exported from Ibo each year. British naval officers from the anti slave-trade squadron were treated with courtesy and hospitality, and made honoured guests at social functions. On the surface, they would have seen nothing untoward, but the more perceptive among them noticed the signs: vessels stealing into the anchorage at night, disproportionate displays of wealth, large barges and 'whalers' with capacious holds – all empty. It was a game of cat and mouse with an elaborate system of subterfuge developed to outwit the British squadrons, missionaries and a few abolitionist colonists. Governors were bribed into silence and a Mafia-style system of contacts grew up. With the markets closed, slaves were held in barracoons away from the towns until a slave ship anchored in a secluded bay, river mouth or mangrove thicket. On dark nights the hapless souls were ferried out in river barges or ships' boats.

Like a slave ship making a midnight call, our dhow crept closer. When we ran the vessel aground in the shallows the drumming stopped which was, if anything, more disturbing. 'Keep your sandals on as you wade ashore,' warned Dave. 'There may be razor clams.' Oh no, not the dreaded razor clams again. As if Satan weren't enough.

We lowered ourselves over the side and Sufu pointed into the darkness. 'That black shape over there is the Portuguese fort. Turn right when you get to it and walk along the beach until you come to a house. It's called Vila Ruben. They'll have beds for you.'

With our bags on our heads we waded towards the beach, unable to make out much beyond the vague crenulations of the 18th-century fortress. The shoreline was all jagged coral and we stumbled towards the villa. A warm drizzle began to fall. The place was right on the beach and had an overgrown garden with crumbling walls. We climbed the steps to find shelter on the veranda while Mike banged on the door. After a long time a woman wearing a night dress and carrying a paraffin lamp opened. Fatima looked frightened. 'Is this Vila Ruben?' asked Mike.

'*Sim senhor*,' she said in a thin voice. 'Is it a room you want?'

It was well after midnight and we had reached our destination at last, comfortably beating the Rio Savane record for late arrivals. So much for 'Ibo before dark'. Even though we'd done everything right, we'd still been thwarted, this time by the tide. Daylight arrivals were clearly not meant to be.

Fatima led us around the dilapidated villa. She explained that she was acting caretaker while the owner, a Frenchwoman called Senhora Janine, was away on vacation. We could take any of the rooms (she and her baby would vacate their bed if we wanted it), including the cottage in the garden. Or we could lay out our sleeping bags on the veranda for a much reduced fee. The rooms were sparsely furnished and the house very old. The garden cottage was the obvious 'honeymoon retreat' for Hayley and David, but it was a bit isolated and Hayley weighed up a possible encounter with the devil against another night with us and chose us. The couple took a room in the house and the rest of us opted to pitch our tents on the veranda.

'Good night children,' called Tank. 'And don't let the razor clams bite.'

I thought the rustling sound was rain, so I didn't emerge from my tent when I heard the others stirring. There wouldn't be any sunrise shots and besides, I was shattered. But soon it grew very bright, so I nosed out of my flaps to find the world beyond the veranda bathed in sunlight. My 'rain' sound was the wind-whipped palms overhead. The others had cleared out, so I went searching, assuming – correctly – that they'd headed for the fort.

Fortaleza de São João Baptista lay at the end of an avenue of casuarinas and was a magnificent, star-shaped building – just what a pint-sized Indian Ocean fort should look like. I found the team in the courtyard where they were watching a group of silversmiths crafting jewellery. It was a painstaking operation which involved melting old Portuguese coins and then moulding each chain link by hand. Who would buy this jewellery? There couldn't be more than a handful of tourists passing through here in a year.

I climbed the walls and circled battlements punctuated with ornate, rococo-style sentry boxes. Cannons guarded the northern entrance to Ibo's anchorage, long deserted since Pemba harbour had superseded it. Dhow sails flecked the blue beyond the shallows and I thought about the generations of Swahili, Indian and Arab sailors who had coasted to the Ibo market under the guns, their menace effectively keeping control of trade in these waters. I figured it would make a wonderful location for a film of J M Coetzee's novel *Waiting for the Barbarians*: a lonely outpost of empire awaiting the invading hordes. How must those early Portuguese soldiers have felt, marooned here to guard a god-forsaken swamp in darkest, fever-ridden Africa? What *saudades*, what yearning they must have felt for the Tagus and its promise of beautiful *raparigas*, fine *vinho verde*, mother's *bacalhau*, bright lamps and a healthy clime.

Exploring the battlements I remembered an account I'd read about the fort under siege. In 1800 three curious-looking vessels – ten-metre, outrigger canoes with sails – were spotted off the archipelago. At first the islanders thought nothing of it, but in time the sight of those dugouts would fill them with terror. Each boat carried 20 warriors and hailed from across the waters in north-eastern Madagascar where the Betsimisaraka chiefs had begun dispatching raiding fleets to harvest slaves. For years they harried the communities of this corner of the Indian, dispersing fishing populations and sending islanders fleeing to the mainland and into the interior.

By 1808 the armadas had grown in size and were sometimes 500 strong, transporting over 8 000 armed pirates. The Quirimbas became all but deserted and the fragmented Afro-Portuguese community encamped under the protection of Ibo's cannons. It was here, in 1816, that the Madagascan warriors were dealt their first decisive defeat. Although raiding continued, the back of the pirate scourge had been broken.

From the battlements I noticed the tide was out and our dhow lay on the sand near the base of the fort. It would be hours before the vessel could be floated again, so there was plenty of time to explore the town. I retraced my steps past Vila Ruben and along the promenade. Although most of the buildings – semi-detached houses linked by verandas to form an ad hoc colonnade – were run down, you could glean a sense of the prosperous, colonial outpost it once was. There were grand buildings with ornate cast-iron work and Marseilles tiles, legacy of trade exchange with French merchantmen. The local commodity: slaves destined for French sugar plantations. As I strolled past the decaying villas, I thought about Mike's comment that Ibo is the perfect place to contemplate the impact of colonialism in Africa. It must have been an efficiently run outpost, with a ferry that left on time, electricity, telephones in every home, cars parked outside, corner shops doing a brisk trade.

But it all started to fall apart when Porto Amelia (Pemba) become the harbour and capital of Cabo Delgado and there were no longer mainland threats to force the Lusitanians onto offshore islands. Besides, the shoals and reefs round Ibo meant that bigger, modern ships had to anchor far out, necessitating cargo transhipment. The advent of Pemba meant the decline of Ibo. Houses were abandoned as they stood, the curtains drawn and unwanted utensils left on the shelves. After liberation locals made homes in some of these shells. Now wires hung limply from telephone poles; fishermen laid out their sails in the streets for repairs, secure in the knowledge that no vehicle would disturb them; the villas of 18th-century traders showed gaping cracks. The whitewash had faded to reveal coral rag, tiles fell from roofs like the leaves of dead trees and strangler figs climbed over the masonry.

The funny thing was, unlike Mike, I didn't register a sense of loss and despair. Of course his feelings were clouded by the devil's presence, but I had to admit I really liked Ibo. It was sleepy, laid back and untrammelled by tourists. Contrary to the first impression, the colonial inheritance hadn't entirely crippled the community. There was industry going on. Admittedly the silversmiths appeared symbolic of the decay of the old colony, their melting of coins washed up on the beach from Portuguese shipwrecks seemed like a scavenging of the corpse of empire. But the town was alive. I met a man building a double-ended rowing boat next to one of the smaller Portuguese forts that guard the old harbour. He was fashioning the wood with an adze and needed no modern tools or measuring instruments – a skill handed down through generations. On the main square in front of the lovely whitewashed Igreja de Nossa Senhora do Rosário (Church of Our Lady of the Rosary) and beside the old *alfândega* (customs house) sat a group of sail makers and menders stitching, whipping and splicing.

I came upon a bed and breakfast establishment that had recently opened and, round the next corner, a man sweeping the gravel road in front of his home, collecting the fallen leaves and making a pleasing pattern in the sand with a reed brush. On a square in the back of the town I found dozens of school children playing a version of hopscotch, and when their teachers called, they ran to queue in the courtyard of a dilapidated, but functioning, schoolhouse. So life was being led, and led productively on Ibo. If there was a devil about, then he was more likely to inhabit those old forts – his legacy was surely the cruelty that happened within their walls and the slave routes they defended.

By now the sun was high and I headed back to Vila Ruben where Sufu and his boatmen were making final repairs to the sail. When they were done, the sailors manhandled their triangle of canvas onto the dhow and bent it to the yard. The rest of us made ourselves breakfast and chatted about our impressions of Ibo. Had the locals lost or gained through independence?

'I think they've been rocked onto the back foot since liberation and this bread-line living must be terrible,' contended Dave. 'We're very lucky that in 1994 South Africa didn't have a massive exodus followed by civil war, like they did here after 1975.'

'I disagree,' I argued. 'Despite the decaying infrastructure and the run-down appearance of the place I think they're better off than before. At least they're making decisions about their future. So what if a few old buildings crumble to dust? Our sentimentality about bits of Portuguese masonry is Eurocentric.'

Upon further reflection I had to revise my thoughts. Tourism was on the rise and those 'few old buildings' were probably the key to the economic health of Ibo. They had to be restored and preserved, but how to do it without turning the place into a museum town? On the other hand, how to have growth and life without compulsory Coca-Cola, BP and five-star hotel with air conditioning? How to preserve the fine old buildings and monitor their restoration without imposing the will of the North ... without mimicking the old imperial act?

Ibo was going to have a difficult future. It's a gem, a mini Ilha, and will need a touch of luck to escape the two faces of the same *diabo*: decay and development. From nowhere in particular, Henrique's smiling face swam into my head like a mnemonic spectre from my unconscious. Oh please don't let him stick his fork into Ibo, I thought.

The dhow was ready to make sail and the moment we splashed aboard, our boatmen began poling us to deeper water. The repaired lateen snared the breeze and soon we were well clear of Ibo, beating through the Quirimbas' mangrove scraps. Woolly-necked and yellow-billed storks monitored our progress from their perches. We passed fishing dhows heading for open ocean, mariners waving and calling to us across the water.

The caulking on our *barco* wasn't great and one of the boatmen had to keep bailing, which didn't prevent our luggage from getting drenched. There was a good breeze and we fetched rapidly through the shallows. Our helmsman was adept, pinching into the puffs and freeing off in the lulls.

We ghosted into Tandanhangui inlet and waded ashore for a quick lunch of stale bread and boiled eggs beneath a baobab tree which Hayley insisted on climbing. But then, like an over-ambitious kitten, she climbed too high and called for help. The boatmen sat watching the *muzungos malucos* (mad whites) with bemused expressions as we instituted a rescue operation, first standing on each others' shoulders, then scrambling into the branches. Eventually, with much grunting and bravado, Hayley was back on terra firma.

We were heading north again, deeper into Cabo Delgado Province, and our surroundings became increasingly tropical. Samango monkeys were everywhere at play and big yellow baboons strutted through villages with the casual arrogance that usually denotes ownership. The AK47s had obviously not been at work up here near the Tanzanian border. We passed two men walking with bed frames on their heads. 'Off to market to sell them,' said Mike. But the markets were possibly days' walk away and what could you get for a wooden bed frame?

Beside the turnoff to Pangane was a wayside shop and bar run by a Chinese man called Chun Sik, known locally as Senhor Suki. 'Old Suki's helped me out a few times when I've been in a scrape,' said Mike as we drew up at the entrance. At first it seemed incongruous to find a Chinese in this part of Africa, but then I remembered Portugal's links with Macau and recalled the 17th-century account of a Chinese man who'd led a war band of 4 000 in Karangaland.

Suki wore a huge smile and was obviously pleased to see Mike. He promptly invited us to his home in Pangane for dinner that evening. 'I have to finish off a few things here, but I'll see you later,' said Suki. 'My staff will help you out.'

'Suki's an intrepid guy,' Mike started as we bounced along the road to Pangane. 'Not many foreigners hung around here when the shit was flying. Back in 1992 he gave me a lift from Pemba to Pangane and I tell you, the road was a lot worse then. Suki was living on the smell of an oil rag, but determined to make a go of business here. His two shops had just been hit by Renamo and were burnt-out shells. He seems to be doing pretty well now.'

Darkness had fallen and we picked our way on a snaking meander through the coconut trees of Pangane Peninsula. Beyond Suki's house the tongue of land began to narrow and soon we were navigating a sandy beach.

'This is it,' said Mike as he swung the Land Rover under a chorus of skanking palms. It was a perfect campsite with a few basic facilities and a boma for preparing meals. But it was the location that excited us: sea on both sides, a tapering headland and pearly sand in the shade of palms. We had the place entirely to ourselves. The camp had been started some years previously by a bunch of young Brits who'd planned to hold fantastic rave parties here. But the trance bunnies had long since departed, leaving their sound equipment behind them on the beach.

'Make sure you don't pitch your tents directly under a palm or you might get bludgeoned by a falling nut,' warned Dave.

'And lock all your valuables in the Landies,' said Mike. 'This place has a reputation for light fingers.'

Tank, Rob and I waited to see where Mike made camp and then rolled out our tents as far from his as was humanly possible without arousing suspicion. It was nothing personal, just that his waking rituals were noisy, premature and distasteful. He's one of those early birds who wants others to share the aurora and the worm with him. To this end he made enough commotion to wake everyone in his immediate vicinity. And then there were the body noises, part of the alarm-clock routine. They consisted of a series of loud (and obviously proud) burps and farts. Having spent some time in, or in close proximity to, lighthouses, I know the irritation of a foggy dawn when nautiphones begin booming. I never managed to work out whether Mike's was designed to irritate us, or a genuine divertissement to start the day on an airy note.

After pitching our tents as far from Mike as possible and asking the guarda to keep an eye on things we headed for Suki's place. Mike hooted and banged on the gate for a few minutes, but no-one emerged. What could have become of our host? We were about to drive away when the gates were swung open by a young man who was all smiles and graciousness. Mike explained that we were Senhor Suki's Special Guests, at which the lad extravagantly ushered in the vehicles.

The place seemed like a compound, surrounded as it was by high walls and inhabited by a family of servants, helpers and hangers on. I was again reminded of Conrad, and the remote Indonesian trading outposts he described so accurately in novels like *Almayer's Folly*, *An Outcast of the Islands* and *Lord Jim*. There were chickens and goats wandering about, children playing and figures milling in the shadows around the yard's perimeter. A couple of scrawny dogs alternated between furious rutting and equally furious barking. 'Possible lodge-dog shot, guys?' suggested Tank.

The enclosure felt strangely feudal: these were Suki's vassals, living off his largesse and owing allegiance to the lord and master. I suppose if your buildings have been torched by Renamo, you resort to traditional means to secure your future, particularly in this out of the way neck of the groves.

'Senhor Suki will be home soon,' said our young host, leading us into a low-ceilinged dining room in the master's 'guest house' adorned with ship models fashioned from tin. 'Make yourselves comfortable. May I get some beers – nice cold Castles from your country? *Estás bem*? In the meantime I will ask the cook to prepare some chicken. I'm afraid that's all we have on the menu.'

Yes, chicken would do fine – we didn't expect anything more elaborate. The heat was stifling and the lukewarm beers went down quickly. Mosquito squadrons (probably the dreaded female *Anopheles* variety which carries the malaria parasite) patrolled in formation, stacked patiently above their victims. Talk was desultory and after hearing a fluttering chase, frenetic clucking and a loud chop, none of us particularly felt like supper.

The boiled and threadbare bird was eventually produced with a proud flourish and our surrogate host stood back to savour the pleasure his dish was sure to give. We made an effort, picking at the meagre grey flesh, but couldn't even bring ourselves to finish it. If he was disappointed in us as guests, he didn't show it. 'Senhor Suki is sure to be home any minute. Wouldn't you like a cup of coffee?' he enquired.

No, sadly we had to decline: a long day behind us and an early start tomorrow. Perhaps next time.

Regrettably then, he would have to ask us to pay. It was all most embarrassing, but there was no other way. Without instructions from the lord, how was he to know we weren't good-for-nothing backpackers trying to pull a fast one on the senhor? It came to R40 a head, an outrageous amount for the sparrow he called a chicken, but we'd pay Suki a visit in the morning and he was sure to refund us. We were, after all, his guests.

As we pulled away the dogs were still performing their blood-curdling double act. 'It's Saturday night and I guess Suki's chatting up the *raparigas* in one of the local dancing or drinking halls,' said Mike. 'He's young, wealthy and single – I bet he strikes it lucky in these parts. Or maybe he just resorts to the *putas*!'

On our way back to camp we passed a reed building on the beach that looked like just the place Suki might be fishing tonight. Local *raparigas*, hair done and dressed in their finest dresses (barefoot though), were queuing at the entrance, eager to be taken by the Latin-African beat. I felt tempted to kick off my shoes and get in there, but it'd been another long day and our beach bedroom promised classic sunrise photographs, so I desisted.

After extracting teeth and brushing contact lenses by the dazzle of the TDi's brights, I crawled into my sack and lay awake listening to the symphony of sea and air. The wind was lashing the palms. The 'trades' are erratic in northern Mozambique, but this looked, felt and smelt like the legendary Kusi, sweeping up towards Kenya and across the Arabian Sea, which drove the ocean-going dhows carrying the riches of Africa in their bellies.

A foot worm had made a home in my sole which kept me from getting to sleep. He probably hitched a ride in one of the cuts I'd sustained walking on coral. You couldn't blame the fellow – just a travelling man with itchy feet like myself. Only I wished he'd chosen another host or vehicle or whatever I was to him. I scratched, but this only seemed to encourage his desire to go walkabout. What a bizarre creature, I thought as I sloshed about in sleep's shore break. At some point the wind dropped and I half-woke into the silent hiatus from dreams of dhows and spice islands and an Odalisque-like Jennifer recumbent in a sultan's harem.

My erotic mind-petting was shattered by a thunderous fart followed by a string of startlingly varied burps. Mike was up and his repertoire was growing. I reflected that his prawn oesophagus had been a blessing in disguise as it had probably spared us many more concertos. Mike was on the mend.

When I drew back the flaps of my boudoir I found the eastern sky ruptured and leaking inflamed colours across the horizon. I could feel the hairiness of the Castles from the night before, but grabbed my camera and headed along the beach to where dhows and dugouts were already making for sea. When Dave joined me to try and set up a few cover shots I noticed that he wasn't looking at all well. His eyes were bloodshot and his face pale. 'You OK, buddy?' I asked. 'You look like shit.'

'Thanks. I'm not doing too good this morning,' he answered. 'Feels like I've been run over by a *machimbombo*. Got a bit of a temperature too.'

The sky was a confusion of dark clouds broken by needles of clear light, making for great photo opportunities. But Dave's heart wasn't in it. We worked a few 'romantic covers' with him and Hayley, but they both looked so run-down – hair unkempt, dark rings under their eyes, Dave gaunt and unshaven – that there was no way these pics would make it into any magazine. We resorted to shooting the boats, careful not to include the squatting figures who were fouling the water's edge.

One dhow caught our attention and we strolled over to talk to the handsome captain who was sitting cross-legged in the prow like a Buddha. It was freshly painted in red and blue with the name *Transmar* emblazoned on the side. It was a *jahazi* dhow, similar to ones I'd seen in Dar-es-Salaam, Zanzibar and Lamu.

'*Bom dia, senhor*! Is this a deep-sea fishing dhow?' I asked.

'*Jambo, habari*?' (hello, how are you) said the captain in Swahili, then switched to Portuguese. 'No, we take passengers.'

'And when do you set sail, *capitão*?'

'As soon as there are enough people wanting to go, we'll be sailing for Tanzania,' he replied.

I wanted to ask him more about dhows like his that still plied the waters of East Africa. I'd managed to hitch rides on them in Maputo Bay, Zanzibar, southern Tanzania, Madagascar, Malindi and I'd sailed their cousin, the felluca, on the Nile at Aswan. But my Swahili didn't get past greetings and my Portuguese wasn't up to pursuing the conversation.

Chroniclers of the 16th century noted the importance of boat building on the Mozambique coast and they identified four main types of vessel. There were the large, ocean-going dhows, or *zambucos*, most of which were built in India or the Gulf, but some were no doubt constructed in places like Moçambique Island. It was on one of these that I had hoped to cross the Indian from Oman to Zanzibar in the re-enactment voyage for the aborted television documentary series *Winds of Change*.

Smaller versions of these vessels were called *bangwas*, which carried local trade up and down the coast. *Transmar*, I guessed, was a modern version of this ancient craft. Before the advent of iron, the planks of vessels were 'sewn' together with rope and the seams caulked with gum. The deck housing was of cane and the sails of matting.

Portuguese mariners also noted *luzios*, decked river boats used in estuaries and inland waterways, and *almadias*, canoes made from hollowed-out trees and sometimes fitted with outriggers. These canoes could be of an immense size and carry up to 20 tons. Indeed, in 1505 Francisco de Almeida's fleet was attacked by such ocean-going *almadias* off Madagascar. Of course there were many variations on these basic craft, their design tailored to the maritime activities of the region, ranging from estuary fishing to the catching of turtles or whales, or from diving for pearls to trans-oceanic trading.

I was happy to see that many modern descendants of these vessels still sailed Mozambican waters, and to find that boat-building methods were still being handed down through families. I suppose it's one of the few 'benefits' of the civil war that fuel, fibreglass and the outboard engine were held at bay a little longer. What's more, I noted that some of the vessels were built along similar lines to the ancient *mtepes* ('sewn' boats). In northern Mozambique it was still possible to see construction using wooden pegs and tightly fitted boards, all caulked and sealed with gum and resin.

Elsewhere in Africa and on the Indian Ocean rim the art of dhow sailing, ancient navigation and traditional construction methods are fast disappearing. Visit the great ports of the Arabian Gulf and you'll be hard pressed to find a dhow bound for the Land of the Zanj. In parts of Africa, dugout canoes are being replaced by fibreglass duplicates, painted brown and gnarled with fake wood textures to look like the real thing and fool the tourists. It's a great loss.

Transmar was a beautiful craft, well-maintained and shipshape. I envied her passengers the voyage north to those evocative places in southern Tanzania that lay just beyond our reach: Mtwara, Lindi and, most of all, Kilwa. The latter was a famous gold entrepot during the Middle Ages, with a magnificent mosque and sultan's palace boasting an octagonal swimming bath and colonnaded halls. Alas this journey would have to wait. Even the lighthouse at the tip of Cabo Delgado Peninsula – the northernmost point of Mozambique – seemed unlikely now. None of us were up for much more northing.

Dave's fever was getting worse and he headed back to camp to have a lie down. I continued shooting the fishing craft. In one frame I could capture *lanças*, double-ended dhows, outrigger canoes and fishing dugouts. A pretty mongrel, the kind of Mozambican mutt we'd become used to, trailed after me as I photographed. As our lot looked so under the weather, perhaps I should rather be snapping portraits for our *Lodge Dogs of Mozambique* book, I thought.

I noticed a group of white-face-pack women wading through the shallows, beating the water with sticks. They were chasing shoals of minnows into a net being dragged by another contingent. I tried to get some photos, but the women shooed me away, shouting and waving their arms at me. I quickly backed off.

Back in camp the guard brought freshly baked bread, relays of fried eggs in pairs, hot water for coffee and papaya straight from the tree. Dave lay in the *barraca* looking positively green and Mike, despite his bullish start to the day, also appeared to be fading. Dave roused himself and called me aside to ask my opinion on our course of action. Should we push on or turn back?

I argued that those symbolic end points, the Cabo Delgado lighthouse and Rovuma River, would only be relevant if they were really the termination of our expedition. Or if we'd set ourselves some sort of mission to explore the *entire* length of the Mozambican coast. But this was not the case. Our end point was Cóbuè on Lake Malawi. In fact, given that we'd end in Gauteng, our journey was circular rather than a linear quest.

In my heart I knew that the Cabo Delgado light would make a perfect emblematic end to our northward trajectory, but I chose to fudge the issue. If we reached Lake Malawi in the far north-west there'd be enough 'symbolism' and we could still claim to have done the length of the country. In truth, I thought we'd all had just about enough. My companions looked awful. They were haggard, drained, exhausted. There was little fun anymore and what with Dave ill, Mike looking grim and me having acquired a foot friend, there didn't seem much point in getting ourselves onto rougher roads and into even remoter areas. No-one wanted to mention malaria, but Dave's fever pointed that way. We all needed a comfortable bed, a shower and some green food, and I needed to have a long and intimate relationship with a telephone that didn't depend on Mozambican operators and fickle celestial bodies.

'Let's head home buddy,' I said. 'We've still got more than 3 000 kilometres to go to Jo'burg with less than eight days to cover them. And let's face it, there'll be some pretty terrible roads between here and Malawi.' That settled it. We'd turn the Landies round and have a day in hand for our homeward journey. It was as though a weight had been lifted and the team were visibly buoyed by the news that we'd be back in the relative comfort of Pemba by nightfall. We broke camp and started loading the vehicles in an upbeat frame of mind.

So Pangane was to be the end of the road. The trek as far as (and beyond) the Rovuma would have to wait for a future expedition. As yet there was no bridge, so overlanders had to exit or enter northern Mozambique via Malawi, an interminable and arduous detour. Rumour had it there was a vehicle pontoon close to the river mouth, but rumours were dangerous things to plan itineraries around. Besides, Tanzania wasn't in our brief and our minds were set.

There were the usual shell sellers and camp-site hangers-on making a bit of a nuisance of themselves around the fringes while we packed. But as we'd hired a guarda, who doubled as camp manager, we felt our stuff would be safe. So when a slightly revived Dave spotted a great photo opportunity down on the beach, we all grabbed cameras and ran without thinking of locking the vehicles.

The aggressive women from earlier were bringing in fish and laying them out on the sand. They seemed to prefer Dave's attentions to mine – it helped that he was offering them cash. One beautiful young woman with a serene expression, bright clothing and white face posed coyly for him, fish laid out in neat rows at her feet. The sky was dark and Dave used his flash to startling effect. I also tried to take the picture and stepped in front of Dave.

'Get out of the way Justin!' he snapped. 'I've set this fucking thing up and here you come blundering in. Go find your own shots ... or at least wait for me to finish.'

I stormed off in a huff, but cooled down quickly, realising it must be hard for him to have me, the rookie, breathing down his neck. After all, the north was his story.

We headed back to the vehicles and, rounding the TD5, I came upon Dave holding a local by the scruff and saying, 'What the hell do you think you're doing?' in a calm, measured tone which I know to be David at his angriest.

The man held my colleague's wallet in his hands and was shouting something incomprehensible in dialect. The guarda came running over, followed by the rest of our team. 'What's going on?' asked Mike.

'I found this guy taking cash out of my wallet,' replied Dave. 'I caught him red-handed.'

'*Não, não senhor! Não é verdade*. It's not true, I was p-p-putting money *back* into your wallet,' stuttered the man, obviously terrified. 'You left the cash lying on the t-t-table when you were p-p-paying for the camp.'

Dave was adamant that he hadn't left any money lying around, but I could see that he wasn't entirely sure of himself. Perhaps the guy was right ... there was just a chance he'd left some cash on the table and we had to give him the benefit of the doubt. The guarda didn't say much, other than that the accused often helped out at the campsite and was an honest guy.

Dave let the man go, apologised, and gave him 10 000 meticais (R5) for returning the money. But the magic had gone out of paradise beach and we packed quickly and left. As we wove between the palms, Dave and I analysed the incident.

'You know, it's our white South African guilt,' I contended. 'Given our upbringing it's almost impossible to accuse a bread-line black man of stealing. If there's even a shred of doubt, no matter how tenuous, we'll give him the benefit.'

'Hey, he could have been a simple and naive chap ... found the money on the table and, seeing no-one around, thought he'd return it to the owner's vehicle,' said Dave.

'But how did he know it was *your* wallet?' countered Hayley. 'And who in their right mind would go rummaging through someone else's luggage, in order to return money? It makes no sense.'

'And what about the guard?' queried Tank. 'He didn't seem too concerned about his clients being preyed upon. It looked like he'd seen it all before. I bet he's in on the deal and gets a cut while keeping his hands clean. Shit, he's probably the guard for the crooks. Senhor Guarda keeps watch while the thieves are at work. In Dave's case he slipped up and wasn't paying enough attention?'

We stopped at Suki's in a hail of barking and caught the dogs *in flagrante delicto* again, still locked in paroxysms of mechanical copulation. *Lodge Dogs of Mozambique* was to be a family read, perhaps even a coffee-table book, so these weren't candidates. I suppose if man's best friend is not getting the kind of love and attention he deserves from man (and in Mozambique this is palpably the case) then strident protestation and protracted fornication are acceptable alternatives.

Our gracious host from the previous night trotted up, parting chickens. He had bad news for us. Alas, Suki was *still* not home. 'Probably sleeping off a hangover under a palm tree wrapped in the arms of a buxom babe,' muttered Mike under his breath.

'Or he's inside hiding so he doesn't have to refund us for last night's hamster,' quipped Tank, even less charitably. We were in uncompromising moods and sped off, scattering feathered rodents.

Chapter 9

We drilled the road to Macomia, then took the Pemba turn. South at last, and homeward. Dave lay on the back seat and Hayley monitored his temperature. I drove the tailing Land Rover and was amazed how pedestrians would step into the road as soon as the first 4x4 passed, having to be hooted back into the ditch. On these remote tracks cars are seldom seen; two consecutive vehicles are unheard of and the sound of the first Landy muffled that of the second. So it was, ironically, often more nerve-wracking driving behind. Pedestrians in the north were also terrible at judging the speed of fast-moving cars. After all, they'd practically owned the road for the duration of the civil war when the occasional lumbering Russian tank was the only traffic. The startled road-owners would whip round wide-eyed, then pack up laughing and wave.

When we hit a stretch of new tar we looked at each other as though something was wrong. The smooth humming and absence of rattle was almost disconcerting. Johnny Clegg, the 'white Zulu' lead singer of Juluka, was chanting on the tape deck and we sang along,

> Spirit is the journey,
> body is the dust,
> I am the driver,
> from dust to dust.

Yes, I thought, perhaps all homeward journeys mimic the act of death, but now that I sniffed home I felt the death of this journey could not come soon enough. To hell with the symbolism of far-flung lighthouses and lakes.

Despite my homeward bent I decided that we had, notwithstanding our gripes and illnesses, eased into a good travelling groove. Places along the way had been emptied of much of their significance as end points, and been relegated to co-ordinates, which is as it should be. Ours had become a different genre of travel to the purely 'destination school'. The journeying was taking on a life of its own and was developing a rhythm – like drumming. The 'sedentaries' – those alien, stay-at-homers – belonged to another world. We were itinerants, at one with other roaders, like the passing Mozambicans with bundles or baskets on their heads bound for who knows where, cyclists with goats strapped to the panniers, and truck drivers camping beside their beasts. The Land Rover cabins were starting to feel like a home with our worldlies piled in behind us, food rolling around our feet and pillows laid out for back-seat sleepers. Squatters of the road.

Approaching Pemba a cop stepped out of a white sentry box and held up his hand. 'He's legit,' said Mike. 'Approach him very slowly and keep smiling. Do everything the ou says and just remember, you don't understand a word of Portuguese – that's crucial.'

'Bom dia, senhor. Onde é que tu vais?' (where are you going?) I could smell the alcohol on his breath.

'Good afternoon, officer, and how are you?' I said in English, following Mike's advice. I could see this was a mean little man. He wore comical red sunglasses and a smile.

'Oh, my friend, where you go?' He tried while peering in the back window.

'We're going to Pemba on holiday. We're tourists ... it's a very nice place!'

'Não fala Português?'

'I'm afraid we don't speak any Portuguese.'

I could see he was linguistically out of his depth and struggling with the realisation that he was going to have to release this fish.

'OK you go!' he said irritably after more peering.

'I'll bet he's wondering what a crash course in basic English for traffic vultures would cost,' said Hayley. It was an investment he couldn't afford to forego if prizes like us started slipping through his net.

'It depends on the cop,' said Mike as we drove off. 'With some of them, the minute they know you speak the language they throw the book at you – and as a hesitant speaker you're at a helluva disadvantage trying to prove your innocence. Also, if you play dumb and they do take you in, you've got a wild card. At a given point you can shock them by letting on that you understand what they're saying. But it's always best to try and laugh or bluff your way out. Keep things friendly and don't let them get heavy.'

With David incapacitated, there were fewer stops for photographs and we arrived back at Complexo Náutilus in mid-afternoon under a brooding tropical sky. This time we were accommodated in Centro Turístico Caracol, brand new chalets across the road from Wimbe Beach – and this time the showers worked. Dave was bundled into bed while Tank and I pulled on costumes and headed for a swim.

'It feels like we're bunking school,' said Tank. 'It's mid-afternoon and we're on the beach. Something's gone terribly wrong. There's got to be a catch.'

'It's our last day on the coast, and we've managed an early arrival,' I said. 'Imagine how much more pleasant this journey would have been if we'd set off earlier each day and got to our destinations before dark.'

The underside of the clouds had turned an ugly purple and rain was starting to spit, but nothing was going to get in the way of our swim. While splashing about in the shallows we noticed a young baboon break free of its street-kid owner on the beach and dash through the posh Náutilus open-air restaurant. The creature leapt agilely from table to table, staying just out of reach of its minder and a half-dozen furious waiters. Eventually the baboon was caught, the boy chastised and the tourists settled down to enjoy the rest of their meal in peace.

But moments later the baboon yanked its lead away from the lad, pulled a mischievous face at him, and raced through the restaurant again, sending some diners into hysterics, others into nervous huddles. A bunch of trinket-selling urchins dressed in rags cheered from the perimeter and were in turn pursued by the guards and maitre d'. It was jolly good theatre. Easily outstripping his pursuers, the baboon bounded from lamppost to palm tree to table, overturning glasses and wreaking havoc. At times he laughed and chattered and looked purposeful in his flight. At others he slackened his pace or perched just out of reach, seeming unsure of his course of action. It was during one of these contemplative lapses that he was finally trapped. Boy and furry friend were both given a cuff and told to *vão embora*. The urchins scattered.

Tank and I dried ourselves and wandered back along the strand behind the boy walking with his arm around his most human of pets. Long-haired jocks were keeping a soccer ball airborne and a reggae beat throbbed from Restaurante Mar e Sol where locals lunched on prego rolls and seafood platters under thatch umbrellas. As we reached our chalet we saw the baboon break free again with the boy in hot pursuit. They were heading back up the beach towards Náutilus Restaurant.

Dave had a migraine, alternating sweats and chills and his temperature was running high. Mike complained of gippo guts and looked white as a beach, but insisted on playing doctor to Dave. 'I'm sure he's got malaria and I don't think we should mess around,' he said over dinner. 'I'm going to give him Fancidar just in case. Better safe than sorry.'

'Don't you think we should call a doctor?' argued Rob. 'Fancidar is a very strong drug. I think we must be sure before we administer it.'

'Look, a doctor is just going to take a blood test which is either going to be positive or negative. Either way, he'll prescribe Fancidar to be safe. Let's not waste time and money.'

We picked at our calamari while Mike went off to deal with his patient. When I got back to the chalet I saw that Dave was turning and twisting in a puddle of sweat. Fancidar is like a depth charge and he was in for a difficult night.

I woke at 03h30 to the sound of Mike's protracted bowel movement. Initially I thought it was semi-automatic rifle fire, but was soon reassured by Mike's groaning. His diet of papaya had finally taken dramatic effect. He spent the rest of the night close to the porcelain and emerged at dawn looking like a ghost; then took to his bed. Rob suggested we delay our departure until lunch to give the two invalids a chance to rest. We all agreed. The back of a jolting Land Rover was no place to convalesce.

It was a muggy, overcast day and I took a long walk. I had Jennifer tramping about in my head again: compatibilities, incompatibilities, possibilities. I was sorting thoughts as I paced along Wimbe Beach, pausing now and then for a beautiful shell or to let a point settle comfortably. In recent days I'd taken to seeing the Mozambican odyssey as a metaphor for my life: ceaseless movement with little opportunity to pause, reflect, maybe deflect. But I could feel a revisionary wind blowing.

Perhaps because the going had become unrelenting, something in me was forcing a rethink. Where did my need to roam, to journey come from? I'd centred my adult life around the notions of restlessness and dissidence, resulting in an inability to slow down, to take stock. This had been partially self inflicted, partially forged by circumstances and, more recently, institutionalised by my job as a travel journalist. Maybe some of it was a manifestation of immaturity and could be peeled like late-summer skin. Perhaps I was, belatedly, growing up. It was not that I had any desire to give up travelling entirely, for that is a form of learning. It's just that other forms of mental wandering could be put to rest. I was also getting the feeling that my desire for a more sedentary existence was a means of imposing some control over Jenny's wanderlust as much as my own. Maybe I could begin to break down the divide I had created between negative stasis and positive motion, forging a marriage of sorts between the two through Jenny.

Whatever the case, for the first time in my life I felt I could countenance some form of 'settling down'. It was a terrifying and, in my nomadic cosmology, heretical notion. Perhaps travel burn-out had brought me to this point, like Crusoe's moments of lonely, island delirium, when his psychological path was drastically altered.

'A cottage by the sea with Jenny.' I said the sentence aloud a few times. It had a certain ring.

Perhaps I could purge myself of this need to take to the open road alone, to quest and conquest. These are implicitly sexual journeys. And in that sense the journeys are circular, a 're-practising' of the stroke – as though perfection were attainable that way. Questing had provided a blueprint for living. It had promised a gratification of the hunger, the opposite of the death (read motionless) instinct.

But on the white sands of Wimbe it all looked quite different. Maybe I'd begun chewing my own tail. Travelling as an end was no longer bearing the fruit I had hoped it would. Maybe there had to be less journeying, certainly less frenetic accumulation, and more cerebral travel.

Looking back over the trip I now recognised a dissident voice in my wanderers' chorus. My desire to slow the journey down, my riling against the tight itinerary and wanting to discover more at each stop, was already a manifestation of seeking depth, rest and 'place', as opposed to the superficial engagements imposed by motion. Perhaps the wells of connection I was inadvertently drilling led to Jenny. Maybe, in one sense at least, I had already stopped journeying, had found a place.

If I came to rest, found a perch with washing machine, mortgage and Labrador (the triumvirate of evil in my nomad morality) wouldn't I go insane? Wouldn't Jennifer and I tear each other to shreds? After all, she had a female version of my disease and was a roving journalist-filmmaker herself. Could we sit on a sofa together watching television without continually glancing at the map (note to self: hang map of Africa in toilet of future home, not living room)? Or could we travel together, finding a balance between our two flighty existences?

A woman with whitened face held up a few silver, trumpet-like fish. '*Não obrigado*,' I said and, snapping out of my daze, found I'd walked a great distance. So I turned back.

Maybe there comes a time when a traveller must try the other tack: investing, nurturing, producing. A leap of faith. Here, at the end of the road, at the end of my travelling tether, I found myself able to open up to the adversary. Now that the heresy was there, corrupting the files of my hard drive, I was quite content to let it go about its business. In due course, I could always administer a dose of Nietzsche, Schopenhauer or travel-prophets like Bruce Chatwin and Jonathan Raban to kill the picket-fence virus.

Remote foreign climes are the place to listen to dissident voices. Even if only as an exercise to renew conviction in one's current course. In that sense at least, I was simply conforming to an age-old, travel-writing convention. Journeying, and African overlanding in particular, transforms people. The hardships and wide-open spaces, the time to reflect, the presence of nature in the raw and alternative ways of life – all contribute to jolting one out of certainties. A close friend, Sarah Penny, had urged on me the catharsis of the African road, wonderfully captured in her travel memoir *The Whiteness of Bones*. Indeed, like an ancient quester, Jennifer had 'discovered' me in Cape Town after a two-month meander down the continent from Kenya to South Africa. Many of the convictions about her glamorous, media-junky London life had been 'o'erthrown by sensual Africa', creating space for the dubious grail that was me.

Crunching the kilometres again on the road to Nampula. The terrain was soft, its grass bowed by a light sea breeze reaching far inland. The acrid smell of charcoal from burning mounds pervaded the cabins. Cotton pickers walked along the road bearing baskets on their heads, bulging with the harvest ... like they were balancing clouds.

Mike was suffering on the back seat of our Land Rover and Dave was out cold in the TD5. It felt like a convoy of ambulances. At one point Mike put up his hand and motioned Rob to stop. Our patient struggled out the door, but only made it a few paces into a cotton field before he was caught short, so he squatted where he was to the great amusement of passing locals. He had no toilet paper with him, but we figured he'd make do with cott'n pickin'. Neither of us – I'm ashamed to say – had the energy to go over with a loo roll.

'Next time, find me a clump of trees, will you,' said Mike weakly as he levered himself onto the back seat before slumping over again. He seemed semi-conscious and clearly didn't have full control of his bowels so we drove with the windows down. At the next emergency stop Mike remembered the toilet paper as he scampered for the bushes. 'At least he's trainable,' said Rob, which was cruel, but we found it so funny that we had to hold onto each other, tears rolling down our cheeks.

It was dark again. An abandoned vehicle loomed in the middle of the road, forcing us to swerve into the brights of an onrushing truck. Delinquent dogs, stupid goats, suicidal chickens leading their young to the slaughter: night driving to Nampula and our nerves were shot.

By the time we reached the northern capital Mike was able to lift his head again and directed us to the relatively upmarket Hotel Tropical which Henrique, bless him, had organised for us. We found it on a tree-lined street behind the Cinéma Moçambique. 'If you want to know why the children in Mozambique think all Americans carry guns and solve their differences by kicking the shit out of each other, then go and have a look at what's showing,' said Mike as we passed the movie house.

Of course the charming young woman at reception had no record of our reservation, did not know who Henrique was and was obviously amused by our request for complimentary accommodation. Her expression read: full board for a measly mention in a South African magazine – you must be out of your mind! The owner was called. He was an urbane, well-educated Frelimo man who quickly smoothed over the difficulties and invited us for a drink in the bar where a bunch of MPs and wealthy investors were fraternising loudly. Over a beer we got the autobiography: after completing a course in business management in Washington DC our host bought the hotel as a virtual shell in 1993 and had been slowly upgrading it ever since.

Mike's face was ashen, so we packed him off to bed as soon as formalities were over. I was supposed to share a room with him, but took the mattress from my bed and went to join Tank and Rob. Mike would probably want to be alone, particularly as he'd be in and out of bed all night on toilet sorties. But (guiltily) I also wanted a good night's sleep and probably wouldn't get one in Mike's ward. He looked like he'd aged 40 years – a balding old man with sunken cheeks and a sheet pulled up to his chin.

Over dinner we spread out a map and looked at the options. There was another difficult decision concerning our route, one we'd have to make without Mike. Should we head north-west for the shores of Lake Malawi, or Lake Niassa as it is known in Mozambique, or cut the journey short by two days and head for home. We had heard great things about Metangula, Cóbuè and Likoma Island, and they would have made good places to convalesce. Metangula was once a slaving port and nearby Chiunga reputedly had a picturesque dhow anchorage and a reed-and-thatch resort set among baobabs. Cóbuè offered fine snorkelling and the chance to view colourful mbuna tropical fish. But none of us could face the extra 20 hours of driving.

'Shortening the trip will allow us to break the last leg – that murderous 12-hour dash from Harare to Johannesburg to catch our flights – in the Northern Province,' suggested Rob.

'I agree,' said Dave, who had rallied enough to take in some food. 'Mike's in a bad way and it would be crazy to take him on the long road to Metangula. As for the track to Cóbuè, we don't even know if it's driveable.'

It was the same issue we had faced in Pangane. The troops were exhausted and the roads too punishing for long detours. Like Cabo Delgado, Lake Niassa would have made a great emblematic end to the journey: we'd have traversed the country from the ocean at the south-easternmost point to the north-westernmost lake-shore village. But symmetry, symbolism and neat denouements were furthest from our minds. A hot bath and a Blantyre Big Mac with large fries and large Coke seemed to tip the scales against the lake.

The lads went to bed early, but I wasn't ready for sleep. A recently popped Larium was going to keep me bouncing off the walls for a while and I knew I'd writhe through a few Jennifer-filled hours if I went to bed immediately. So I opted for a stroll around town. From our previous visit I knew that Nampula didn't have much to offer – well, anything actually, but I couldn't face lying in wait for Mr Sandman while Rob and Tank harmonised their snoring. As I left the hotel two young women rose from their table on the terrace and followed me. Out in the street one of them came up and grabbed my arm, '*Como se chama, muzungo*?' (what's your name, whitie?).

'Justin, *e você*?' I answered, a little taken aback.

'Carla,' she said and showed me a flash of teeth in the darkness.

Women don't initiate this sort of thing where I come from. I often rue the fact that they don't, so I didn't want to appear churlish.

'*Onde é que tu vais*?' (where are you going?) she asked.

Oh, I was just wandering around, I explained, and thank you for asking. I didn't know how to say 'anti-malarial prophylactic complications' or 'kite flying courtesy of Larium' in Portuguese. As it happened, it was probably a good thing I didn't bring up the word prophylactic as it would probably have got me into trouble.

We had stopped beneath a street light and I could see they were both very young, mid-teens. 'Amigo, why don't you come with us to a party?' suggested Carla.

'I don't want to stray too far from the hotel where my companions are sleeping,' I said.

I now noticed that Carla's friend – the silent one – was quite beautiful. She had Swahili features – vaguely Asian eyes, full lips and high cheek bones – and was dressed in a tight-fitting, ankle-length dress. One strap had fallen off her shoulder.

Carla noticed that my eyes had wandered slightly and, no doubt in order to regain my attention, placed her hand on my groin and with one deft movement used her thumb to undo my fly. Surprised, you might think, and you'd not be far off the mark.

At this point the pouty friend ran her hand lightly over my bum and said, '*Vamos foder, muzungo*' (let's fuck, white man).

As a travel journalist I've learnt to take pains not to offend people from different cultures ... just because they say and do things differently. One doesn't want to be indelicate. In California I had to bite my tongue when my hosts served dinner at 17h30. Why!? Living in Oxfordshire for a period and not being a tea drinker regularly got me into awkward situations. The English don't take lightly to a nice cuppa being turned down, and never ask whether you'd prefer coffee. They simply can't conceive of someone with all their faculties not liking tea.

Similarly, there have been many times when I've got myself into trouble misinterpreting the good intentions of foreigners. In Egypt, for instance, one develops a defensive coldness and rudeness in response to ruthless baksheesh hunters, but sometimes you can be caught out. Wandering the back streets of Cairo I was at first abrupt to perfectly friendly people. I had to restrain myself from telling them where to stick the soapstone sphinxes I was sure they had secreted under their galabias, to be produced as soon as they'd won me over with false friendship. But away from the tourist route the people were genuinely friendly, and I had to eat my unkind words.

So you roll with the punches in foreign parts and try to tread as culturally correct a course as possible. It's not always easy and often requires a bit of ingenuity. The way things were going with Carla, I felt one of those sticky situations coming on. I cursed Mike Slater. His guidebook was sorely deficient in this department: 'All forms of unprotected sexual contact (i.e. without a condom) should be avoided, as well as any other situations in which exchange of body fluids could take place (for example sharing razors or toothbrushes).' We hadn't got to the razor and brush part yet, but things were moving pretty smartly in that direction.

Carla's forefinger was running along the elastic of my jocks and her other hand was behind my neck pulling me closer. She was terribly attractive ... Her lips were parted and I could smell more than one Dois M on her breath. It was time to mention the existence of Jennifer. Then again, maybe having a girlfriend was OK in her Weltanschauung and thus not a valid excuse for avoiding a roll in the cassava.

But she pre-empted my reluctant confession – for she was very pretty indeed – that there was 'someone else' with one word. '*Pão*?' I got the picture immediately. *Pão* means bread and Mozambicans use it liberally meaning a 'tip' or *cadeau* (gift). Clearly she wasn't only attracted to my Dutch-tulip/English-rose looks. My bulging trouser pocket, filled with hundreds of thousands of meticais, was an added allure.

I took another approach, explaining that there were two other men in my hotel room who wouldn't take kindly to our cavorting on the mattress beside them. So we couldn't go back there and, besides, I was awfully tired.

Carla looked mildly interested at the prospect of *pão* from three muzungos with bulging pockets, then thought better of it. She slipped her hand from my underwear, gave me a peck on the cheek and said, '*Ciao, muzungo, até à próxima*' (bye, white man, until next time).

I turned back to the hotel and Nampula's two sirens sauntered up the street from pool to lamp-light pool.

Over breakfast Hayley said that Dave had hardly slept at all, but that Mike, whom she'd looked in on a few times during the night, was a little better. Henrique had painted an ugly picture of the road to Cuamba, suggesting it may take up to 20 hours, so we needed to make an early start. But the invalids were moving at underwater pace. We convened at 07h30 – bags packed and ready in the lobby – and I made a bet with Tank that we wouldn't get away before 09h00. He and I had made similar bets on previous mornings and I had invariably won with the later estimation, but this time Tank knew he had me on the rack.

Of course I won, largely due to David's slow start. Unfortunately, Dave heard Tank congratulating me on my astonishing victory, and was furious. We both felt very guilty. Then Hayley refused to talk to us in the vehicle as we drove around looking for a place to change money and buy groceries. When we got out, she strode ahead of us, not acknowledging our presence. The bank wouldn't change rands, which only added to the tension, and it was eventually an Indian corner shop that obliged (with an excellent rate).

Standing in the queue in a cloud of curry powder and listening to loud Hindi music, I was suddenly struck by how few Indians we'd seen on our journey. There had been a time when the Indian and Afro-Indian community were a dominant elite in parts of Mozambique. Of course there had been Muslim and Hindu traders along the coast long before Da Gama arrived, but after the Portuguese had established power bases in Malabar, Goa and the northern ports of Cambay, Indians began to arrive in larger numbers and soon filled important positions in commerce, administration and the military. What had become of them all, I wondered. I guessed that, like many Jewish families in Africa, Indian traders cease to function in a political climate inimical to commerce. They'd simply moved on.

Back on the street Tank finally asked Hayley what the matter was and she admitted that, apart from being pissed off at us for irritating Dave, she was getting tired of always organising meals, buying the food and then having to prepare it. She had a good point. Part of the problem was Mike's indecisiveness. Things hadn't been properly planned for this leg and the situation was exacerbated with the two decision makers partially out of action. Another problem was that Hayley was good at it – efficient and resourceful – so we'd left her to her own devices, merely contributing money to her food kitty whenever she requested it. We apologised as best we could and resolved to change matters.

The Landies headed west for Cuamba on a road far better than expected. Huge inselbergs, hundreds of metres tall, rose on either side, often forming characterful formations. There were pyramids, slumbering maidens, Pinocchio noses and giant's fingernail scratches in the granite. Some looked like outsize versions of Makonde sculptures – grotesque depictions of ancestral spirits.

Our trek through the waist of northern Mozambique ran along a slave route, a well-trodden path which led from the southern shore of Lake Malawi, through Yao territory to the ports. David Livingstone estimated that for every slave who reached the coast, four died during the raids or the forced march. How many tales of misery could be told about the ancient highway; and how many footprint palimpsests marked this road to a lifetime of captivity?

It was not only slaves and their captors who trod the paths from west to east. Great Yao caravans of over 1 000 porters also brought ivory to the coast. They passed through Makua territory and ended up trading with agents of the Portuguese *moradores* ... or Swahili smugglers ready to whisk the ivory northward in fast, shallow-draft dhows.

This has always been great bandit territory too. During the liberation struggle, Frelimo fighters – and later Renamo – enjoyed free rein in many parts of the region. But these were just the latest heirs to a long tradition. The Makua used to range from well-fortified stockades using armies of slaves acquired through trading in chattel. The matrilineal configuration of Makua society allowed for the men to be away on extended raiding expeditions while agriculture and village life continued undisturbed, as these had always been the preserve of women. Slaving, trading, warring and raiding for 'wives' were boys' business, and they all involved being mobile, which made the bands difficult opponents to pin down or subjugate.

In the 19th century one of the greatest Makua bandit leaders was, ironically, a Swahili-speaking Muslim called Marave. All attempts to crush him failed. Finally a Portuguese army was sent into the interior accompanied by a Goanese military band, but they were no match for Marave.

Around the turn of the century there was an accidental meeting between Marave and the British consul, Maugham, who was visiting the region on a shooting party. Upon returning to camp one night Maugham found 50 warriors waiting for him. 'All were armed with guns,' he wrote.

> Their woolly hair, grown long for the purpose, was twisted into innumerable thin, long tails or plaits carried backward and reaching to their shoulder-blades. Their cheeks were slashed with deep longitudinal cicatrizations several inches long, and so deep in some cases, as completely to penetrate the flesh, their upper teeth being visible through the gashes ... Slung over their shoul-

> ders were bags of monkey or cat skin, which contained their ammunition, snuff and other necessities.

Maugham was taken to Marave's stronghold where he found that 'nothing could have exceeded the dignified courtesy of my reception, or my surprise to find this terrible chief so refined and considerate a host.'

Appropriately for this country of renegades, Marave – bandit of bandits – was never captured. This in an era of modern artillery, machine guns and early aeroplanes.

We stopped near Ribáuè for lunch on a bridge. The Landies were quickly surrounded by a group of children who stood staring at our food. Hard-boiled eggs were peeled, bully-beef, cucumbers and tomatoes were sliced, but our hearts were not in the eating and the kids ended up with most of our meal. Dave was trying to do an interview on the Iridium phone, with Tank inciting the locals into fits of loud laughter, which was taken in good spirit by Dave and his interviewer (and hopefully the South African listeners).

Things had been tense between David and I for a couple of days. He came over to where I was eating a piece of papaya and sat on a boulder. 'Hey Just, sorry 'bout snapping at you yesterday on the beach.'

'Not a problem, Dave. I *was* getting in your way and I'm sorry too.'

'You know, this trip has been a great photographic opportunity, but such a strain. I find it really hard working with you and Rob around. It's exhausting. Whenever someone grabs a camera you panic that you might be missing out.'

'Ja, I know what you mean. Even as the rookie photographer I sometimes feel it.'

'Taking pictures is such a personal thing for me,' said Dave. 'I try to develop a relationship – albeit fleeting – with my subject. I get so passionate about the process. Like yesterday. Yes, I gave the woman with the fish a few coins. But it was more about establishing a moment of trust. It takes tremendous energy and it's delicate. It was soul destroying having you step in the way to grab your snap. I hated feeling the rage. Guess it was a bit of malaria and a bit of Larium talking too. Sorry buddy.'

Soon we were on the bounce again and our minds wandered to places where the world wasn't moving: oh for hot and cold running telephones, satellite food, buttered babes and ice-cold pillows. Juluka was playing their brand of '80s Zulu pop on the deck again (only Mike had brought tapes) and dust filtered in clouds through the air vents: 'We are the scatterlings of Africa, each and every one. We're on the way to Pelamanga, where the world began,' sang Johnny Clegg.

The afternoon wore on and the landscape became increasingly beautiful, and improbable. The proportions and shapes of the inselbergs seemed all wrong. Fields of gay sunflowers stretched all the way to the granite bases and a polarised sky domed above the peaks. Hardly had we got up speed from one photo call, than a photographer would yell for another stop.

'When I eventually get down to writing my travelling tales, I'll call it *Memoirs of a White Kaffir*,' said Mike from the back seat. He'd got a bit of colour back and had eaten most of his lunch.

'Why on earth?' I asked, roused from mind-numbing road stupor.

'Well, when I was doing national service, all the *troeps* used to call me *kaffirboetie* because of my politics. As you know, 'kaffir' also means 'non-believer' in Arabic – and, in a sense, I've been a non-believer of one form or another all my life. And a nomadic one at that.'

The drone took over again, but Mike had got me mulling. It was an intriguing way of viewing this travel virus we all seemed to have contracted. Ours was a sort of secular faith, a belief in enlightenment through motion. As 'journeymen' we were learning the ropes of life through the performance of travel, a *Cole's Notes* or short cut to the ways of the world. Or so we told ourselves. And what better way to learn the scriptures of kaffirdom, of agnosticism or chronic dissidence or scepticism, than through travel. Journeying with an anthropological and soul-mining bent; indeed, mind-bending at times.

Mike and Hayley were in the front seats talking about marriage and the notion of settling down. Hayley had recently parted from a boyfriend of seven years, a relationship that came very close to marriage before she backed away. Now she and Dave had grown very close and I was beginning to wonder about what track they were on. They both seemed to be wondering too. The fact that Dave had been a wanderer like me for so long, and that Hayley had just come off a marriage-like relationship complicated matters.

Mike was telling Hayley about his experience of wedlock and having children: 'I reckon you only truly become adult when you've had a kid. Children bring with them a kind of passivity. It's sobering stuff for rovers like me. Hell, it makes us more human, more caring.'

I was listening, but not participating. In the past I'd have made some conceited comment about the manacles of marriage. Instead I shut up. What Mike was saying made some sense and, given my feelings for far-flung Jennifer, were ringing true in an unfamiliar sort of way. Perhaps I was becoming 'more human'. Whatever the case, I passionately wanted Mozambique to end and to get myself to Covent Garden, even if I had to walk up the west side of the continent, swim the pillars of Hercules, trot through *rioja* and *Beaujolais* country and breast the Channel. I was in homing-pigeon mode.

After dark we crossed the Lúrio River again, this time hundreds of kilometres upstream. This brought us into Niassa, the last of Mozambique's ten provinces, bar Tete (which we'd dip into on our homeward leg from Blantyre to Harare). If we couldn't make it to the Rovuma, we could at least claim all ten provinces in the space of 20 days.

Our Landies rumbled into Cuamba, bound for the local missionary's home. The town became a backwater when the railway line from Malawi fell into disuse during the war, but was experiencing a revival as a link in the Nacala Development Corridor. After making some wrong turns on the wide avenidas, we found another of Mike's men of the cloth, this time a dominee.

It always amazes me how Afrikaners turn up in the strangest corners of the continent – often doing good works in their own humble way. Here was a South African minister living with his wife and baby in a remote part of Mozambique, helping to run a host of community projects. They'd had to learn Portuguese and cope with considerable hardships. Contact with South Africa was difficult and Gauteng lay four days' drive and four border crossings away.

The dominee greeted us warmly and pointed out where in his garden we could camp. We pitched our tents in the chilly night air. Here in Mozambique's highlands was the first occasion we needed jerseys. Mike's prawn oesophagus had returned and he was looking grim again.

Three friends of the dominee from Stellenbosch University were also encamped in the garden beside a fuel tanker-truck. We introduced ourselves and discovered that they had driven all the way from Cape Town to a settlement on the Rovuma River where they'd helped with the building of a missionary church. After spending only a week in the region, they were about to embark on the epic, 4 000-kilometre drive home. We thought *our* trip was crazy.

We walked to a nearby restaurant past a graffito that filled a whole block: *Abaixo o Imperialismo* (Down with Imperialism). The television was blaring some irritating Brazilian soap opera and we sat silently waiting for *frango zambeziano* which took an age to materialise. Fortunately the three Stellenbosch boys – all clean shaven, polite and charming – arrived to jolt us from our apathy. We felt like the poor relations and were fascinated by their exploits. It turned out the leader of the trio had recently finished his studies and was running a trucking company in Maputo. Trucking and the Lord: an odd combination, but not, I considered upon reflection, an incompatible one. In order to make a bit of pocket money for the long trek home, the lads were delivering jet fuel to airstrips in northern Mozambique for the electoral commission. National elections were to be held later in the year and voter-education teams, ballot boxes and the like had to be transported to some of the remotest polling booths in southern Africa.

The young Afrikaners were idealistic and intrepid. I envied them their single-mindedness and devotion. They knew their way with equal ease around vehicle engines and darkest Africa, and they had a hotline to the Lord. The latter might have been what got them out of trouble earlier in the year when they tackled Dondo to Caia during the wet season. Such a journey would rate right up there with my worst nightmares. They did the trip in an old SADF Samil truck, a rugged vehicle well suited to the job. Despite its high clearance they often had water coming over the bonnet and kept passing stranded or drowned lorries abandoned until the water subsided, which may have been months in the future.

I woke early the next morning to the sound of a town stirring and the loud drone of bees. Evidently I'd pitched my tent directly beneath a busy hive. Bother. At breakfast both Mike and Dave looked a lot better, but not enough to convince us that heading north to the lake was a good idea. Dave claimed that he had his 'spurt' back, but we were sceptical. When Mike bragged that he felt he could once again 'fart with confidence' we began to feel nervous. As long as he didn't try it in the vehicle, we cautioned.

'Last night I had the weirdest dream,' said Mike. 'I can't think what it meant. I was in a subway station in New York and there was this fire. For some reason everyone was panicking because a train was about to pull into the station.'

'Well I'm afraid if you go with Freud on an anal interpretation, you might not be over your gippo guts,' I ventured. Fortunately I was wrong and there were no express toilet needs for the rest of the day.

Border-bound we rattled down a flame-tree lined main street where bicycles were the ruling orthodoxy. Our team was in high spirits, not so much due to the imminent departure from Mozambique, but the promise of warm showers, comfy beds, fast food and the rush of tar under our wheels.

The locals seemed poorer than elsewhere and this got us talking about the foreign aid that had poured into the country towards the end of hostilities.

'Aid is another form of enslavement,' said Mike controversially. 'The foreigners are often more of a problem than a help. Aid agencies send in $1 000-a-day consultants, but the projects they initiate aren't sustainable. Missionaries like the dominee do far more: they're operating at grass roots and stick with it through thick and thin, sharing their adopted community's trials and tribulations.

'I once came across a group of do-gooders who had each paid an organisation £3 000 to come out to Africa and do their stint. They built a school in six weeks. Then, at the opening, an MP came to tell the locals how great this bunch of foreigners were. "Look at these whites: they come from Europe and actually *pay* to work their asses off – for you!" he harangued. This just makes the foreigners look like wizards and the locals feel even more helpless.'

Mike had a point. The aid phenomenon skewed the whole picture. In the early 1990s foreign aid accounted for more than three-quarters of the Gross Domestic Product. Countries like Mozambique have to learn to help themselves. As long as foreign powers keep sending aid (often with unwanted strings attached), the problems continue. There are, perhaps, exceptions, like natural disasters and the reduction of national debt. But so often the West, and formerly the Soviet bloc, got it all wrong. A starving child on a television screen galvanises do-gooders, but the aid, when it comes, causes more harm that good. In the case of famine, for instance, food often arrives too late. Just when the country is starting to feed itself again, there's a massive influx of provisions, sending prices tumbling, thus crippling farmers.

When Mozambique was driven to signing an agreement with the World Bank and International Monetary Fund in 1987, Frelimo was forced into allowing in many NGOs that they saw as undesirable. Control of foreign projects and aid money was quickly taken out of Mozambican hands and well-intentioned aid workers often blundered in, causing harm through their own ignorance – or arrogance.

The aid circus was also a breeding ground for corruption. Mozambicans working for these agencies always seemed markedly better off than their fellow citizens. Many locals claim that corruption was almost unheard of during the early post-independence years. Now it's everyone for themselves and 'aid' had contributed to this corrosion of values. Indeed it was hard to find a rural market where aid goods weren't on sale – no doubt having 'fallen off the back of a truck'.

Although Mike felt that people like the dominee were doing more good at village level than the aid agencies, I couldn't but feel that missionaries and religious charities were often yet another form of enslavement Mozambique could do without. There were stories of priests dipping into the young flesh at missionary schools and cases of nuns distributing food only to Catholics among the starving. Christianity has also had a bad track record in south-east Africa …

By mid-morning we had reached Entre Lagos border post. As we crawled into 'town' Mike told us one of his border-crossing stories. He and two friends had been camping on Ilha when their Kombi was broken into. The passport of the woman in the party was stolen. This was in the bad old days when South Africans were not to be trusted and a South African without a passport could only be one thing: a spy.

They considered their options and decided the best solution was to try to smuggle her through all eight border controls (Malawi, Tete Corridor, Zimbabwe and South Africa). There was a makeshift cupboard underneath the bunk in the back of the Kombi and she crawled into this tiny space as they approached Entre Lagos.

'*Porra*, it was nerve-wracking stuff,' said Mike. 'Fortunately none of the guards searched the vehicle and by the fourth time we'd done this we found her snoring loudly when we opened up … which could have been a bit of a give-away had a custom's official been poking around.'

As we stepped from the vehicles, money changers swarmed around us, fanning bills in many currencies as though they were decks of cards. The men offered us appalling exchange rates into kwachas: they had a captive market as it's illegal to exchange meticais in Malawi. Dave tried to set up an intricate 'money-changing' sequence of shots (he'd obviously got his photography spurt back) while I took the passports to be stamped. There was no queue, which didn't deter the moronic official from taking 20 minutes to apply the stamps. He had a Neanderthal face and stared at Rob's (upside down) US passport for an age.

When it came to my turn I held out a little pile of South African passports. He looked at me scathingly, but his attempts at questioning me in Portuguese met with practised incomprehension. He mumbled something to his subordinate from which I deduced that he didn't believe we'd come all the way from Ponta do Ouro in only three weeks. 'Look at us,' I wanted to say, 'look into our eyes and at our vehicles. Can't you see the journey etched there, plain as daylight?' He paged slowly through each passport, not missing a single blank page lest it held the key to our incarceration or his enrichment, or both. Finally he brought his stamp down like a guillotine. Five merciless blows with his right arm and we were free to cross.

'You're lucky it was softy and not old snake-eyes on duty today,' said Mike as I emerged from the darkness of the office into the blinding light. 'He'd have had us and the vehicles stripped. No namby-pamby rubber gloves here, mate ...'

Our Landies waded through the thick sand of no-man's-land. On the Malawi side chaos reigned. There was a traffic jam, or at least what we considered a jam after days of empty roads, and a full train waiting to enter Mozambique. The TDi was leaking gear-box oil at an alarming rate and we'd need to get to a garage quickly. I sat on the bonnet with a Coke and let Hayley and Dave do the passport thing. There was a rugby scrum around a counter where officials remained courteous and spoke the Queen's English, but efficiency was not their watchword.

Although the border looked to be a long wait, I was pleased as punch. It would be quick going now: a day to Blantyre, another day to Harare, one more to Messina and by Saturday evening we'd be in Jo'burg. A piece of cake. Four easy driving days on good roads and only 2 500 kilometres to go (to complete our 9 000-kilometre quota – in other words nearly Cape Town to London). We were as good as home, I figured. And I was right. Once out of Mozambique everything happened faster and the roads seemed smoother, gentler, easier. Even Tete Corridor, the Civil War's hellfire run, was a breeze with potholes filled in, landmines cleared and easy border crossings. Travel decadence.

To pass the time while waiting for our passports to be stamped I flicked through Mike's guidebook for the last time. Despite its faults, it had been our Bible (even Mike had found it useful) and had served us well enough. Where we'd followed the written word, we'd been fine. Where we'd improvised, we'd got ourselves into trouble. I came upon a humorous, from where I sat anyway, piece of advice which I'd previously missed. It read: 'If you are planning a "whistle-stop" tour of the entire country in your own 4x4 vehicle, you may anticipate an average speed of 80 km/h, which amounts to at least a six-week journey.' A beautifully crafted sentence with not a word out of place.

I was sitting on the bonnet of the TDi and Mozambique spooled through my head. Words we'd learnt along the way were triggering memories: the deadly flysquito spray, the life-saving *Sempre Coca-Cola* signs that appeared out of the dust on lonely roads, the cobra-mamba of Gorongoza, and the untranslatable exclamation *'É pá!'*, uttered in unison at each adversity.

Sitting there musing, I suddenly felt a surge of anger at the unfair hand Mozambique had been dealt. The country was cursed by its climate, position, topography and history ... and its many plunderers. Damn it, these were good people (*boa gente*). Some of the goodest I'd ever met. Despite decades of civil war and the devastation of famines, floods and droughts, the country had come through remarkably. You had to put it down to the spirit of the people, to their capacity for forgiveness and their optimism. They were pulling the country up by its bootstraps. Civil wars, particularly in Africa, are usually fought along tribal or ideological lines. In Mozambique this was not the case, but rather the product of the heinous foreign policies of two neighbouring states. Perhaps that's why the country has so readily embraced peace. Or maybe the *gente* simply couldn't face any more nightmares.

I was thinking this way when a young American couple wheeling bicycles passed me. They looked stressed and exhausted. Their pannier bags were overflowing and both carried big backpacks. How would they keep their balance on the uneven roads, I wondered? Their superfluous gear and dejected expressions spoke of inexperienced cyclists, maybe inexperienced travellers. Who in heaven had advised them to take a cycle tour round northern Mozambique? They appeared beaten before they'd even crossed the border.

The man stopped, looked at me, and wheeled over: 'Have you guys come from the other side?' He made it sound like the fourth dimension.

'Yes,' I said. 'It's been a long road for us. We've come from the far south.'

'What's Mozambique like?' he asked.

Where to start? What to say?

It was like nothing we'd ever experienced before, like no road we'd ever taken. We'd seen some of Africa's finest buildings, met some of its bravest, most forgiving people. We'd microlighted over reefs, snorkelled through coral gardens, climbed the dunes of Bazaruto, sailed the night dhow to Ibo. We'd scaled the ancient walls of São Sebastião and watched fishermen mending their sails in the street. We'd done Dondo to Caia. We'd savoured molten prawns, cashew nuts lightly peri'd and too many chilled Dois Ms. We'd chased nightjars and cobramambas, stalked sunsets by the dozen, and been buzzed by flysquito-resistant mozzies. We'd found perfect, palm-rimmed beaches, forgotten Portuguese forts and crumbling cathedrals. Mozambique had opened us up, disembowelled and disheartened us ... laid us out on a bed of concrete on an Alto Molócuè roof ... and one of powder sand at Pangane.

It had taught me to see differently ... plunged me into depression, and made me soar. It had done everything a journey should do.

'It was tough and great,' I said.

'What are the roads like between here and Moçambique Island?' he asked.

My God, you poor lambs, I thought. From here to Ilha, by bicycle!

'Not very good, I'm afraid, and there aren't many towns along the way. Stay at missions or churches – they're your best bet. And carry lots of water.'

There's a word the locals use for a backpacker: *pachiça*. It refers to those who carry their baggage or bundles on their heads. In the old days it applied to slaves – the dispossessed who were forced to make the long trek to the coast. Just then it seemed as though the old word had found a perfect match in these coast-bound, tourist slaves.

I realised too that I had been slave to the nostalgic dream of a prewar Mozambique passed down as family lore. I had been a *pachiça*, carrying a pack of *saudades* handed down through grandparents, parents and siblings. Along the way I'd shed much of the baggage and forged my own relationship with the place, bred a new set of experiences to feed my progeny, or those who cared to listen.

The two backpacking cyclists had trudged 50 metres down the sand road into no-man's-land and, to the great amusement of locals who'd stopped to watch, were trying to mount their beasts. After a few false starts they were both up and wobbling at tortoise pace towards Mozambique. They didn't get very far before one toppled over. The backpacks were making them hopelessly top heavy. Perhaps, in time, they'd take a leaf out of the charcoal vendors who strapped bundle to pannier. Maybe the muzungos were trainable.

For them, 'a journey through Mozambique' was just beginning and whether dream or nightmare, their grandchildren were sure to hear all about the antediluvian odyssey, about prawns the size of crayfish, deserted tropical beaches and ancient towns of haunting beauty. About hardships beside the steaming, iron snake at the Malawian border, then a descent into Eden …

We rumbled into Malawi past a group of Mozambican children heading east. They gave us the two-hand wave as if to say, 'In our future we will carry no weapons, will mean no harm.' Suddenly I was all choked up. I stuck both hands out the window and waved.

O Sul

Dhows are the mules of the western Indian Ocean and provide a living link to this corner of Africa's rich, and at times tempestuous, maritime past.

Legally 4x4s are not allowed on Mozambique's beaches, although exceptions are made at some launching spots, like here at Guinjata Bay. But 1x2s are a different story.

The TD5 took a berth near the bows of the Catembe to Maputo ferry, a rusty craft with a gung-ho helmsman whose idea of mooring was alarmingly close to ramming.

Inhambane has an eclectic mix of architectural styles, ranging from ornate Portuguese villas to mosques, and from cathedrals to socialist-era monstrosities.

O Centro

At Benguerra Island the men swim out to their dhows before threading them through the sandbanks to the archipelago's rich fishing grounds.

The basic elements of dhow sailing have remained unchanged for centuries: a triangle of lateen-rigged canvas, an open deck with salt-worn thwarts, an alert tillerman playing the breeze with instinctive skill.

A warren of reed stalls crammed with capulana shops, pyramids of tropical fruit, open-air hairdressers, tables of spices and the odd drinking den ... Vilankulo market.

The beaches of the Bazaruto Archipelago (Benguerra pictured here) live up to the old timers' tropical paradise dreams.

O Norte

As is the Makua custom, the women of Tandanhangui smear their faces with powder ground from the bark of the nciro tree, which acts like a moisturiser.

The TDi drew up outside Murrupula Cathedral near Nampula where the priest was continuing a tradition of Catholic education established by Portuguese missions over the centuries.

Cotton pickers walked the road to Nampula bearing baskets bulging with the harvest ... balancing clouds.

On Ibo Island the sail makers and menders lay out their canvas on the main street, secure in the knowledge that no car will disturb them.